MORE PRAISE FOR
HELLO, HE LIED

"If this book's publisher has any sense at all, it will set up tables at all entry points to Hollywood, stack them high with copies of this witty, gnomic guide to making it as a producer in La-La (or is it Lie-Lie?) Land and wait for a scene straight out of *Day of the Locust*."—*People*

"The best insider's view of Hollywood in years—a wickedly funny, engrossing account of how movies get made, by a successful producer and one of the smartest people in Hollywood."—Richard Preston, author of *The Hot Zone*

"One of the most unusual 'other truths' to come from the showbiz trenches of the West Coast . . . what resonates is Lynda's unusual take on what being a woman in Hollywood means . . . A life work on how to survive."—Liz Smith, *New York Post*

"If I had read *Hello, He Lied* when I was running Paramount Pictures, I might have lasted a while longer. On the other hand, after reading it, I might not have taken the job at all."—Brandon Tartikoff

"Obst's book offers practical advice to would-be movie-makers."
—*Washington Post*

"If you've ever wondered how Hollywood got to be so brilliantly stupid, beautifully ugly, thoughtfully mindless, and uselessly important, quit wondering. It's all in *Hello, He Lied.*—P.J. O'Rourke, author of *Age and Guile*

"When it comes to Hollywood, and matters pertaining to it, you couldn't be in better hands than Lynda Obst's. She's funny and she's smart, and she knows the town, the players, and the deals in a way that only an insider can. I laughed a lot and I learned a lot more reading her book."
—Dominick Dunne, author of *Another City, Not My Own*

"A useful primer for hopeful producers, as well as a model for writers of future I-was-a-female-producer-and-lived-to-tell-about-it books."
—*Entertainment Weekly*

HELLO, HE LIED –

and Other Truths from the Hollywood Trenches

HELLO, HE LIED —

and Other Truths
from the Hollywood Trenches

LYNDA OBST

Broadway Books   New York

The author is grateful for permission to include the following previously copyrighted material:

"Swing Song" from *Now We Are Six* by A. A. Milne. Illustrated by E. H. Shepard. Copyright 1927 by E. P. Dutton, renewed © 1955 by A. A. Milne. Reprinted by permission of Dutton Children's Books, a division of Penguin Books USA, Inc.

"Comment" from *The Portable Dorothy Parker* by Dorothy Parker, Introduction by Brendan Gill. Copyright 1926, © renewed 1954 by Dorothy Parker. Reprinted by permission of Viking Penguin, a division of Penguin Books USA, Inc.

Excerpt from Crystal Awards Speech by Barbra Streisand given at the Women in Film luncheon. Copyright © 1986 by Barbra Streisand. Reprinted by permission of the author.

"Make New Friends" from the *Ditty Bag* by Janet E. Tobitt. Reprinted by permission of the Girl Scouts of the United States of America.

BROADWAY

A hardcover edition of this book was originally published in 1996 by Little, Brown and Company. It is here reprinted by arrangement with Little, Brown and Company.

Broadway Books titles may be purchased for business or promotional use or for special sales. For information, please write to: Special Markets Department, Bantam Doubleday Dell Publishing Group, Inc., 1540 Broadway, New York, NY 10036.

BROADWAY BOOKS and its logo, a letter B bisected on the diagonal, are trademarks of Broadway Books, a division of Bantam Doubleday Dell Publishing Group, Inc.

First Broadway Books trade paperback edition published 1997.

Library of Congress Cataloging-in-Publication Data

Obst, Lynda Rosen.
    Hello, he lied : and other truths from the Hollywood trenches /
Lynda Ost.
        p.   cm.
    Originally published: Boston : Little, Brown, 1996.
    Includes index.
    ISBN 0-7679-0041-3 (pbk.)
    1. Obst, Lynda Rosen.   2. Motion picture producers and directors—
    United States—Biography.   3. Motion pictures—Production and
    direction.   I. Title.
PN1998.3.O28A3   1997
791.43'0232'092—dc21
    [B]   97-25218
                                                                    CIP

ISBN 0-7679-0041-3

For Oly, of course.
My trenchmate.

CONTENTS

PREFACE

A FRIEND OF MINE once described me as a Polish producer, because I was the only producer she knew who wrote for extra money. Over the course of writing this book I discovered that I also write for extra career options, extra outlets for my frustrations, and extra work: What would I otherwise do on Sundays or on planes? Relax? But it was only after it was completed, over the course of three years of excruciatingly frustrating work, that I realized why I had felt so compelled to write it: Through it I refound the joy of producing, and remembered the reasons I had started producing at all.

I have a kind of hybrid world view: I ended up in Hollywood accidentally, so I arrived with a reporter's eye and an anthropologist's distance. Slowly, inevitably, I've gone native. Fifteen years of day-to-day exposure turns anthropology into sociology. My perspective swells and shrinks in the daily drama. Often I lose it entirely. Writing is my tool for getting it back. Sometimes it even works.

What on earth is this thing variously called producer, executive producer, coproducer, associate producer, scrolling before the film begins? What is this endlessly qualified job that seems to be done by so many and yet is actually done by so few? The *Oxford English Dic-*

tionary defines *produce* well: "To lead or bring forward, bring forth into view or notice; to offer for inspection, consideration, exhibit." This is what we do. We lead and bring forth: our work, our worth, our products to be exhibited. We start movies and then we finish them. We bring them forth to you, the viewer, our audience. How we actually bring something forth — out of the daily mayhem that annihilates the best of our intentions — is the subject of this book.

I've watched Hollywood change radically over my tenure, the "baby boomers take Hollywood" years. It has undergone systemic changes, personality changes, changes in opportunity for gender and race, changes in technology. Yet in many ways it never fundamentally changes: Its unwritten rules have stayed the same as they were during its founding-mogul golden era. But interestingly, in the past few baby-boomer years, the inner workings of Hollywood, not just the glamorous goings-on of its movie stars, have become news, worthy of reportage. Why? Somehow it is intuitively clear that what goes on in the deep, dark recesses of the movie business tells us something (scary) about the process of work mixed with power in the latter days of this millennium, in every venue. Success is sudden; defeat is swift. Reinvention remains an option.

Over the course of my education in the movie business, I've seen my peers crash and soar; I've seen the system create and destroy; and somehow, despite the drama and the sideshows, I've learned how to get movies I love made. There is, I've discovered, a peculiar logic that underlies the seemingly arbitrary customs and traditions that have evolved in Hollywood. I observed, theorized, and wrote it all down. It may not all be exactly right (rightness being an elusive thing), but it's how it looks from where I sit. It is my manual for surviving the havoc in the modern trenches of work.

This is not a mean book, so if that's what you seek, seek elsewhere. I love what I do, at least a good deal of the time, and have few axes to grind. Those I'm still stuck with I've tried to ignore. This book tells everything I know about Hollywood. It's a pretty funny place. Funny like hell.

I'd like to thank three gifted editors: Fredrica Friedman, Andrea Cagan, and Ingrid Sischy. I am indebted to each. Only an editor knows what a treasure a great editor is.

Chapter 1

NEXT!

"Do your work, then step back.
The only path to serenity."

— *Tao Te Ching*

"They won. We lost. Next."

— *Barry Diller*

I REMEMBER ONE EVENING in 1994, steaming in a hot bath, when it suddenly occurred to me that I might have finally run out of Mondays on *The Hot Zone*, a movie I'd been working on more or less constantly all year. Every Friday, after I'd spent a full week keeping the package — the director, script, and stars — together, it would fall apart again. Every weekend I had to hustle to put it back together. Every Monday morning the press would call to ask (for example), "Is it true that Ridley Scott [the director] is dropping out?" "Of course not," I would reply, relieved not to be lying (at least for the moment). Then the package would threaten to fall apart again, I would put it back together, and another Monday would come. "Of course not." "Of course not." "Why would you think that?" It was the most unstable project I'd ever worked on.

Getting any picture mounted is a Sisyphean task, but this one was complicated by a closely observed struggle between studios and rival producers. In one corner of the ring was a very large sixty-year-old male producer from Warner Brothers, and in the other corner was me, a short female producer from 20th Century Fox in my early forties. The press and each side's self-interest had turned what began as an auction for rights to Richard Preston's now-celebrated article in *The New Yorker* called "Crisis in the Hot Zone," about an outbreak of the deadly Ebola virus in a U.S. Army facility, into a frenzied competition between studios and rival producers that soon escalated into a pitched battle.

Fox and I had won the initial skirmish by convincing Preston of our sympathetic intentions. He had elected to interview all the interested producers and choose from among them. As an ex-reporter, I was attracted to the true story. As a working mother, I was attracted to the heroism of Nancy Jaax, the army veterinarian and mother of two who was at the core of Preston's article. We did not want to make an exploitative horror film. Credible argument. We won the auction. Credible victory. That was the last moment any of it made sense. To our astonishment, the losing producer from Warner Brothers decided to proceed regardless of the fact that he had lost the auction. His idea was to make his own knock-off version of the Preston article. He called it *Outbreak*. So much for honor among thieves.

I was exhausted. Fifteen years before, when I had begun developing my first movie, *Flashdance*, I had no way of knowing how hard it is to make movies. It had taken me six years to become a producer and probably three more to know what I was doing. After producing two important directors' debuts, those of Chris Columbus (*Adventures in Babysitting*) and Nora Ephron (*This Is My Life*), and having two near brushes with the Oscars and two homegrown flops, I thought I had seen the extent of the joys and disappointments that Hollywood had to offer. But none of it had prepared me for the highs and lows and lower lows of *The Hot Zone*.

Like Atlas, I felt like I was balancing all the issues of the movie on my shoulders: the director's fear of the studio, the studio's fear of the director, all of our fears of the potent movie stars — Robert Redford and Jodie Foster — who could make us or break us at any juncture. But all of these opposing forces could have been tamed with the proper amount of time. In the context of a race to production — everyone believed that there was a place for only one such movie in the marketplace, but no one was folding — time was a luxury we didn't have. All of us — director, studio, stars, and me — were deeply concerned about how the race would compromise the movie. Keeping each party from fatally losing faith as we conducted a speedy, expensive rewrite was a juggling act that took everything I had learned during my long apprenticeship. Every movie I had ever made, every struggle I had fought, every alliance I had forged, had been necessary to teach me how to keep the balls in the air. And yet, the movie remained elusively out of my control.

The press was eating up the story, and the coverage of the race had been affecting the basic process of putting the movie together — a kind of media Heisenberg uncertainty principle. The volatile but extraordinary package we had assembled included the brilliant English director Ridley Scott (*Alien, Thelma and Louise*), Robert Redford to play virologist Karl Johnson, and Jodie Foster to play Nancy Jaax. Redford and Foster had their own strong points of view about the script. Because of the race, everyone felt destabilized and feared that the script would suffer from lack of time. The last draft had been written by Redford's writer from *Quiz Show*. By the time Jodie read the script and had to formalize her commitment, her part had subtly changed. She decided to pull out.

Now the project was dangling out there for everyone to see, without a costar for its male lead. Great copy. High stakes. My ego was engaged. I was charged to win this race for my studio and for the writer and the key participants in the story, whose life rights I'd also purchased.

My job as the producer was to breathe life into the movie — from its infancy as a *New Yorker* article through its adolescence as a script being written against a tight time clock, and finally into its adulthood — by finding a director and choosing and securing the cast. Each phase had been critical and perilous, and the movie was now on life support. This is the greatest crisis for a producer, the threat of watching your baby die. I had to keep it alive, hour by hour, day by day.

On one particularly bad but typical morning, Bryan Lourd, Redford's agent at Creative Artists Agency (CAA), and a close ally and friend, woke me to tell me that the director and screenwriter of the Warner movie were flying to Sundance to meet with Redford. "You're not serious," I say, staggering pre-coffee. "Can't you stop him? Don't they understand that he's going to do *HZ?*" Next line is ringing: head of the studio. "How's the rewrite coming? I want it for the weekend." Next call: Jodie's agent. "She's flying to Paris and won't be reachable. You better send the draft today." Try to find the writer: no answer. Writer's agent: "He'll be done when he's done." Then the worst call of all, Mike Fleming of *Variety*, the best trade reporter in the business. Now I'm really screwed, I think. Because somehow, I reason, I can clean this up with Bob, but only if no one knows about his meeting. If it's reported, it could unravel Jodie. Two actors gone, no movie. Heart pounding, softly: "Hi, Mike, what's up?" His even tone: "I hear Wolfgang's flying to Sundance, trying to talk Redford into doing *Outbreak.*" "Don't be absurd, Mike. You know Redford is committed to Fox. Just a rumor. I'll check it out and call you when I get in." Then I down my Starbucks and fly to the office. Relaxed. Another Monday at work.

Bosnian Muslims were under genocidal siege, Hutus were slaughtering Tutsis, the prospect of national health care was falling to pieces while O. J. ran, and I wish I could tell you that I was aware of any of it. But this kind of pseudodrama shrinks perspective, rendering us (or at least me) myopic to the rest of the world. All news becomes the trades' industry news, and you are it. The race to make the movie — and the coverage of the race — had revealed in me an almost Joan of Arc–type complex. I felt like I had to win for the good of mankind. (Or at least for the good of my team, which, by this point, I had mistaken for mankind.) I had to win. I thought of what Sumner Redstone had said in the wake of finally winning his publicly waged, prolonged battle with supermogul Barry Diller over the purchase of Paramount Studios. "The prospect of losing was simply incompatible with living the rest of my life." These battles fought with blinding passion often dim in the light of day when the damages are assessed. But let's face it: I'd rather have a Pyrrhic victory than none at all. But finally, I thought, I had to face the prospect of losing. Hating it, I realized that I had to come to terms with the possibility.

Then I remembered the lesson offered by Barry Diller in the wake of losing the same battle against Redstone for Paramount. For Barry the stakes must have been as personal. He had run Paramount a decade prior and had been ousted in a coup d'état planned by his arch nemesis, Paramount CEO Marty Davis, who was supporting Redstone's bid. The stock market was watching; all of Hollywood was watching. And what did Barry Diller say to the rapt audience when his much-rooted-for bid was finally defeated? "They won. We lost. Next." He was soon trying to merge his QVC with CBS in his never-ending pursuit of his own network. A player is a player is a player. This is where all Zen wisdom in Hollywood begins and ends. And I had learned it, I realized, by watching the masters.

This is the amazing thing about "Next:" The bath that inspired the preceding ruminations took place on a Sunday. Six weeks later, on a Monday morning, the movie pulled back together and in the weeks that followed returned to the same brink of destruction and rehabilitation no less than four more times. After Jodie left we went to Meryl Streep. Her agents thought we had a great shot, but then came *The Bridges of Madison County*. She chose Clint. Redford finally dropped out, and we died. No actors, *Outbreak* shooting. (They shot second-unit monkey footage for weeks on end, as they were raced into production without a script too. But cameras were rolling.) The race had started without us.

Yet I am alive.

The pressure can crush you or turn you into the diamond version of yourself: hard and brilliant. Finding the former alternative unacceptable, I've tried to teach myself the rules of attaining the latter. It has been sink or swim. From the beginning, I instinctively understood that there were operating principles behind all the ad hoc strategies, manipulations, and potential sandbags. *They were like secret rules.* Every business has them. I had to find out who would take aim at me and when and why. At least if I knew what people were up to, I could function: Forewarned is forearmed. I started writing about what I saw as a form of therapy and investigation. The results, after fifteen long years, are these principles, my personal techniques for surviving the process of trying to get what you want when those around you are trying to get what they want instead.

The course of making movies is strikingly instructive about all forms of collaborative work. It is a petri dish that grows through its high stakes and public adulation every imaginable type of cell, both healthy and malignant. Ego problems are endemic in every walk of life, but in the movie business egomaniacs are megalomaniacs. Greed is a universal factor. In Hollywood it's the whole factor, a way of life. Every business is hard to break in to. In Hollywood there's a Darwinian hazing ritual. Competition is the impulse of capitalism; in the movie business it's the impulse to homicide.

Hollywood looks glamorous because it is populated with the faces that play out our fantasies on screen. But never forget that those faces have been through four hours of hair and makeup. When they wake up in the morning they're full of pimples and dread, just like you and me. In most fields of endeavor there are no easy jobs; there are only graceful ways of performing difficult ones.

My goal has been to learn how to get movies made without losing sight of the reasons I began. I have had to learn to recognize the insidious nature of the beast without becoming one.

FORESHADOWING

I had no idea I'd ever end up in the movie business. From a Hollywood perspective this sounds absurd; it is assumed that everyone wants to be in the movie business, ipso facto, and anyone who denies it is either lying or has tried it and failed. But the truth is that originally I was in love with the newspaper business and in love with journalism and in love with the *New York Times*, which is where I was in 1978 when all this began.

I had a lot of false starts before I was happy at work. I was a frustrated graduate student in philosophy at Columbia; I had a brief, failed stint trying to be a classical music disc jockey; and I was a copywriter for rock and roll artists I didn't like. I was always driven, but I had no idea where I was going. When I hooked up with David Obst, my life changed. David was at the center of a whirlwind of optimism; everything was possible. He was the literary agent of Bernstein and Woodward, John Dean, and a host of writers and reporters across the country. He was Johnny Appleseed, tossing out book contracts to young and talented journalists, who were thrilled to pursue their dreams. He and Jann Wenner allowed me to try my hand at putting together a book called *The Sixties* for Rolling Stone Press. By the time I had finished transcribing hundreds of interviews and condensing them into punchy little pieces, I had become an editor. I had developed a skill; I was ready for a job. David encouraged the *New York Times Magazine*'s new editor, Ed Klein, to meet with me.

From the moment I began working at the *New York Times Magazine*, I was in hog heaven. My excitement inured me to the back stabbing of the news floor, a lot of which was directed at my good fortune, as I was a young woman of twenty-four, married to a successful literary agent (read: not dependent on my paycheck), with entrée to the old gray lady, the *New York Times*.

Executive editor Abe Rosenthal became my mentor by admonishing me during our first interview not to "button up my vest." I seemed somewhat irrepressible, and he didn't want the august *New York Times* to stultify my enthusiasm. I had just brazenly characterized the magazine as a "beached whale," which made him smile broadly. "Have fun," he told me. Because I didn't know enough not to, I took his advice. I had a wonderful run as an editor of the *New York Times Magazine*. Fresh from having edited a book on the sixties for *Rolling Stone* magazine, I was the *Times*'s "man" on the counterculture beat. I was lucky; I had access to great writers through my literary agent husband and so I soared. I found good stories, I assigned pieces — even from the maternity suite when I was giving birth to my son — and I edited in my dreams.

My idyllic life didn't last long. I was furious to learn on my son's three-month birthday that my husband had made plans for the family to move to Hollywood. He had been making deals on the West Coast for a few years and had grown up in L.A., and he had come to believe that his future was in the movie business. I had never taken the possibility of living in L.A. seriously. I harbored no Hollywood fantasies, although it was one of my beats at the paper and I knew (at least peripherally) a lot of powerful people in the movie business.

I had always enjoyed my time in Los Angeles. Who wouldn't as a visiting *New York Times* editor and wife of a hot literary agent? It is always best to meet Hollywood people when they want something from you, as opposed to the other, more familiar way around, and so I found Hollywood glamorous in a kind of madcap, remote, impersonal way. We were wined and dined, treated like exotic out-of-town dignitaries. We were invited to the Hefner mansion and to Bob Evans's home to join him for dinner and shots of Stolichnaya. My sense of Los Angeles was very New York provincial, as in "all those people are crazy out there" (which they are), and stupid (which they're not), and immoral (it's more interesting than that). It seemed like a brave new world, but still not one that I could imagine as mine.

But I had to get over my ideas about Hollywood and my nostalgia for the gray lady. Get over my smug dependence on the prestige of my company logo. Get over my desire to be national news editor. Get over the feeling of contentment I had finally earned in learning that I was actually good at something. I seemed to have no choice. The ship was sailing. I had to find a house, a nanny, get a job, and move.

Now I was facing the job part. I couldn't join the L.A. bureau of the *New York Times,* because I had an infant and would be useless covering fires, earthquakes, and riots. The thought of any other newspaper depressed me. The movie business beckoned in a kind of "when in Rome" way, but the actual prospect filled me with dread.

"Join Casablanca! It's a candy store!" enthused Peter Guber, its then chairman. Casablanca was the unlikely name of the multimedia film and record company he had recently formed by merging his production company with Neil Bogart's successful record company, then at the forefront of disco. I had met Guber while at the *Times;* he and his wife were among the most interesting of our L.A. friends, young and hip, wildly successful and ambitious. Peter is a natural teacher, a brilliant business theorist, and as such had been a helpful source for me at the *Times,* patiently explaining the ins and outs of the changing movie business. When he heard that David was planning to move, he offered me a job.

Across a table from me at my house on Sixty-fourth Street sat my future boss, his knee bouncing to an inaudible rhythm track, as my

New York life crumbled around me. This man is wearing a ponytail, I thought. (I tried to picture Abe in a ponytail. No go.) Peter was frenetic. So am I. (Later we made quite a team: clamorous, exhausting. We overwhelmed the opposition.)

"But I don't know anything about making movies," I admitted sheepishly. Peter looked at me as though I were raising the dumbest of trivialities. He talked to me at these times very patiently, as though I were a bright foreign exchange student. He explained that my concern was not relevant, that my experience with writers was all I needed. "A producer is as good as the script in his mouth," he said. I suspected that what he meant was we're only as good as the writers we know. (This has become a credo for me.)

Peter was extremely nice, in fact he loathed conflict, but he understood the adversarial nature of everything when it came to business. He was fond of saying things like "This is show *business,* not show *friend.*" I stared at the multicolored logo that ran down half the page of the Casablanca stationery on which he was outlining my options. I'll have to design new stationery, I thought.

"If you want to do books, do books. If you want to do magazines, do magazines," he said. What he actually meant still eludes me, but I've come to learn that this is called "blowing smoke up your skirt" — pretending he's on your agenda in order to get you on his. The truth was that he had no intention of indulging my passion for magazines. He wanted me to be in development, that is, buying and developing scripts, picking the movie ideas, picking the writers. On the face of it, it seemed similar, or at least a distant cousin to the work I loved at the magazine, that of selecting and assigning story ideas to writers. So I accepted the offer of a job I didn't fully understand.

Unbeknownst to me, the era had just dawned in Hollywood when there was one "girl" at every meeting to read scripts, write notes, and dispense mineral water. The people doing this job, the first nonclerical one widely open to women, have come to be known as "d" girls, short for development girls. And this is what I became: Peter Guber's "d" girl at story meetings, the sessions in which we worked with the writers, fashioning the stories, structuring the scripts-to-be.

My point of view and skills, such as they were, were now in service to Peter Guber. He was going to teach me the ropes. Peter was
a "whiz kid." When he was twenty-five he became the youngest
person ever to be head of production of a studio. Peter was famous
for his ability to dazzle; he dazzles right off the top of his head,
spinning impressive story notes and corporate plans to an ever astonished audience. His credits include *Batman* and *Rain Man* and
a number of other movies with *man* at the end. But before he'd ac-
cumulated all these credits, he dazzled with charts and facts. He understood how the business was changing — he was the first person
I ever heard use the word *synergy*. Long before Bill Gates, Peter understood that information was power and he had the most. He used
to say that "whoever has the most information wins," and humbled
every grown-up around him with the spectacular display of what he
knew. At the beginning of his career he literally carried the largeness
of his knowledge around with him. (Physically, on a big board. Seriously.) He was P. T. Barnum, young Hollywood style. At pitch
meetings, which we attended together, Peter was a moving target,
never sitting still. He'd assemble an impressive audiovisual package
to accompany his presentation. "You have to spend money to make
money," he used to say, though he *never* spent his own. (An important Guber lesson: Never pay for *anything* yourself. How does this
work? You get others to pay for you. Lessons 1, 2, and 3.) He made
sure the buyers knew there were many other buyers clamoring for
the project and therefore they were privileged to be there. It was in
these early days, while studying Guber's pitch meetings, that I
honed my pitching skills.

There I was, bound (you could say dragged kicking and screaming) for the brave new world of Hollywood. Soon I was ensconced
in the former office of Donna Summer's manager, working at a
desk covered in organza lace, staring at leopard-skin walls, occasionally being called into Peter's office to dispense exotic bottled
water for three times the salary I was making as an editor of the
New York Times Magazine.

Now I was a "d" girl for Peter Guber. Director of Creative Affairs. Peter had given me the option of making up my title, a concept so alien to a *New York Times* veteran it embarrassed me. I

picked this curious combination of words as my title because it seemed the least fraudulent (and most amusing). If this option is given to you, skip the humility and pick Vice President, the sine qua non of titles.

Immediately after my move west I noticed a precipitous decline in my popularity with my former Los Angeles friends. I was no longer the *New York Times* editor. A famous woman agent with whom I had dined regularly in New York said exactly that to me when I called her for lunch during my first week of work. "Why should I talk to you, Lynda, when I can get Peter Guber on the phone?"

This was a big lesson for me. In retrospect (I hate retrospect) it taught me the realities of the suddenly transformed playing field. As an editor at the *New York Times Magazine,* I was significantly different from who I had become as "d" girl for Peter Guber — that is, significantly less exciting to everyone in Hollywood. Before I left the *Times,* while working on an article about women in Hollywood, I had become impressed with one woman, then a studio VP, now a prominent producer. When I came to town I called her. My reception (or lack thereof) made it clear to me that my call was presumptuous. I hadn't yet earned the value of her friendship in the currency of Hollywood. I'd had value as a *New York Times* editor, but now I could presume to trade nothing. It was apparently silly that I, a lowly "d" girl in town (she could see right through my seemingly august title), would think I could be friends with her.

The other thing I noticed early on was how differently people behaved toward one another here than they did in New York. It was as if they didn't care if they ever worked together again. The lack of a common ethic scared and disturbed me, coming as I did from the *Times,* which suffers from a notorious sanctimony about these things. People seemed to lie to each other as a matter of course. No big thing. "Hello, he lied" was a joke I heard about someone I knew during my first month at work. Here I had no one to look up to, nowhere to go for counsel, no safe haven, no turning back. But I couldn't bury my head in the sand — I don't like the quiet. Or the sidelines. So I had to learn to navigate the mainstream, where many are willing to lie, cheat, and steal for any opportunity.

In the early days I was in a panic most of the time. I had no idea what my job was and there was no job description. No manual, no models, no mentors, no *Premiere* magazine, no one to turn to for advice. I remember going to a shrink in despair over my work.

"What exactly is expected of you?" he asked me.

I had no idea. I sat glumly, drowning in regret at having left my dream life in New York.

"Well, what do you do during the day?" he asked.

"I talk on the phone," I answered.

I left his office realizing I would have to make up my job out of whole cloth.

Life had become a series of tightrope walks over utterly unfamiliar terrain. The stakes seemed enormously high, and I didn't understand the rules or the players. It was in my first week of work that I experienced firsthand Barry Diller's adage, "Next." It has become my most critical survival skill.

PRECIPITATING INCIDENT

On the last day of my first week at Casablanca, I found a manuscript on my desk from my New York counterpart, who retrieved manuscripts from unofficial sources for a living. The agent selling the book was the notorious and venerable Jeff Berg, the then president, now chairman, of the International Creative Management (ICM) agency and certainly one of the most formidable advocates and adversaries in the motion picture business. To this day, when Jeff Berg calls it hits me like a nicotine alert, and I reach for a cigarette before I pick up the receiver. So on my first week of work, to be called by Jeff Berg and taken out of a meeting for an "emergency" was very dramatic. Berg began, "I demand that you tell me who slipped you this manuscript!"

I froze, not knowing how to reply. But I had my training as a journalist: Never give up your source. From some previously unknown depth in my soul (which I hoped later to find again in moments of extreme stress) came my response: "Well, Jeff, I can't tell you who gave me that manuscript. You know that!"

He said, "If you don't tell me who gave you that manuscript you will never get another manuscript from ICM as long as you work in this business!"

This was a substantial threat.

"Furthermore," he added, "I'm calling Peter Guber."

I responded (from the same mysterious depths I'd suddenly accessed), "Jeff, does that mean if I *do* tell you who gave me this manuscript, you'll give me *all* of ICM's new books?"

I don't know whose feisty spirit spoke through me at that particular moment; sometimes I think it was that of Ida Lupino (whose house I'd bought in Los Feliz), the brave and remarkable pioneer director, actor, and producer who championed the cause of women on and off screen. Much to my astonishment, my response stunned Jeff also, and he hung up. I sat there decompressing. Wrong? Right? As it turned out, I *had* done the right thing, though I had no idea at the time. The clue I might have read had I known what I was doing was that he was off the phone in an instant, on to his next crisis.

I had had the last word. But who knew? I was just surviving the moment.

Then I was seized by panic again. I ran to see my boss because I thought Jeff Berg was about to get me fired. Peter was sitting at his massive desk as usual, Midas-like, reviewing his list of projects — his golden inventory. I blurted out, "Peter, I need to speak with you. I need to speak with you. It's an emergency. It's an emergency."

Finally he said, "What is it, Lynda?" And he looked up, giving me his fleeting but full attention.

Speak quickly, I thought, here's your moment. It's your dime. Phrase it well. Don't be emotional. Spit it out; try to explain and don't trip on your words. "Peter, I've just had a very difficult confrontation with Jeff Berg, who's threatened to get me fired because I wouldn't give him the name of the person who slipped us a manuscript. I'm sorry, I didn't know what else to do." I squinted my eyes, ready for a barrage of anger.

"So what's the book?" he asked.

"What book?" I said, opening my eyes again.

"The book Jeff called you about."

I knew the answer to that one. *"Little Gloria, Happy at Last."*

"Is it any good?"

"I don't know; I haven't read it yet," I told him.

Peter actually stopped what he was doing. "What do you mean you haven't read it yet?"

"Peter," I said, choking. "You don't understand. Jeff Berg may try to get me fired."

"So what? You stepped in dog doo. Clean it up."

"So you won't fire me?" I asked him, incredulous.

Peter gazed at me with a mixture of sympathy and exasperation, as if he were indulging a hopeless remedial student. "Read the book. Tell me if we want to buy it. NEXT."

I'd survived. It wasn't about Jeff Berg or slipped manuscripts. Peter had taught me in his Zen-like fashion to think about the doughnut (the potential movie) and not the hole (the posturing personality junk). He had taught me not to be distracted by the skirmish — and miss the battle. What if a bidding war had been going on while I was worrying about my career? I would have gotten into much more trouble for missing the auction than for having done my job. Check. I got it.

Next. No single movie or event makes or breaks your career. Everything can be undone, including success.

TAKING IT AS A GROUP

"This script sucks. Nothing personal."

— *United Talent Agency agent*

Hollywood has an idiosyncratic theory of language. Nora Ephron, our director on *Sleepless in Seattle,* once told me that someone said to her about a particular rejection, "Don't take this personally."

She answered incredulously, "How am I supposed to take it? As a group?"

Yes, that is the answer, as it turns out. You have to take it as a group. This sounds odd, but you take it as a group by saying "Next." Personal humiliation and career-dashing confrontations are endemic, impersonal, and constant. This is the flip side of ambition: debilitating exhaustion and the constant threat of defeat. Therefore every crisis can't be taken too seriously or you won't survive.

Making movies, like all high-stakes careers, resembles sumo wrestling. Five-hundred-pound gorillas try to push you out of the box, and you have to hold your ground. You must not let incident transform into drama. Even when your feelings are hurt; in fact, particularly when they are hurt. Hang tough. Don't budge. The only way they know you're a player is when you respond to disaster by behaving as though nothing devastating has happened. Denial also works. It's a terrific advantage if you actually feel nothing, as opposed to having to anesthetize. This is clearly why the best full-time deniers of all — sociopaths — do so very well in Hollywood.

It is just as important to move on in the wake of stunning success as in the wake of disaster. You must keep on moving your guy around the board. Getting stuck on Payday or Opportunity Knocks may look good to the occasional passerby, but what does he know? It is critical in the wake of a hit that you move past talking about it and pick up the next day's business. Nothing is more pathetic than a filmmaker holding forth about some hit from seasons ago, unless he's Billy Wilder. Then it's charming. But the borderline is a thin one between statesman and dinosaur. If you try and ride for too long on a good opening weekend, you run the risk of acting like a dinosaur — stuck, defined by last week's grosses. Clinging to something that everyone else has let go of. The pace of change is often rude, which the *Sleepless in Seattle* team experienced firsthand on the weekend that *Sleepless* had its spectacular opening.

I had gone to bed that night with the number $4 million dancing like a sugarplum fairy in my head. This is what TriStar had estimated (guessed) our business would be on its first night of a national release, based on prerelease testing and awareness polls conducted by the distribution division. Statistically, the first night is used for modeling the weekend, and the weekend is used to predict the entire domestic box-office life of the picture. (It goes like this: If the picture does $3 million on Friday, it ought to do $5 to $6 on Saturday and someplace between $4 and $6 on Sunday. If Saturday is not appreciably higher than Friday, or Sunday collapses, there is bad word of mouth and the picture will die. If the numbers reach the high end of the model and build, there is good word of mouth and the picture will have "legs.")

Distribution executives can predict exactly the amount of business a film will do after the first weekend. On your first and second movie you don't believe their predictions. You know your movie will defy convention. You hope against hope. You tell them they're wrong. You fight and rail against this hideous piece of determinism, but it's pointless. The accuracy is unerring.

Distribution execs at TriStar were predicting the following formula for *Sleepless:* If we made $4 million Friday, we could expect $6 million on Saturday night and something in the middle, like $5 million, on Sunday. Fifteen million cumulatively for the weekend. It was amazing, huge, and the highest projection that the studio or any of us was willing to utter out loud.

At seven o'clock Saturday morning the president of production at TriStar called with the astonishing number — $5.4. This earthquakelike number had a meaning of epic proportions. We were a gigantic hit. A smash. The tether between a person and the world is pretty tenuous on these mornings. There is a danger at these moments of slipping out of control altogether. Just rocketing out of the zone. I've seen it; it's not pretty.

Five point four million was one point four more than we — the whole *Sleepless* team — had dared to dream. This portended blockbuster status: $17 million! It turned out to be the largest opening for a romantic comedy in history, bigger than *Pretty Woman* or *A League of Their Own*, the movies used as the criteria to predict our potential grosses as they had the same target audience. (As a result the distributors of *While You Were Sleeping*, which was released three years later, ended up using our grosses to predict theirs.)

The week *Sleepless* opened was one of the best weeks I've ever spent at work. It was "huge," as we say. A hit movie is the brass ring. Everyone's telling me it must be the best week of work of my life almost made it true. I got lots of flowers, faxes, and telegrams from people letting me know they were cheering for me, some of whom I barely knew. Yet I didn't sleep very well. I discovered a tiny layer of anxiety unsettling the feelings of celebration. It's so fleeting, that success, you feel a tendency to cling. It's the terror of knowing that although you own Monday, you may not own the whole week even through Tuesday, let alone Friday.

Which is what happened. Flying high on Monday after a day in a town where the cleaners knew my grosses, as did all the better maître d's, I figured I'd make it to Friday before abdicating the joy. But no. By Tuesday, somewhere in my bones I knew that this delicious feeling couldn't last. Maybe it was the enormous marketing campaign for *The Firm*. But till Friday? Couldn't we hold it till Friday?

Just. We owned the week until Friday, when *The Firm* opened. By nightfall, it was Sydney Pollack's weekend. Regardless of the fact that our movie kept playing and playing (like the Energizer bunny) for the whole remarkable summer, I had to move on to new business. *Sleepless* has been thus far the biggest hit I've worked on. It grossed upward of $120 million domestically and close to $100 million foreign. The sound-track went triple platinum, and romantic comedies were back in vogue. It was great, but if I had believed that the success of *Sleepless* would last forever, I would have taken a mighty tumble. Time to move on.

I was lucky. *Sleepless* was not my first movie, and I had suffered both bad and good opening weekends before. As with failure, I tried not to take the movie's success at all personally because too many other people were also responsible. So the heady aftermath of its opening was not dizzying to me because I knew it wasn't about me. If success happens early, right out of the gate, it's a mixed blessing. For a newcomer, for whom the tendency to gloat and float is natural, this exposure without a thick skin, without alliances and without commensurate power, is particularly dangerous. It feels almost due you, preordained, automatic, and as such is addictive. The radiation at these heights is toxic, both from your new hotshot neighbors in the higher firmament and from jealous peers below. The handling of this moment is critical.

SOME RULES ABOUT SUCCESS I JUST MADE UP

1. Don't float too high. Humility, faux or otherwise, is great protection.
2. Keep some sandbags stabilizing the balloon. Don't lose your bearings, leave your spouse or lover, fire your accountant, spend your financial underpinnings, or dump early allies.
3. Let yourself get off the ground. A contradiction to number 2, but grace is made of this. Don't be scared and you can soar.
4. Be wary. Look around you for potential ego collisions and avoid them. They will exhaust you through proliferation. (The friend of your enemy is now your enemy.) This falls under the voluminous "life is too short" category. Fights distract, they distort one's perception of the field, they poison everything they come in contact with, and eat up crucial time and energy. Worse yet, they earn no income. Transcend. *Next.*

I consider any big boosts in the form of hits as temporary. So are big plunges. Long-term boosts are subtler. I find that if I start thinking that the lift that comes from my hard efforts and a stroke of luck, like a hit or a new job, is permanent, I am likely to lose my edge. As soon as I feel entitled the rug is pulled out from under me, if for no other reason than overconfidence. Perspective helps me remember the temporal nature of any good fortune. It's up to me to sustain it, with hard work, hungry as ever. While I'm up things run smoother and people are that much easier to convince. Then, as in football, I try to capitalize on a turnover, maintain momentum. But we can always fumble. When we fall there are those people who are thrilled we are back in the muck and mire with them. So be it. Next.

Late at night this "Next" stuff worries me a great deal. I miss old friends I've given up, regret the passing of alliances I couldn't sustain: the writers I struggled with who couldn't go all the way and were replaced, the friends who became competitors and then much worse than that. I fear for the loss of the qualities a person needs to stay in tune with the human race — empathy, and worse, more expendable, sympathy. Does it all get diffused into abstract political causes? Does the impulse to loving-kindness in Hollywood become teaching a UCLA extension course? Stints at homeless shelters over the holidays? I know a studio executive who routinely lies, then returns home for weekend religious services. He lets you know too. He may have to excuse himself early from lying to you so he can go home and pray.

Chapter 2

NEVER GO TO A MEETING WITHOUT A STRATEGY

"Prevent trouble before it arises.
Put things in order before they exist."

— *Tao Te Ching*

"What were you thinking?"

— *my shrink*

I LEARNED what meetings were all about when Peter Guber, in his inimitable mentor mode of giving me enough rope to hang myself, encouraged me to "get into television." I was armed only with the number of the William Morris agency (our company's television agents) and our inventory of underwater projects, most of which were spin-offs from *The Deep*, the 1970-something actioner starring Jacqueline Bisset and her bikini. This was Peter Guber's first movie as producer, a project he had taken with him from Columbia that was dear to his heart. I believe he could have merchandised it into perpetuity. The list of potential TV spin-offs included: *The Making of* The Deep, *The Making of the Documentary on* The Deep, and a TV series that featured "the shark from *The Deep*," starring the science consultant from *The Deep*. (You see, we did market this property forever.)

What I didn't realize was how little access Casablanca's television agents actually had to Peter Guber himself. Each agent was dying, literally, it seemed, to speak with him. Every phone call I made to generate business I got the same response, "I need to talk to Peter." So I delivered him. I actually got him to attend a meeting in a large conference room in which ten William Morris agents got to jump down his throat and ask him every question they had ever dreamed of.

"Why didn't you return my phone call?" one barked.

"Are you replacing Bill Tenant?" barked another. My ears pricked up. Bill Tenant was my direct, nutty boss. Peter ducked the question.

"Did you like the script I sent you yesterday?" insisted a third.

In football they call it "piling on." The agents were panting, all seizing the rare moment of access to the guy who actually had the power to say yes. Peter slipped like Houdini out of the building. I remember standing on El Camino minutes after the near gang bang with Peter practically hyperventilating.

"What the hell was that all about?" he asked me.

"They all wanted to meet with you," I answered.

"And what did you want?"

"Me?"

"Us. What did we want? What were we trying to accomplish?"

I looked at him blankly. I guess I should have brought a list of our projects they could have packaged their actors with, huh? He spoke to me with less than patient exasperation. "Lynda. Get it. Never go to a meeting without a strategy."

I was embarrassed at how dumb I had been, how unprepared. My job was to be Peter Guber's first line of defense, and as a first lieutenant I had failed. I got it. If I didn't know what we wanted to accomplish, we couldn't accomplish anything. If we weren't there to score, we couldn't win. It had been their meeting, not ours. I never forgot this lesson. It goes like this: You are a salesman, so bring your sample case. A meeting is either won or lost, so you need a strategy. A strategy implements a plan or an agenda.

Strategies are devised by intersecting your agenda with that of the other person at the meeting (i.e., "Let's talk about you. What can you help me with on my agenda?"). If you have no strategy and just attend a meeting blindly (lunch is your most socially demanding meeting of the day as you have an hour and a half to cultivate a relationship), you lose your edge because you can count on the fact that your lunch date has a strategy.

Every chance encounter is a meeting, and each meeting is part of a larger series of actions that, when taken together, accumulate into an overall agenda. Agendas can shift, change, and adapt, particularly with a new job. But one must always have one. Each move either furthers or obstructs an agenda. Think of it as a board game.

Sometimes meetings, because they are often held in such delightful places (e.g., the bar at the Four Seasons), can be mistaken for high teas at which people forget what they're doing and start thinking they're merely having drinks with a couple of well-dressed people with great haircuts. But the truth is that each of these well-manicured charmers is, in fact, ruthlessly pursuing his or her agenda. If he is a studio executive, he wants big summer pictures. A producer wants his script to be that summer hit. The most wide-ranging fishing expedition of a meeting has its agenda, even if it's only information gathering, friendship building, or propagandizing.

At lunch with an agent, a producer's strategy would be to win her over and make her aware of his projects. Or simply to go fishing for new hot properties. This is called "tracking," and people are paid to do it. When he has her rapt attention, it's critical that he doesn't bore her to death.

The following is a sample lunch conversation between a producer and a reluctant literary agent.

Producer: So how was your New Year's? . . . Aspen?[1]

Agent: Hawaii. I was sick the whole time.[2]

Producer: How hideous! Did you get a lot of reading done?[3]

Agent: Had to. When I finally felt better, it was pouring.

Producer: What you need is a great big auction over your new favorite script.

Agent: I did read a really terrific new writer over vacation.[4]

Producer: You know how I love to work with new writers! Why don't you slip it to me early[5] and I'll make your first bid?[6]

---

1. It's never boring if he talks about her.
2. Shut down — or an opening?
3. Lead the dance.
4. BINGO!
5. A descendant of "sock it to me," slipping a spec is giving a time advantage to one buyer with plausible denial to the rest of the buyers. As in, "I have no idea how she got it!" A gift.
6. He can't really guarantee this but why should he? He hasn't read it!

Agent: Great idea!

The producer wins. If the script is any good.

Now let's look at a sample conversation between a producer and a preening studio exec over Chinese chicken salad.

Producer: Congratulations on this weekend! Twelve million! You guys creamed 'em.[7]

Exec: It was my picture, you know.[8]

Producer: Of course. Everyone knows.[9] Your stock must be pretty high this morning.[10]

Exec: I guess so.[11] I'd sure love to bring in a big spec this week.

Producer: You could sell anything this week!

Exec: You think so?[12]

Producer: I'm getting a terrific script slipped[13] that no one has seen. Spielberg is tracking it, but I think I have it exclusively.[14]

Exec: I heard about it! I definitely want it.[15] When can I get my hands on it?

Producer: Friday. It's yours.[16] In fact, Darren[17] has been asking around about it, but I'd rather give it to you. You're my main man.[18]

Exec: And you're mine. Even though you're a chick!

The producer wins again. If the script is any good.

RED LIGHT/GREEN LIGHT: THE BOARD GAME

Getting a movie made is like playing a board game. Your location on the board, who's ahead of you and who's behind you, determines your strategy. Of course, you must know where you're going.

---

7. Locker-room talk.
8. This is true whether it is or not.
9. Flattery will get her everywhere.
10. Hoist them on their own petards.
11. Fake humility. A new standard.
12. This is her setup. She goes in for the kill. Now.
13. A verb, to slip. See 5.
14. Spielberg tracks everything, so this lie is borderline safe.
15. He's salivating now, despite the chicken salad.
16. After she gets *her* hands on it.
17. His chief competitor.
18. Bonding, flirting, joking — depending on gender relations.

You mustn't just follow. The purpose is to win — that is, to get a green light to get your movie made. To do this, your goal is to move your piece around the board until you're home free. The board consists of the following boxes: constant no's, soft yesses, firm maybes, yes for an answer, yessed to death, and development hell.

The goal is not to win popularity, not to see your name in the trades, not to get the best table at Morton's. These perks are trading cards in the game and as such are concomitants to success, but they are not the goals of the game. They are the equipment with which to play the game. Many people forget this and as a result they miss their turn. A wildly popular producer with forty dinner engagements and no green light might as well release *himself* in twelve hundred theaters. With no product at all and no script in your hand when opportunity knocks, it doesn't matter how good your seat is at the table.

But first you have to get to "the table." The table, the mythical entrance point to the board game that provides access for a producer to set up an idea, is purposely elusive. No one who has earned a seat wants to give up his place. He must be elbowed out or must choose to share his spot through alliance or mutual agenda. Getting to the table is a survivalist trek of natural selection that hones out those too weak to function once they've arrived. The question people always ask: How to begin? This has been made preternaturally difficult. It's a hazing thing. It's been like this for generations and it is pervasive in all aspects of showbiz.

The most famous entrance paradox in the world of jobs is the policy of Actors Equity, the stage actors' union. That is, you can't become a member without working in a show and you can't get a job in a show without being a member. Dealing with this kind of paradox is part of the freshman ritual, because when you complain about this, people on the inside smile. It sounds like an ironclad policy and from the outside it is, but from the inside it's who you know. That's why the easiest way to the table is through nepotism — you can literally share your father's or mother's, your brother's or sister's, or, in a recent update, your husband's or wife's seat. The next best thing to being there is being close personal friends with someone whose father/mother is at the table, ad infinitum, ad nauseam.

Think of it in terms of six degrees of separation. Everyone is six people away from someone at the table. Find the beginning of the chain of arms, the people in your life who are closer to the table than you are. They are your first allies. Find something they want. People at the table often grab hands with those farther out who have something to offer: a script, the rights to something interesting, an idea. Before you hand off to the nearest well-connected arm, however, find an entertainment lawyer to protect you. You must be legally attached to the underlying rights to any material you trade up with so that it isn't grabbed out of your hands altogether.

Once you have secured a place at the table, you must do a lot of favors for immediate and not-so-immediate family members. Although this is sometimes a tedious responsibility, it's well worth your efforts, because occasionally you hit pay dirt (and also, at least in my family, it's the modern day version of filial piety). The quintessential example of this in my life is when I did a favor for my favorite uncle, Carl.

"I need you to meet with the daughter of my biggest customer," he said, invoking the family perk. "She wants to be a producer [so what else is new?] and is dying to get your advice."

I knew the drill. "Tell her to call my assistant and say that she was referred by you." My assistant could take it from there.

On the appointed day, Karen Spiegel arrived, twenty-six, well put together in an upper–New York kind of way, nervous but graceful, totally prepared for the compulsory fifteen minutes. With her father's backing (this helps), Karen had optioned the rights to an unpublished novel called *Absolute Power* — a tale of despicable goings on in the back bedrooms of the White House. She had done her homework well and had prepared a synopsis of her project and well-designed promotional material so as not to blow her fifteen minutes at the table. Not a moment of her fifteen was wasted, and I was impressed. I offered her a job on the spot as my production assistant on *Contact*. But even better, Karen took that lead to find out from me how she could submit her manuscript to publishers. I was one-stop shopping. I appreciated the sincerity of her hustle and decided to help her out.

"Here are the names of three literary agents in New York," I offered. "You can use my name but make sure you tell them I haven't read the book." I had nothing to lose helping out my uncle's best customer, giving his daughter entrée to a literary agent without risking my credibility. There was no downside with a possible but unlikely upside. I asked for nothing in return.

Cut to: three months later. I arrive at work one day in the middle of *The Hot Zone* misery, and my then "d" boy, Eric, says, "Guess what's the biggest book in New York? Guess what sold this morning to Warner Books for two million dollars?" Dumbstruck, I knew the answer. It was Karen's *Absolute Power*. The movie auction had already begun. The Warners producer I was fighting on *Hot Zone* had received an unofficial (slipped) copy of the manuscript and was making a bid. I didn't even want it, but I wanted it. Karen Spiegel was on the phone.

"Did you hear? Can you believe it? It's all because of you. The movie rights are yours. Tell me how to handle it." This is how alliances are born, how you pay back your mentors, and she did it with no prompting. What a natural! I called the head of my studio, because although this book was not on my agenda, it might have been on his. As it turned out, my studio never made a bid, but you can bet Warner's *Outbreak* producer didn't get it either. It went to Castle Rock, Rob Reiner's company. When Karen Spiegel protected me, she had unknowingly created a strategy. This made her a factor in the auction and gave her leverage at the only moment she would control the property. Then she became executive producer with an excellent fee. This was brilliantly played to her own advantage, while her sole intention had been to work with allies.

Here's the biggest p.s. of all time: It was announced in January 1996 that Clint Eastwood would be starring in and directing *Absolute Power* from a script by William Goldman (*Butch Cassidy*, etc.). And coproducing with Mr. Eastwood is none other than Karen Spiegel. (Let's hear it for the novice who hung on for the ride!) Too bad it hadn't been on my agenda, or to my taste. Hindsight makes fools or geniuses of us all.

PITCH ETIQUETTE

Let's start from the beginning. A pitch is an idea. A development deal is a project. A script approaching the bull's-eye during packaging is a script (quaint, no?) and after the green light it's a show. In wide release it's a hit or a flop. If it's a flop, it's "Next."

Pitching is the red-light phase of the game. The purpose of this phase is to find a yes in the sea of no's all around you. There are, let's say, ten buyers. One of them has got to say yes. A writer should bring a producer to a pitch meeting for social savvy, political leverage, and simultaneous translation for the artistically challenged. A producer should always bring a writer unless she wants the studio to choose the writer for her. Some producers are irresistible to some studio executives. The writer should know this and not bring the wrong producer to the wrong studio. (It's like planning a dinner party.) Some producers are wonderful at relaxing executives, creating a casual, partylike atmosphere. Others are not.

I recently set up a pitch at Fox by bringing in the stars — Meg Ryan and Rosanna Arquette. They were coproducers on the idea and were acting as saleswomen as well as artists. Rosanna wanted to do a screenplay loosely based on her very romantic love affair with the rock star Peter Gabriel — romantic comedy as catharsis. Meg, one of her best friends, had helped her through the traumatic denouement and attendant nervous breakdownette, and by now the two had found the humor in the story. They wanted to produce it and star in it; Meg would play Rosanna and Rosanna would play her own best friend.

They wanted to partner with me and bring this cautionary tale about losing yourself in a love affair to the screen for all vulnerable women. They were here at the pitch meeting without "hair and makeup" — no one had wardrobed them — and they looked better for it. They are both so smart and engaging, what studio president could resist these two beauties laughing, bonding, and pitching their hearts out? We could have sold tickets to the pitch. My then studio president couldn't say no and he didn't. Pitch as party often works.

Some producers are taken seriously intellectually (whether or not they deserve to be), and it's important to know which ones they are in case the writers are pitching a drama, also known as a movie with a downbeat ending. Anyone can pitch a comedy, including a smart person, partly because rawness counts in comedy, partly because it's easier to cast (always say Jim Carrey). And you can successfully cast it out of television, i.e., Bill Murray, Eddie Murphy, Woody Harrelson, and recent examples *Saturday Night Live's* Chris Farley and Adam Sandler. Classically, producers "wind up" the pitch meeting, that is, prep the group for the right mood and intrigue them with the "area." The writers do the "pitch" — the actual telling of the story. Producers should try to navigate the meeting for the writers, save it from dangerous twists and deviations from their mutual intentions or from annihilating political blunders by jumping in when, for example, the writer is about to refer to the exec's biggest bombs. Producers cannot wrest control completely, though, as the real control is always with the buyer — on the other side of the table.

When I first came to town, I wrote the ontology of a pitch meeting in order to figure out what they really were and to provide some tips for novice screenwriters. Nothing has changed in the ensuing decade.

ONTOLOGY OF A PITCH MEETING

FADE IN

INT. FEMALE EXEC'S OFFICE — DAY

The office is lined with sports paraphernalia, reflecting the general gender confusion in Hollywood. An EXEC in Armani suit, fishnet stockings, and cowboy boots is glancing at the trades and talking on the phone to her shrink, lover, or boss.

EXEC (*to* GIDGET, her assistant and future "d" girl) Who's next?

GIDGET You can't cancel these guys. They're downstairs.

EXEC Bring in the troops.

ENTER TROOPS

Fleshing out the creative assemblage are two more EXECS: one JR., one JR. JR. The JR. EXEC has read half of the script sent by the agent as a writing sample for this pitch. The JR. JR. has read all of it. He says nothing.

EXEC Who read these guys' script? Can they write?

JR. EXEC They did *Hollywood High* for Lorimar, *Cheap Thrills* for Kings Road, and *Trust Me* for Guber/Peters.

EXEC I've never heard of any of those movies.

JR. EXEC That's because none of them has been made. But they just did a rewrite for Grazer and they're fast.

EXEC Good. That means they'll pitch fast. Bring 'em up.

CUT TO: *Your classic comedy team: two writers and a PRO-DUCER. The writers, PHIL and BILL, are dressed in 501 Levis, college or Lakers T-shirts, and well-worn sneakers. BILL sports a baseball cap. The PRODUCER is easy to pick out: He's dressed like a cross between Miami Beach and Miami Vice, and the resemblance doesn't end there.*

GIDGET Can I get you something to drink?

PHIL Perrier?

BILL Ramlosa?

PROD Pellegrino?

GIDGET distributes Evian water all around. Everyone looks pleased. The PRODUCER whips out an Emergen-C Pack, tears it open, and fizzles it into his glass.

PRODUCER Ever since I've been going to AA I've been hooked on this stuff.

The writers shift awkwardly in their seats, hoping the PRODUCER will get them through this crucial small-talk section of the pitch.

PRODUCER (*to* EXEC) So — how's your divorce?

EXEC It's fabulous. I got the Nautilus equipment, so I'm in good shape. And yours?

Now that they've touched on the intimate aspects of both their lives, the PRODUCER must execute the critical segue into the pitch.

PRODUCER I still have my wheels — and that's all I need in this town. In fact, that's how I got this idea. Here I am driving down PCH in my new Ferrari at two A.M.[1] — and it's riding high — all of a sudden, I realize the car is my date — I'm bummed because I can't bring her upstairs. It's then I realize my fantasy. A Ferrari that turns into a woman. Car by day, woman by night. I call it *Hard Drivin' Woman.* (*He looks at* EXEC.) That's why I brought it to you; it's right up your alley. It's a cross between *10* and *Splash,* with a touch of *My Mother the Car.*[2] I see two videos already.

Everyone is stunned. The EXEC reaches for an Evian and lights up a Camel.

EXEC Have you got the story worked out?

The writers respond to this moment of pressure by speaking simultaneously.

BILL Phil, why don't you start?

PHIL Bill, why don't you start?

BILL I don't really have this down yet. I mean, it's not engraved in stone.[3]

---

1. The windup: Generally there are two kinds. One is the first-person fake, a media-related, quasi-intimate anecdote, a version of which is here. The second is the so-called true story, the true-to-life incident that inspired the story. This is vital in television and actually useless in movies, but few buyers know this. Often they are impressed with the mere fact that some aspect of the notion has been verified by reportage . . . giving it the illusion of life or importance. Either way it is a very handy transition technique.

    Tips on the subtle aspects of the windup: The windup anecdote is a common and opportune place to name drop casually: parties, people, restaurants, vacation spots, or critical screenings. Naming famous people present when the idea you are about to pitch suddenly occurred to you is standard.

2. The peak of the windup, and the mark of a truly gifted pitcher, is the presentation of the high-concept "miniaturization" of the idea. It must be said succinctly — as in its seminal influence, the *TV Guide* log line. The tag line of the windup occurs when the producer (usually) combines the names of past solid hits to form a genetically engineered new movie idea. This is a neat trick and is preferable when only two movies are hybridized — the third here is too much.

3. Listed are some of the clichés habitually given as excuses for half-baked, shoddy thinking. The glibbest can "wing it" through unprepared story pitches, but this isn't necessarily a good sign for the eventual script. Being quick on your feet isn't the same as being good on the page.

PHIL *(interjects)* We're not married to it, but — we open with a dream sequence. . . .

PROD *(interjects)* This is the first video.

BILL In it we see Norman[4], a nerdy twenty-five-year-old unfulfilled dreamer, fantasizing a parade in which every woman he has ever desired becomes an exquisite car. We see that Norman has a long way to go to make his fantasies real. He's not popular with girls and he's a terrible driver too. He's planning to buy a Ferrari tomorrow to change his life.

JR. EXEC How can he afford the Ferrari?

BILL Inheritance.

PHIL Life savings.

PRODUCER Tax refunds?[5]

EXEC You can work out the back story later.

PHIL Then one day . . .

PROD Here's where we suspend disbelief. . . .

PHIL So then one day Norman figures out that no matter how wonderful his car is, it's no substitute for the love of a woman. That night Norman pulls into the garage, goes up to his bedroom, and there, parked on his bed, is a fully equipped, sleek, dynamic woman dressed in a custom-colored, candy-apple, metal-flake, Ferrari red negligee.[6]

EXEC How did it turn into a girl?

---

4. Introduce your character to humanize (read: cast) the pitch. The right age for your protagonist is critical. Here "nerdy" is selected because it is an easy route to "character change." Whatever condition you choose for your central character, it should contain within it the seeds of his evolution. This is your critical "character arc" — all characters improve their lot, unless they are the antagonists, in which case they get theirs in a big scene called the "payoff."
5. Wrong. Terrible error not to have anticipated this question and worked out a mutual answer at least on the ride over. The Jr.'s are clever and are listening carefully to score points on mechanical details.
6. Hyperbole is an excellent indicator of potential ad copy. Used sparingly, it can be effective on executives so they can imagine the poster.

BILL Fairy godmother.

PHIL Remote-control garage-door opener.

PROD Special effects?[7]

EXEC You can work out the device later.

PHIL Now Norman runs to the garage and the car is gone. He runs upstairs and realizes it's true. His fantasy car has become his fantasy woman.

PRODUCER This is our second-act crisis.[8]

EXEC What is the issue?

PRODUCER Does he go for the car, or does he go for the girl?

JR. EXEC Sounds like *Let's Make a Deal.*

EXEC So, what does he do?

PHIL He picks the car.

BILL He picks the car.

JR. EXEC What's his motivation?

BILL He has to get to work.

PHIL Lack of emotional maturity.

PRODUCER It's a coming-of-age story.

EXEC Coming-of-age stories are over.

PRODUCER *(sweating)* It's not a coming-of-age story exactly; what I mean is it's a Bigger-than-Life, Fish-out-of-Water Action-Adventure — you know, like *Beverly Hills Cop.*

EXEC Perfect.

---

7. Try to avoid internal disagreement on central points at all costs.
8. This notion of the second-act crisis has become common in pitch meetings since a certain popular story-structure class became the rave in Hollywood. Everyone knows about the three-act structure, borrowed from theater, which implies that our hero is in desperate shape — the farthest possible distance from his goals — at the second-act break.

PHIL So. Norman picks the car, but he isn't happy. It's not work-
    ing well. He tries diligently to fix it and fails. He takes it to the
    best Italian mechanic in L.A., who keeps it for months. Norman
    goes to the mechanic to retrieve her, but no go. The mechanic
    bawls him out: "What'samatta with you? A high-performance
    machine like this, you ever tune her? You gotta take a baby like
    this to the limit, you know, torque her three, maybe four times
    a week minimum, to keep her happy. She's happy now."[9]

JR. EXEC Is this a triangle?

BILL Yes.

PHIL No.

PRODUCER It's a beat, a subplot.[10]

BILL Then we cut to the chase scene.

PRODUCER (interjecting) This is a very realistic sequence, cut to a
    driving sound track. . . . ZZ Top is wild for this.

EXEC I get the general picture here; what kind of casting do you
    see?

PRODUCER Daryl Hannah and I have been looking for something
    to do together.[11]

---

9. Don't go into excruciating detail in telling the plot. Remember this is a condensation.
Think of it as the *Reader's Digest* condensed-novel version of a screenplay. These people have
short attention spans and they hear stories all day. Also, the people they turn around and sell
your story to have even shorter attention spans. Tell them the salient points, the series of
beats. Do tell about subplots if they involve hot or surefire, of-the-moment casting like Jim
Carrey, George Clooney, Alicia Silverstone, or Whitney Houston. It's common for some
pitchers to break into dialect when describing plot. This seems to replace character description. Fortunately, this is most frequent in comedy, and comedy writers do funny dialect, but
a funny meeting does not guarantee a funny script.
10. Beats: Epistemologically this is a curious notion. It has something to do with the rhythm
of the plot — those consecutive moments in the plot that create the structural underbelly of
the story. Beats are related to one another by both narrative and emotional causality. A subplot: a bunch of beats carried by actors other than your star.
11. Notes on casting: Imagine all of the roles in your story cast by big-box office stars.
People over forty-five do not count unless it is a "drama," and then only a few stars count:
Harrison Ford, Robert Redford, Sean Connery, Gene Hackman. Know which stars are basically unattainable and/or unavailable to save yourself from looking dopey. But under no circumstances ever allow a pitch to hinge on the casting of one particular person. This is the
easiest route to a pass. Also, know what actors your studio has standing deals with and what
ideas those stars are looking to develop. The studio needs to justify the astronomical fees paid
to keep these stars off the market and gobble material for their commitments like candy.

JR. EXEC I bet you have.

EXEC Daryl is unavailable.

PRODUCER Anyway, this is a director's picture. Ivan Reitman and I have been trading phone calls all week.

BILL And now we come to the emotional payoff.

Phone rings. GIDGET bops into the office with enthusiasm.

GIDGET I hate to interrupt, but Spielberg is on line two.

The EXEC bolts. The meeting comes to an abrupt standstill. There is an awkward silence as GIDGET distributes a second round of Evian to everyone. The EXEC returns.

EXEC Well, I guess we've wrapped it up. That was terrific, thank you. I know how busy you are; I'll call you first thing in the morning. . . . I think this is very fresh. Let me speak to my people and get back to you.

PHIL, BILL, and the PRODUCER leave. They do not know what to think. They share a shocked silence only broken in the parking lot, where they discuss the EXEC's ridiculous outfit — three-part Azzedine Alia special to showcase her pecs.

Back at the pitch table, the three EXECs push back their seats and exchange glances.

EXEC Who's next?

THE THREE STAGES OF PITCH

Pitch is transactional theater. The quality of its performance is an important factor in its outcome. Regardless of the nature of the story we pitch — historical drama, cartoon adventure, police procedural, inspirational coming of age, brainless comedy, classic remake — there is a customary structure to both its content and its performance. Each pitch has three stages.

1. THE PREP

Before the segue into the pitch, the producer has to prep the room. We do this by talking about the spouse, the boy/girlfriend or lack thereof, Gymboree, yoga, diets, the playoffs (if it's the right season; any playoff will do), or whether some mogul is going to Sony or MCA or Disney or anywhere at all. Gossip is currency in prepping the room. Charm rules.

2. THE WINDUP

The job of the windup is to warm up the room. No self-respecting producer should ever rely on the writer for personality and ease. (Notable exceptions are some comedy writers, who are like stand-up comedians. This brings to mind the perennial question: If the pitch is funny will the script necessarily be funny? Hard-learned answer: No.) First of all, the writer is likely to be the only person in the room more nervous than the producer. Second, his talent is often in inverse proportion to his ability to pitch — read: schmooze. Consider the almost axiomatic observation: Good writers pitch badly and bad writers pitch well. The exceptions — the good writers who pitch well — are a function of gifted personality. They're charming. They are often the most highly paid, more often future directors. A tip: Writers for whom solutions come too quickly are suspect. This is "producerthink." The writer should know that the solution to a story point is supposed to be harder than that.

3. THE CONCEPT

Then the wired producer must meet his optimal challenge, the mark of a truly gifted pitcher: He must present the concept whole — the miniaturization of the idea. It must be succinct. This is the famous high concept. Its seminal influence is the *TV Guide* log line. The most common (and banal) form of the high-concept idea is the hybrid: as in "*Pretty Woman* meets *Friday the Thirteenth*" (a great-looking whore is dismembered by a horrific, hockey mask–wearing creep). It requires virtually no imagination. By combining the names of past hits, one forms genetically engineered new movie ideas — sort of.

The appeal of these ideas is that they appear to reduce the risk level for the buyer. And they don't take deep concentration to grasp. No limb jumping here. Just by referencing these past hits, we share their patina of success.

Before the meeting the producer should have prepared the writer to be able to tell the story without going into excruciating detail. Members of a pitching party should have resolved among themselves any major plot disputes. This sounds obvious, but I can't tell you how many pitch meetings I've seen go awry through internal debate. Like an escalating marital rift, these meetings dangle perilously on the precipice of collapse unless grand synthesis is quickly found. This is your job. Subtle theoretical issues can remain tactically open as these minor snags often invite debate from the buyer, intriguing and involving him.

KNOWING WHAT TO PITCH TO WHOM (AND WHEN)

Recently I pitched a remake of *Anna Karenina* to Fox, my home studio. This book, my favorite, was clearly on *my* agenda. Selling it was an uphill struggle, and it was a project I couldn't have dreamed of setting up in a dry spell. I had to convince my guys that there was a viable commercial movie to be made out of a nineteenth-century tragedy in a week that was driven by the box-office hits *Casper* and *Batman Forever.* In these cases, movie stars are our friends, because the only people who are brave enough to commit to a commercially questionable literary masterpiece are those who can afford to survive it if it doesn't work. It has to be a big star. What's in it for him or her? You guessed it: awards, reviews, credibility. I needed to make a movie star, figuratively, my friend on this project. Casting is everything.

I scanned the movie universe for the biggest female stars in the cosmos, because in the end, as critical as Vronsky is to Anna, *Anna Karenina* is *her* movie. Anna was first played by Greta Garbo, then Vivien Leigh, and to justify a remake I needed a star from the new generation of actresses worthy of the role. When you imagine the characters of Vronsky and Anna played by the best of this exciting generation of stars, the movie starts to feel fresh. Michelle Pfeiffer,

Uma Thurman, Isabelle Adjani, Geena Davis, and Annette Bening are some of the actresses who had come to mind.

The other natural ally for such a picture is an A-list director. He too can survive any outcome, though with more bruises. It was possible for me to approach talent of this order because my writer, Cynthia Cidre, had accomplished a remarkable script, deeply emotional and highly castable. In pitching *Anna Karenina* to my studio, I argued (stretching a point) that the success of *Bridges of Madison County* boded well for us. "*Bridges* is about adultery too, and they don't get together in the end either." This approach is called "whatever works."

Literary period pieces are expensive, presumably. (I had to tell them I would and could make it for "a price" — this implies a reasonable one.) But I was on a roll. After seeing the studio's initial reluctance, I started intelligence gathering. I learned that my studio was courting the hotter-than-hot director of *Four Weddings and a Funeral*, Mike Newell. So signing Mike Newell was on Fox's agenda. Here, I thought, we might intersect. If he said yes to my movie, Fox's agenda would be congruent with mine. Newell was intrigued, but just long enough for me to set up the pitch. By the time I had a script, he was committed to another movie. I was okay anyway because I had heard that Alan Pakula (director of *Sophie's Choice*, among many others) was interested and had wanted to do *Anna K* for fifteen years. He is probably the premier women's director, and I knew I could get a movie star if he committed. Bingo! Potential movie. Very potential.

My strategy was to find a way for the project to work for my partners as well as me, not being entirely selfish, at least in my approach. Let's face it: My studio is not financing me in order to underwrite my fantasies. They finance me in order to use my best skills to find movies that *they* want to make. If I could put together a movie star–Alan Pakula version of this movie, then I would be doing my job and eating my cake too. Alan Pakula's interest drove the project for six months, until one day he slipped away on a "go" Harrison Ford movie (who can blame him?) and left us with four interested movie stars and no director: my version of *Four Weddings and a Funeral*.

Soon after, CAA's Kevin Huvane, one of the most agile and

strategic of agents, called me with a message. "Great news! I have another movie star for *Anna Karenina*," he enthused.

"Great," I said, my heart sinking. "Does she direct?"

Within months I had three new directors interested and the studio teetering between a big yes and a quiet no. Driving it home, turning the maybe into a big yes, is the job of the producer. I must make them feel that it's too much trouble *not* to make the movie! Incredibly, like some horrible Jungian shadow, another *Anna K,* not stellar in either script or cast (in my humble), recently assembled itself under the leadership of a very aggressive producer. It is shooting. I am waiting with a truly stellar package in the damned wings.

There is always a small area of convergence between what the buyer wants and what you want to sell him. When they are looking for an action movie, your Native American love story suddenly sprouts five action set pieces. The point is to find this area of convergence, meld your agendas, and convince the buyer that your love project is the blockbuster he needs for Christmas. In the case of *Anna K,* I want to do classic Russian tragedy. They want a movie-star vehicle. A small area of convergence if I hit the right exacta ticket. I'm working on it.

There are well-worn techniques for selling a project a producer loves to her boss: She does not say that it speaks to her personally; she does say that it speaks to her in a way that is universal. She always says that it's what *he* is looking for. As in, "This is the great romantic comedy you've been looking for," or, "This is the Brad Pitt vehicle we talked about," or, "This is the summer tent-pole movie [the movie that leads the summer roster] you needed." She doesn't let her boss believe that the adored project is only a personal fascination. To me *The Fisher King* was a masterpiece about the healing power of grace. To Peter Guber (then chairman of Columbia TriStar) it was a summer buddy comedy. Fine. We were both right.

A key aspect of blending agendas is getting to know the personal tastes of particular buyers (executives) at the studios. When you take them to lunch, learn about their passions, favorite writers, directors, movies. Gleaning this information, getting it right and using it, is the most important intelligence gathering you can do.

When serendipity strikes, you find your key allies: those with the same taste as you — those with taste at all — those precious few buyers with a point of view and a willingness to express it. These people are rare gems, and cultivating them is the secret to getting your own passions realized.

Studios try to pack their staffs with people of different strengths. Typically they will have a guy whose specialty is comedy, a girl, usually Ivy League, who is on books and important writers, a very commercially minded whiz kid chasing action scripts, and someone who has been around long enough to know some good directors. Figure out which one is the most appropriate for each idea.

CLASSIC RESPONSES TO THE PITCH

1. GETTING A FIRM MAYBE (MOST COMMON AMONG MIDDLE-LEVEL EXECS)

Take the buyer at his word even if he doesn't want you to. Do not oversell. (Desperation is always a pass.) If the buyer says something cryptic, typically, "Let me speak to my people," or, "I'll get back to you," it's important not to read too much into it. It's not a good sign, true, but it's not necessarily a bad one either. Maybe he's being political. (Maybe? Definitely.) Or maybe he's passing the buck. Maybe he's not paying attention altogether. The most likely explanation is that he can't say yes by himself, and you'll have to press to go through it all again with the boss. Try to leave the meeting with the best of good intentions at the least. If the meeting ends with a firm maybe, nothing has been lost. (Nothing gained, I admit, but nothing lost.)

The key to moving a maybe to a yes is to make the buyer feel as though other buyers have already said yes. "Warners has an offer on the table," or, "Steven is interested." It helps if it's true, but it never is. No one wants to be the first yes. Why is this? I don't know, but I think it's anthropological.

2. BEING YESSED TO DEATH (THE SPECIALTY OF BOTH AGENTS AND PRODUCERS)

A. This is wonderful! We can't believe how well executed it is. Unfortunately, there is no room for a piece of this quality in our current production plans.

B. I love this. My boss loves this. We're sending it upstairs where we're sure they'll love it too.

C. Great! If you get Julia Roberts we're a go!

3. GETTING THE DOORS SLAMMED (PAINFUL, AVOID AT ALL COSTS)

A. This is too broad for our taste. (A profound insult: "There's a buyer out there somewhere.")

B. This is too subtle for our taste. (A humdinger of an insult, as is "No hard concept": a phallic defeat. In the locker-room ethos of Hollywood, there is nothing worse than a phallic defeat.)

C. We have too many stories just like this. (An out-and-out lie, indicating profound lack of originality. You don't want to work with them either.)

D. This is too unique. (Read: "You're a kook!")

E. Great! If you get Julia Roberts we're a go! (Classic jerk-off. Like you're too dumb to know that Julia's unavailable.)

Yesses often have to be excavated, dug for. (Not begged for, a critical distinction.) But if a no is a no is a no, you have to find a way to try elsewhere. (See "Next.")

4. TAKING YES FOR AN ANSWER (MORE DIFFICULT THAN IT APPEARS)

Know your buyer's mood. By and large, these people have short attention spans, are forced to listen to bad ideas all day long, and the people they must in turn pitch to have even shorter attention spans than they do. Rule of thumb: The greater the mogul, the shorter the attention span. Since sometimes yesses are fleeting, they must be seized. You can find even the smallest yes in any point of convergence, agreement, or identification between that person and your idea. He already knows you like it. What you have to do is identify the moment *he* likes it. The moment it becomes — his. The ineffable second when it happens. Then you must bore a hole into it, larger and larger, that lawyers can fit through.

The dumbest thing you can do is turn a yes into a no. People actually do this all the time. It may seem self-evident, but it is not. You can't be enthusiastic for both of you. If you argue your point ad nauseam once you have achieved consensus, you can exhaust your boss or buyer back into a no. *Do not do this.* Less is more.

KNOW THY BUYER

"I wouldn't go near Warners this week. It's scary over there."

— *anonymous literary agent*

Every studio has a flavor. A personality. A mood. Clearly it derives from the flavor, mood, and personality of the boss, so it changes with personnel and the season. Many lunches are spent speculating about the nature of these moods, and these are profitable discussions. A mood would be, for example, Sated — as in, we ate too much recently (too many high-calorie spec scripts bought); or Hungry — rapacious needs in the distribution schedule to fill (because this is the agent's favorite, this mood quickly transforms into its opposite, Sated). The producer's favorite is Needy, when the studio or its head has been the recipient of bad publicity or bad box office (our version of bad body odor) and has to make a big splash (deals as PR). A common mood, one I see all the time, I call Opaque. As in, "You guess 'em." The following list of flavors is arbitrary, as the mood at a studio can shift from month to month, boss to boss, season to season. At any given time, any of these descriptions could apply to any of the studios.

MGM: *Quirky*
Paramount: *High concept*
Fox: *Meat and potatoes*
Columbia: *Closed*
TriStar: *Hungry*
Universal: *Grumpy*
Disney: *Jumpy*

Studios are truly anthropomorphic. They have bad moods brought on by flops. I've had to deal with a studio in a bad mood and trust me, it's no fun at all. Everyone fears for his job, and no one will go out on a limb and express an original thought. Execs look for "no-brainers," scripts that have value because someone else wants them. As a rule, they only like you if they don't own you; they only want what they can't have. What they already own displeases them, just like a rejecting lover. Time to move on.

Studios often respond to bad moods by developing a defensive (or offensive) strategy. As in, "We're not buying anything. So there." But how can a studio have a strategy? Doesn't this imply a metaphysical absurdity? Isn't a studio just a collection of a hundred hierarchical agendas? (Or at least six.) Or is it the whim of one boss? There may be no distinction between a studio's strategy and the strategy of its chairman. In fact, if that studio head is really a leader, there *is* no distinction. Then the proposition is not at all absurd, and the studio can act strategically. A great leader has coalesced all the agendas under his and can function unilaterally. Sadly, this is not often the case. Strong leadership is rare.

Does a studio have a collective mind? I would argue yes. Just as it has moods and needs and streaks of good luck and bad. A studio's collective mind is its agenda, which, like yours, is often in flux. Often if you don't like a studio decision, like the weather in Texas, if you wait another hour, it will change.

GOD AND AGENTS HELP THOSE WHO HELP THEMSELVES

Bulletin to all Cinderellas, female or male: There are no rescues here. No fairy godmothers. No princes. No white horses. *You have to do it yourself.*

At the exact moment you know exactly what you're doing and you can do it without them, powerful agents come to your aid. When you can get scripts without them, they send them to you. When you no longer need them, they're there. This is the Darwinian reality. This is the survival of the fittest, and you don't get "fit" by riding on someone else's coattails. You need to develop your own leverage. Run the laps yourself.

Literary agents control material, and material is your lifeblood. You need them much more than they need you. An agent with a hot script, based on either hype or quality, is the hottest ticket in town. His phone list is a mile long with friends, 98 percent of whom will be foes the following day if they aren't the ones given the opportunity to submit that script to a major studio. This hysterical dance — the sale of a big "spec" script — is hell week for producers, making wallflowers out of some and belles out of others.

Agents (naturally) take the path of least resistance. If an agent helps you before you can survive on your own, his client can go down with you — and then he will lose his client. He will champion you to his clients when you are a champion. He will sell you when you are easy to sell. Every project is a lifeboat. He is afraid to let his client step into a lifeboat with someone who doesn't pull his own weight. For the agent to need you he must feel that with your paddling the project is less likely to sink.

You have to give the agent confidence that when he passes the baton of protection to you, you can run with it. This takes experience on your part, the knowledge of how to protect the writer from meddlesome studio notes that might upset him, the vicissitudes of studio transitions, the pitfalls and tastes of the buyers. If you know how to navigate among all these obstacles while keeping your own point of view (merged with that of the writer) intact, the project won't incinerate during its spell in development hell. In other words, you have to know how to get a movie made, and the agent is correct in waiting until you do.

If you're not yet fully navigational, find a partner who is — another producer, a director, some significant player who can give you a boost. And relax. There's a lot to learn. If you're fun to be with, she just might want to teach you. This is where charm is an indispensable asset: Agents take pity on breaking baby producers with successful personalities or obviously good instincts. It's the little grace that lives here (apart from nepotism) that greases the wheels of the process for the young and inexperienced. You are helped only by those above you who take a special interest. Apart from these rare and precious alliances, you must bond with your peers.

When agents won't submit scripts to you, you must have them "slipped," given to you by friends, unofficially — that is, seize them from the marketplace. At the baby/entrance levels of the business, you will get your scripts from your friends or allies via the Xerox machine. If someone more official has passed on the script and then you bite down hard enough, you may be able to get attached to it. But this is a fifty-fifty proposition at best, because the agent selling the script is responsible to those to whom he first submitted it. Like ambulance chasing, this form of script chasing relies on good information as to where the action is. This you get from your friends, so it's good to have some.

TANDA MIA

There is a tradition in the Salvadoran army called the *tanda* — the class each soldier enters becomes his permanent set of alliances, his power network. Members of the class share a code of silence, protecting each other from any human rights abuses, sharing in the spoils of the capture of all contraband, promoting leaders from among themselves, and secretly disciplining one another. It is similar in Hollywood.

You must remain very aware of the class of peers who began with you because they are your allies as well as your competitors. They are your generation, the ones you clawed with. My *tanda* of boomers is impressive. Many are now running studios and agencies, or are premier producers. Right behind us is an equally formidable *tanda*. CAA has a *tanda* of its own: the Young Turks. You measure yourself in your own *tanda* and mentor with someone in the *tanda* ahead of you. As you (dare we say) age it's critical to make alliances with the *tandas* below. They are the youth who keep you informed of breaking new scripts, music, trends, filmmakers, potential employees. Cardinal rule: It's a youth business. Stay young.

AUCTIONS CAN BE FUN

These days I hear about new hot scripts from my development executives. When my "d" person reads a script she loves, we submit it to our studio so they will buy it for us. If a bunch of buyers (more than one will do) all want to buy the same script, bingo! It's an auction. This pumped-up, adrenaline-charged ritual really gets the Hollywood testosterone crowd going. There's nothing more desirable than something someone else wants.

Manuscript auctions, as they're called in publishing, or bidding wars, as they're aptly named in Hollywood, make me anxious and exhilarate me. Often in the wake of a fractious bidding war that I've lost, I try to analyze their sociology as a way of coping with how irrational the whole thing feels. The sociology of crowd hysteria prevails where an opening bid of a hundred thousand dollars is like screaming "Fire!" in a crowded theater. There are a thousand varieties of auctions, all with an enormous psychological component. Hype, in all its glory, is in full swing. (Think Jackie O. Sotheby's auction.) There is no true intrinsic market value (as Marx would say) to any material except on the basis of precedent. You pay a writer at least what he has been paid most recently. For an unknown writer on his first sale, there are no parameters. Price is determined solely by market forces at a given moment as they affect a given idea executed in a given way.

The most fun I've had in an auction this year was when I set up a script with Fox to which Woody Harrelson had tipped me off. Some friends of his, who had an expertise in bank robbery, were writing a kind of "virtual reality–Thomas Crown Affair" heist movie for him called *Ten Percent Man,* and he wanted a partner to help him produce it. It was the right concept at the right time with the rightest possible star. Woody has many friends, studio heads bond with him, he's a guy's guy and a gal's guy too. A rare bird.

When word got out that he was attached to star in a script with a commercial idea, the town went wild. (Heist movies are big this year in development — I have no idea why, except that young movie stars like them. They're fun to do. The guys get to run around in trench coats in dark, wet streets at night shooting at each other. And they always get the girl.) I knew my studio wanted it and I had the inside track. I was determined to win it. I had covered my bases with Woody, his agent, the writers, and their agents. I needed to win it quickly because if the auction got out of control and every studio got into it, the price could soar so high it might price my studio out of the market. This required a delicate balance on my part. I couldn't inhibit the auction price to my personal advantage to the financial disadvantage of my partner Woody. If I did, I could lose control as well as allies. Fox preempted the market with a healthy three-hundred-fifty-thousand-dollar offer, so the writers were well paid, Woody was happy, and my studio didn't overpay in the process. We won. A rival studio president whom I like a lot wouldn't speak to me for a week.

The same script in a different month or even week can attract wildly different offers, or perhaps none at all. A new writer (assuming he has an agent or other access to the table) could make a million dollars if he hits the bull's-eye: the right idea, the right genre, original style, castable parts, and a couple of studio bidders looking for a summer tent-pole movie. And if his agent has given you the script to take into the winning studio, then you become the engine of a moving train.

Once you get to the table, by hook or by crook, under the auspices of either your *tanda* or your uncle, you must be able to articulate what you want and really want it more than all of the other people who will pursue it just because it's hot. (This is circular, as the material is hot when someone desperately wants it, whether or not it's good.) This can often work against you but endears you to literary agents.

Being the person who heats up the auction and then loses it due to having driven up the bids by your own enthusiasm creates a kind of planned obsolescence. I've developed some strategies to mitigate this. Often I can get an agent to give me an exclusive time period to get my studio to buy the material, but this happens only when it's intrinsically hard to sell — never the case with supercommercial no-brainers, everyone's favorites. Agents will give you an exclusive submission only under the following conditions, listed in order of ascending importance:

4. They like you.
3. You're considered to have "good taste," so you can heat up the project.
2. They know you have the clout to buy it.
1. They know you have the money to buy it.

These now-legendary supernova, rags-to-riches stories that stoke the fires of many a starving writer really do occur, probably three or four times a year. Hooray! You're flavor of the month! But much more frequently the auction is a bust and the script is never sold. I've seen the same piece of material fluctuate over twenty-four hours from a potential six-figure bidding war to a dud, a party nobody comes to. In a recent auction of a *New Yorker* article, there were four interested buyers on Friday and none by Monday because two studios passed, deflecting the heat. What happened to Friday's passion? What would have happened if someone had offered a lot of money on Monday morning? Why didn't someone offer a little bit on Monday when it was no longer an expensive auction? Where does this come from? Is this some kind of primitive alpha-male behavior? Is everyone afraid to dip his toe in first? Is it fear of holding the hot potato, or, more appropriately in this case, the cold potato? I find it completely mysterious, but nowhere near as mysterious as does the writer who spent the entire last year writing the bloody article!

How do you avoid becoming a victim of the market? Even the writer needs a strategy, albeit a small one. Richard LaGravenese emerged brilliantly from the success of *The Fisher King* to be among the most sought-after writers in Hollywood. Even with the albatross of several options for Disney (their pound of flesh for buying *Fisher King*), Richard's movie choices displayed a remarkable range. His first option for Disney was *The Ref*, a dark domestic comedy. His second was the critically acclaimed children's classic *A Little Princess*. Next he wrote *Unstrung Heroes*, the quirky family drama that served as Diane Keaton's directing debut. Then he wrote the mature and wonderfully rich and romantic *Bridges of Madison County*. Little if any of this was tactical. It was instinct and talent. His strategy was creative; he only selected material truly suited to his particular sensibilities. (No *Crimson Tide* rewrites for a hundred thousand dollars a week.)

Beware of the writer with too big a strategy. He's either a bad writer, a closet producer, or a future director. Do your research. Don't tread where everyone else is, but don't go too far astray. Feel the currents of the culture and flow with them.

The corollary to never going to a meeting without a strategy is never getting off a jet without a strategy, never going to a screening without a strategy, never going to dinner without a strategy, never going to a breakfast without a strategy. There are grave implications of this way of thinking for your personal life, i.e., never going on a date without a strategy (see "Chix in Flix" chapter).

It's hard to sleep with so much strategy.

Chapter 3

HITTING THE BULL'S-EYE

"Fundamentally, the marksman aims at himself."

> — *Zen in the Art of Archery*

"Where's the bull's-eye?"

> — *Peter Guber*

MY FIRST MOVIE hit the bull's-eye. *Flashdance.* It was 1980 and it was also my first year in creative affairs with Peter Guber at Casablanca. I had taken Peter's advice to heart and was pursuing the kind of writers I knew well and had access to: magazine writers. Early on I discovered that waiting around for a great script to plop on my desk was a pipe dream. If there were any plopping anywhere, they'd plop onto much better connected desks than mine. I had no track record or credibility with which to pursue the industry's top screenwriters, so the only scripts I got from agents were retread rejections from seasons past or unsellable white elephants (à la: A moving story of two circus midgets on their long trek across the Alaskan tundra). Destiny knocked in the form of Tom Hedley, a former *Esquire* writer. He too had just arrived from New York and felt like a stranger in a strange land. He had written one movie that had gotten made in Canada and was armed with some great new ideas. Being able to attract a magazine writer because of the familiarity in our backgrounds was my first genuine advantage in Hollywood. Hedley trusted me implicitly, and though he was being wooed simultaneously by execs with more experience and status than I had, my background and the similarities of our sensibilities gave me the edge. It was using what I uniquely brought "to the table." This was my advantage, due to the specific skills I had before I came to town.

Over drinks at Le Dôme, a Sunset Strip restaurant that is no longer happening but was then the unofficial industry commissary, he told me about a group of girls in Vancouver who danced in strip bars with music, choreography, and costumes of their own design. The men in the audience had almost stopped ogling to actually watch them dance. Many of the girls had blue-collar, guy-type day jobs in construction, day labor, maintenance. They seemed to be inventing themselves as dancers out of whole cloth, without formal training, access to dance companies, or money. I was transfixed by the seemingly dissonant elements of self-invented feminism and self-exploitation. It felt completely contemporary and mythic to me, a woman's *Rocky*.

Bingo! This was a movie: an exercise in the American Dream expressly for young girls. I envisioned Bob Fosse. Dance numbers. A hit. And that it was, although it took five long years of connecting upward with more and more powerful allies until it turned out, as often happens in your freshman outing, I had aced myself out. Effective downward mobility. The well-trod process of getting replaced on your own project worked like this for me:

Initially I sold the screenplay I had developed with Tom Hedley for two years to Dawn Steel, a remarkable young executive who had just begun her first season at Paramount. Dawn had gotten her start in merchandising; she was the whiz behind the *Star Trek* ashtrays immortalized in the *New Yorker* cartoon (STAR TREK: THE ASH- TRAY!). With her now-famous crown of thick, brunette hair, her purposeful stride, and her natural bravura, she resembles nothing so much as a lioness perusing the plains below. From the moment we met (a mutual friend, manager Keith Addis, introduced us at one of his wonderful parties), I was galvanized by her. I had never met a woman with the same kind of overt ambition as a man. It never occurred to Dawn to hide her intentions under a bushel, which both thrilled and terrified me. The encounter changed both of our lives. Dawn had to fight inside the studio to get *Flashdance* made with her then boss, Don Simpson, until he was suddenly made a producer, partnering with Jerry Bruckheimer. When they were told they could pick any picture out of development as their first, they picked *Flashdance*. They replaced my writer with the now notorious Joe Eszterhas (*Basic Instinct, Showgirls, Jade;* thought by many to be the most overpaid writer in Hollywood today) and, with Dawn, brought in Adrian Lyne to direct. Lyne was then known for his stylish, award-winning British commercials and for *Foxes,* his directing debut starring Jodie Foster about young girls in trouble. He is now the illustrious director of sexy dramas like *Fatal Attraction, Indecent Proposal,* and also *Lolita.*

This team made the movie. And they made it a hit. Even my bosses, Peter Guber and Jon Peters, were mostly out of the loop, apart from some input they provided to the music and choreography team. I was low man on the totem pole (remember the words of Bob Dylan: "He who comes first will later come last") and ultimately reduced to my lowest possible contractual credit: associate producer. (This almost always happens when you're starting out because you have no leverage to protect yourself. Nor additional skills to provide. But I got lucky. Because I had worked so long on the project, its enormous success couldn't help but reflect on me, even as "associate" producer.)

Ultimately, three writers, four producers, and a new studio later, the movie still worked. It didn't need Fosse. It didn't need stars. It didn't need me. The concept itself was the star. It didn't depend on the excellence of the final draft to work (the script never really worked that well). It didn't depend on perfect casting. Its entire principal cast hasn't been in a hit picture since. But it worked. And I think it still does. *Flashdance,* like its progenitor, *Rocky,* is a paradigm bull's-eye movie in that any movie where the hero reaches for and achieves his or her dream, particularly one with dance numbers, is bound to connect with, at the very least, the American public.

Think of getting a movie made as a game of Zen archery. Every movie has its own bull's-eye, which is the goal. Knowing that there is one, where and what it is, is the point of the exercise. The farther away you stand from the target, the more the arrow decelerates along its path and the less likely it will hit the target at all, let alone the bull's-eye. A movie idea's potential can be evaluated by determining whether it is a big bull's-eye or a small one (these terms are borrowed from Peter Guber, the master of the big bull's-eye idea — to wit: *Batman*).

A big bull's-eye idea — *Die Hard, Speed* (*Die Hard* on a bus), *The Addams Family* or any old television series that most of the audience grew up on — does not have to be perfectly cast, perfectly directed, or perfectly written (although good casting, etc., helps, as ever) to hit the bull's-eye. A small bull's-eye is one that's easy to miss. *Forrest Gump* is a great example of a potentially small bull's-eye movie whose talent expanded it into a great big bull's-eye. Based on an obscure novel that scanned the life experiences of a successful American innocent, *Gump* was not an obvious movie idea by any stretch of the imagination. It has since earned a best picture Oscar and more than $400 million. Such a film has to be perfectly cast, perfectly written, and perfectly directed to work. It was. With a small bull's-eye movie, often a love project (or why work so much harder?), you must compensate for your distance from the target. You need the help of physics in the form of speed (momentum) and force. Speed in this equation is timing, the cultural conductive medium in which the hit is forged. In the case of *Gump*, the culture was hungering for its theme of return to innocence; people were reeling from a loss of faith with nothing to replace it, and *Gump* spoke right to this nostalgia for American virtue.

Force is determined by the presence of stars or A-list directors. In the *Gump* equation, that was Tom Hanks and director Robert Zemeckis. When you combine speed and force successfully, you get a pop-cultural phenomenon, something even larger in impact than a hit movie: People were compelled to go to the theater to watch Tom Hanks undergo their own spiritual crises. A movie as cultural pilgrimage.

Hitting the target, i.e., getting a movie made, is hard enough, but that in itself is not a victory. Victory comes from getting a bull's-eye, getting a movie made that works. If you get your small movie made and no one sees it, have you won anything? If a tree falls in the forest and no one is there, etc. . . . No. You must hit the bull's-eye.

Hitting the bull's-eye is the purest form of pleasure Hollywood has to offer. In fact it may be the best feeling in the world. It's why we do this: to tap into the mainline of popular culture, to see our ideas speak directly to the masses, hearing them mirrored on *Oprah* and *Nightline*. This may be the one truly unadulterated feeling of joy that producers get, the hit that addicts them forever and ever.

The ineffable part of hitting the bull's-eye is timing. Timing is in large part luck, some part skill. The hard part, reading the culture by predicting the crests of interest — the needs of the collective unconscious — is a God-given gift. It's almost magical. It's easier to read the culture by following the box office, cloning past hits into newer versions of themselves. *Flashdance* originated from a combination of the two: Hedley's reading of a subculture combined with our instinct that a girls' *Rocky* was due. But none of us knew how powerful new market forces would affect its fortunes.

During 1980 to 1983, when Hedley and I were developing the script, we were under constant self-inflicted pressure, believing that the timeliness of the idea would evaporate because the real phenomenon, these blue-collar girls who danced in bars at night, we thought was a local one that was vanishing. That's magazinethink. We didn't know that its continuing existence was utterly irrelevant to the movie market. What we also didn't know, what no one could have known or predicted, was that by taking as long as it did to get made, the movie would become the first MTV movie. It debuted with full-on rock production numbers just as this infant network was looking for multimedia opportunities to exploit. This magical convergence, a female empowerment–themed dance musical and an underprogrammed and much-watched MTV, hit the bull's-eye. Part skill, large part luck.

Thinking bull's-eye is the secret to getting movies made. You cannot kill a big bull's-eye movie with a stick. Big bull's-eye movies, again, *Die Hard* (terrorists in a high-rise), *Cliffhanger* (Stallone hanging from a cliff), are movies that sell in a sentence, for which the advertising poster practically designs itself. Big bull's-eyes are commonly called no-brainers by the studios. They are summer or winter tent-pole movies, that is, movies around which a studio's release schedule can be built.

Sometimes the addition of a big star in the right genre (action, usually) reads like a big bull's-eye. But these are often small movie ideas disguised as big bull's-eyes by the dazzle of star power. The best example of this is *Last Action Hero,* a notorious and instructive flop of the summer of ninety-three. The industry commonplace at that time was that an action movie with "Arnold" (he is *never* referred to otherwise) was a combination sufficient to break all previous box-office records, regardless of content. But its mix of childlike fantasy and hard action (a comic-book character joins forces with a real kid to fight the forces of evil in one of those two worlds, I can't remember which) pleased neither the kids nor the heavy action audience. The idea is king.

Small bull's-eyes are the hardest to get made, naturally. (These are the ones about which we always hear at Oscar time: the years of unending rejection, the winner notes, except from the following people . . .) These are ideas that when pitched are considered "small and soft." This particular insult, being considered "small and soft," is the gravest one in Hollywood. Think about it. (There are a lot of explicit phallic references in Hollywoodspeak. This is neither accidental nor peripheral. Subtext here is text. Don't be shy about it; embrace the vulgar in your clothes and in your speech. Subtlety is wasted in Hollywood. People wear and say the most outrageous things. No one will notice if you don't, so you may as well have fun.) Famous examples of "small and soft" besides *Forrest Gump* include *Rambling Rose, Driving Miss Daisy,* and *The Crying Game.* The box office showed us why these ideas were worth fighting for. *The Crying Game,* made on the extended credit of its determined producer, Steve Woolley, on behalf of its gifted director, Neil Jordan, hit the timing bull's-eye. It plunged to the heart of the gender confusion permeating the culture and fed our hunger to see what had not yet been illuminated — a man totally convincingly living as a woman — but was alive in the darker corners of our collective consciousness. When movies permit us to do this they hit the bull's-eye. But no one who made this movie, even the brilliant Miramax marketeers, could have known how big an audience there was for

The Crying Game. Sometimes box office reveals a little of who we are.

It takes a great deal of leverage to get a small bull's-eye movie made. *Rambling Rose* was driven by Renny Harlin, a powerful director acting here as executive producer. *Driving Miss Daisy*, a Pulitzer Prize–winning play, was carried to the screen by the considerable force of Lili and Richard Zanuck, its producers. The makers of *The Crying Game* begged, borrowed, and fought. It was Jordan's best work; it had to be. In archery terms, he had to stand so close to the target he couldn't miss. When I later worked for the Geffen Film Company, from 1985 to 1987 (they had no titles, but I was their production executive, one *giant* step up from a "d" girl), we could make an occasional small bull's-eye picture, if the conditions were right. (Read: if David felt like it.)

When the script *After Hours* came to us, David green-lighted it because he simply couldn't say no. A green light, by the way, is just that: permission to go ahead and start hiring people to prepare the movie for production. It was budgeted at $4 million, paltry considering that it was to be directed by Martin Scorsese, who was available and willing to shoot it that minute. Even if the movie flopped, any financier would lose very little and make new, important best friends. The script was weird, surreal and fresh, a very small bull's-eye with two dazzling elements: Scorsese and a budget of only $4 million. These elements took a quirky comedy by an unknown writer so close to the bull's-eye it actually couldn't miss.

As with *Last Action Hero*, which cost $85 million and grossed a modest $55 million, big flops are usually small bull's-eye movies that buyers were snowed into believing were big ones. This is achieved by the movie stars whose presence inflates the target. If the movie would not have been green-lighted without its stars, it is usually a small bull's-eye in disguise. *Bonfire of the Vanities* (cost: $38 million; gross: $15 million), a treatise on the eighties in Wall Street society, was a small bull's-eye that was treated like a big one because it had been such a big bestselling novel. Category mistake. Big book does not necessarily equal big movie. *Ishtar* (cost: $55 million; gross: $12 million) and *For the Boys* (cost: $55 million, gross: $32 million) were classic miscalculations. No matter how much the audience liked the stars of these flops, the ideas (*Ishtar* — a "road" movie set in the Middle East; *For the Boys* — a World War II musical) were still too weak to sustain the audience.

Movie-star power is the single most distorting lens in evaluating a bull's-eye. It is also the single most effective element for moving closer to the bull's-eye. Herein lies the trick. You can get closer to the bull's-eye and then find that you're getting closer and closer to a small bull's-eye. Which means that in order to have a hit, you have to be exactly on target. Don't get caught up in thinking that the bull's-eye grows when you get closer to it. It doesn't. The closer you get, the more possible it is to get the movie made, but this doesn't make it good.

SURVIVING AND ESCAPING DEVELOPMENT HELL

Have you ever noticed that you know a bunch of people who call themselves producers, but they're never in production? How about most of suburban Los Angeles? That's because they are stuck in development hell. Development hell is being so far from the bull's-eye that you can no longer see the target. This is when your screenplay is owned by a studio and there is no apparent road map out of continuous rewrites until turnaround.

Turnaround is a good news–bad news joke in reverse. It means the project is dead — the studio that owns it has expressed its lack of interest by abandoning it, often when a new regime has taken over. Then the property reverts to the temporary ownership of the producer who has requested turnaround rights in his contract. (Sometimes we choose to share these rights with the writers.) This means that the project instantly becomes available to its producer to set up elsewhere. A script in turnaround is both a rejected wallflower and the new girl in town, as many a passed-on project has become suddenly desirable upon reentering a sympathetic marketplace.

Three of the movies I've made — *Adventures in Babysitting, This Is My Life,* and *The Fisher King* — were put in turnaround by their original studios before another studio took them on. Turnaround can be a blessing if you seize the moment and spin. You must take advantage of timing before your maiden project looks like an old maid. In any case, it is wildly preferable to development hell.

My first experience of turnaround is my pep talk for all my friends who unhappily find themselves in development hell. Debra Hill, my former producing partner, and I had developed our first movie together at Paramount, *Adventures in Babysitting*. This was the story of a beautiful high school student who, after being stood up on a date, is relegated to babysitting two teens and a kid sister. When her girlfriend calls, abandoned at a bus station in the city, the four naïfs take off on a nocturnal adventure in the streets of Chicago. Starring Elisabeth Shue and directed by Chris Columbus, it was the actor's, the director's, and my first picture.

Instead of being given a quick start date, we were put into turnaround the day we were expecting a green light. We were essentially told, "Thanks but no thanks. We're not going to make this so you have another chance to set it up elsewhere and refund our costs." Debra and I were completely stunned, so we did what we did best together: We whipped each other into a frenzy and swung into action. We called all our allies: agents, studio executives. We told them we were taking the package out for bids in the afternoon. The town was abuzz. We headed (where else?) to Le Dôme for lunch, where our apparent confidence spread through the room. We ordered raw meat for lunch (okay, steak tartare). On our return, our incoming phone list contained the names of no fewer than four studio heads. Disney, then Hollywood's most ardent courters, won. The movie went right into prep: green light.

You get close to the bull's-eye in turnaround or in development by packaging. That is, by bringing in a star, director, or some element with such drawing power that your financiers have little breathing room in their decision making. In the case of *Babysitting*, our element was the genre, teen, with Chris Columbus, then known as a Spielberg protégé and writer of *Gremlins, Goonies,* and *Young Sherlock Holmes* (and since then of *Home Alone* 1 and 2, and *Mrs. Doubtfire*). Studio heads who were considered prescient about talent believed in Chris and they obviously turned out to be right.

In the even more elusive (but arguably more accessible) world of independent financing, elements such as stars, directors, or hot ideas are king. (Actually money is king, but "elements" raise money.) Certain prestige directors, successful action-movie directors in particular, can make a project "bankable." International rights, cable, pay, and network rights can be sold on the basis of a star's name to raise financing. Many stars are so popular overseas or in a particular market (cable, for example) that those markets can be sold individually for large enough numbers to finance certain productions. This gives stars enormous power in naming their deals and their projects. In this extremely Byzantine (to me at least) world, deals are patchworked together by banks and insurance and bond companies, tied ultimately to a U.S. distribution deal at one of the major studios (banks are unlikely to finance movies that can get made but not marketed or distributed).

The advantage I've found in working inside the studio development system is that through it I gained access to the talent way before I could ever expect to be on a first-name basis with it. Before you get to dine and party with the movie stars and directors who are giant steps toward the bull's-eye, you can get to know their agents and development executives. Many movie stars are contracted to studios wherein they behave as producers. Sort of. Inside the system, the six degrees of separation rule — getting close to the table through friends, family, and allies who are already seated — holds, and fledgling producers can pitch their projects to an executive who has access to their dream cast or dream director. The key skill here is to make the project appear real, inexorable, a moving train. This is the M quotient in the equation $P(ower) + M(omentum) = G(o)$. You have to make your movie inevitable, whether or not it is. This is not a game of Mother, may I. Never ask permission. It will *not* be granted. On every level there's an ally out there who can help you get close to the bull's-eye. Figure out who it is. Find her. Cultivate her. (Refer to chapter 7, "My New Best Friend.") These people are critical to your survival because apart from them, you can assume everyone else wishes you ill. Particularly if you're doing well (although this is when they act the nicest).

Make no mistake about it: Development hell is a form of purgatory. This is when they yes you to death and you'd give anything for a solid no just because it's solid. What separates the players from the participants, the actors from the acted upon, is knowing how to get yourself out of this helpless, dependent, useless state.

The same thing always happens whenever I'm packaging (pardon the inexact adjective) a very good (or hot — these are neither mutually exclusive nor predictive) script. First I call my co-captains, Jim Wiatt, my agent and captain (read: president) of ICM, and Bryan Lourd and Kevin Huvane at CAA. I alert these well-connected players to the existence of a potential movie, which mobilizes their various armies of actors and directors. I try to create a kind of red alert. All of a sudden I begin to hear from all the great actors' agents. Ed Limato, the czar of actors' agents at ICM, always calls me first. He is the harbinger of a great property. As I talk on the phone with Ed I allow myself to fantasize about combinations of his clients in my projects: Richard Gere and Michelle Pfeiffer, Mel Gibson and Goldie Hawn, Denzel Washington and Marlon Brando. All within his grasp. Each a green light. When sharing a new script with Bryan Lourd or Kevin Huvane, the great talent agents at CAA, I can hope for Robert Redford, Woody Harrelson, Ralph Fiennes, Elisabeth Shue, Annette Bening, or Brad Pitt. Dreamy leads, all of whom get a picture made.

These agents are the aperture to the other side — and if you're lucky they're your allies. For a moment (because soon none of these questions will be directed to me, except as a funnel to my director) I do what I'd always thought a producer got to do. Nix and yea actors, package in my mind's eye, undistracted by conflicting opinions. But beware: If you get too committed to a notion your director later disagrees with, you lose, sometimes big. You are out on a limb with the agent, and a tough director (which the successful ones are) will often neglect your creative opinion from that point forward. But if the director doesn't agree with you, who cares? This is a deeply humbling fact, good practice for the enormous humility required for working with A-list directors.

More often you are pitched terrible ideas when you have a great script. Arnold for Vronsky? I don't think so. In order to handle this onslaught of options, good fortune, and hype, you develop a standard repertoire of responses to the inquiries, especially the ones whose very names make you gag. For example, "How interesting. I'll talk to the director as soon as we have one." How's that for conviction?

FROM FLUIDITY TO SOLIDITY

At what moment does a movie become real? In other words, when can you call your accountant and tell him to relax? A clue: Never when you think. In each project it's slightly different, but it always has to do with money and momentum. It happens when the project has chugged to the tippy top of the hill and can only move downhill hence. This is the fluidity that leads, hopefully, to solidity.

SOME RANDOM EXAMPLES OF FLUID MOMENTS

1. *Flashdance* was green-lighted when Dawn Steel finally got Adrian Lyne to direct it. She asked him eight times. I was asleep when he said yes; I awoke to find Dawn and Simpson/Bruckheimer already making the movie.
2. *Adventures in Babysitting* was green-lighted after Disney won it in the bidding that followed its being put into turnaround at Paramount. First-time director Chris Columbus was already attached.
3. *Heartbreak Hotel* was green-lighted the fastest. Too quickly, if there is such a thing. Virtually as Chris Columbus turned in his script, Disney said "Go!" We never had time to think. It was a reward for *Babysitting*, with a tight budget of $8 million.
4. *This Is My Life*, Nora Ephron's directing debut, went into a sluggish turnaround from Columbia. It was green-lighted in a speculative casting meeting at Fox. Nora suggested Julie Kavner, and much to our astonishment Joe Roth said "Go" at a price, a tight budget of $11 million.
5. *The Fisher King* began its road to a green light when Debra Hill and I attached director Terry Gilliam, whom we knew Robin Williams would approve. That Robin was interested was our long-fuse green light. ("Robin is interested" was our mantra for a year.) When he committed, we were "go."

6. *Sleepless in Seattle* was green-lighted when Tom Hanks committed. That's the short version; the longer follows.

7. *Bad Girls* was green-lighted before we got there — when the cast and budget were approved.

8. *The Hot Zone* was green-lighted when we still had the commitments of Redford and Foster. It stayed green-lit past Jodie's defection and until it was clear that no appropriate costar could be found for Redford in time. Our fluid phase never solidified.

9. *Contact,* based on Carl Sagan's bestselling novel about a female radio astronomer who intercepts the first extraterrestrial communication, got its first blinking green light when George Miller committed. When he left the project, its solidity dissolved. It is now set for fall 1996 under the direction of Robert Zemeckis.

10. *One Fine Day* was green-lighted when Michelle Pfeiffer, with whom I'd developed it, said yes to the first draft. This is what passes for a miracle around here.

Let's face it, the solid moment is the moment of the commitment of the star. You say you have a director? That's good. Blinking green light. Now get the star!

WHAT STARS LIKE

Parts that can win them Academy Awards, where they play crazy people, great political leaders, saints, martyrs, criminals, psychopaths, serial killers, famous writers, or unsympathetic, outsider-type weirdos.

WHAT DIRECTORS LIKE

Film noir, downbeat endings, movies that can win them Academy Awards, literary masterpieces that enhance their stature, visually exciting backdrops, gangsters. All things dark. These days, frighteningly, they all want Grisham. What's a producer to do?

WHAT STUDIOS LIKE

Buddy pictures, action vehicles, romantic comedies, presold blockbusters, upbeat endings, sympathetic characters, American Dream stories, unfettered optimism.

Your job, should you accept it, is to navigate along a straight channel among these competing and conflicting agendas. That film noir thriller the director wants to make is the buddy picture the studio wants (well, two guys are in it). That psychopathic loner the actor wants to play is the same guy as the crusading cop the studio wants (well, he changes). You must convince every party that you want what they want and that what they (the big "they") want is what he wants, and you must march all of them toward the goal line more aware of what they have in common than what they will later discover they don't.

This will be your job for the rest of the show. (For the rest of your life.) The danger here is obvious. If you're papering over an abyss too wide, if there really is no convergence, you'll fall through. You will spend the rest of the show fighting these competing notions and stretching yourself like a human canvas over the gaping chasm. Believe me, this is an extremely unpleasant sensation.

Peter Guber was convinced when he green-lighted *Fisher King* that it was a buddy comedy. So what that to me it was the Holy Grail? It was also a buddy comedy. But the process, when stretched past credulity, results in a hybrid that pleases no one. (Let's be honest. No one is ever pleased unless it's a hit. The box office is the ultimate arbiter of the industry's historic debates.)

HOW TO GET A DIRECTOR

The modern equivalent of *How to Marry a Millionaire,* the getting of a director is a great seduction in every way but sexual. This is the big time, the high stakes, the moment that separates the men from the boys, the women from the girls. I don't mean just any director, because wanna-bes are a dime a dozen. It is a cliché that everyone in Hollywood wants to be a director, and I think that it's half true. The other half want to be studio heads. But film is a director's medium, even when studios are in financial control, so no one says yes to a movie until he knows who is behind the lens. The big directors can do anything they like. (It is a truism that no one but Spielberg could have gotten the profound and searing Holocaust book *Schindler's List* off the ground.)

The "breaking" directors, the newest, hottest ones with fresh hits under their belts, are the toast of the town. There is probably no greater rush in Hollywood than being declared "enfant auteur terrible." Witness Quentin Tarantino, phenomenon-director of *Reservoir Dogs* and *Pulp Fiction,* who has been lofted on such a plume of hype and expectations one only hopes he can descend gracefully and get back to his work.

Directors didn't wield this much power in Hollywood's golden years because the studios had everyone under contract and told them what to make and when. Now an A-list director (one who has a big hit or two and a solid critical reputation) is the crowning prize of a winning script, and every two-bit, second-rate script and its master are trying to get the same fifteen people. These guys (and recently, thankfully, gals) are payday, they are the sine qua non of a green light. They are the difference between development hell and production hell (which of course at first looks like heaven). Most big directors are "pay or play," which means if you commit to making their deals they get paid whether or not the movie is made. (Can you believe this? In what other business can you get paid for merely intending to do a job? Thus, their power.) A $6- or $7-million fee, an average that has doubled in the last two years, is a lot of money for the studio to toss away. It's as close a guarantee that the movie will be made as you can get. This is why most studios endeavor to postpone the pay-or-play component of a director's deal until a budget and cast have been approved.

Producers are never pay or play on our own because we're never the reluctant party. We always want to make the movie by definition, so getting us is no big thing. (We've initiated and nurtured it to this point, but so what?) We become pay or play when someone more reluctant does. (Legally we are pay or play at the approval of budget and cast.) We are the beneficiaries of a chain reaction begun by their leverage. This is why we must learn to reel in a director and turn a flirtation into a full-blown romance.

The selection of the director is the last critical creative decision the producer makes about the movie without the director, and she makes it in tandem with the studio. It is the most important creative choice as well as the gravest production choice the producer will make on the film. How well the studio collaborates on this decision defines the producer-studio dialectic. As the producer, you must maintain active participation, if not leadership, or your leverage will be usurped. Many producers are so hungry for their fees or a go picture, they will go with any director the studio approves. This is the producer version of hackdom. I can't tell you what terrible directors we were offered that could have gotten *Fisher King* made earlier. But what's the rush? *Use up a great script on the wrong director and you may toss away your chance at the brass ring.*

Once your director of choice says yes, the die is cast. He is in creative control (if he is worth his weight) from here on in. The nature and extent of your collaboration — therefore the nature of your entire experience on the show — will be determined by the admixture of your personalities. Pick correctly or forever hold your peace. Because once the director takes the helm, it's a whole other deal. You just hang on for dear life and ride the wild beast.

MARRYING TERRY, OUR FIRST AUTEUR QUA WILD BEAST

Debra Hill and I were at a meeting at CAA, which at fluid moments is for me the nexus of my packaging activity because it represents a disproportionate number of A-list directors: Sydney Pollack, Steven Spielberg, Mike Nichols, Dick Donner, Joel Schumacher, Ridley Scott, Robert Redford, to mention a few. I was surrounded by five agents named Mike, none of whom was the famous (now long gone) one, and stellar director-agent Jack Rapke. We were going down the list of available directors for *The Fisher King*. A name would be mentioned and I would imagine the script through each lens. None clicked. Then one of the Mikes, Mike Marcus, said, "Here's a crazy idea. What about Terry Gilliam?"

Debra and I looked at each other and knew immediately that it was the boldest, most insane, most perfect idea that we could strike in this room. We also knew how dangerous it was. *The Fisher King* concerns a cynical disc jockey (Jeff Bridges) who drops out and is befriended by a visionary tramp (Robin Williams). Together they seek the Grail, which is secreted on Fifth Avenue and will bring romance and happiness. But for all the grand mythic and comedic framework, the film is essentially a chamber piece. Everyone was seduced by the serendipitous link between Gilliam's Monty Python past — *Monty Python and the Holy Grail* — and the *The Fisher King's* Holy Grail.

Creatively the only hesitation was that historically Terry only directed his own material. But his agent, Jack Rapke, was encouraging. Terry was interested in reading new material that he didn't write, Jack said, if it was strong, smart, and commercial. Later, when I got to know Terry better, I guessed that he wanted to show he could do an intimate love story. We seized the great notion. We weren't scared, even though the studio was scared for us in triplicate. The idea of two girl producers and Terry Gilliam was one of the most frightening propositions they had ever heard. Terry's last venture, the $41-million venture *The Adventures of Baron Munchausen*, a surrealistic period fantasy epic, had been a bloody financial mess for the same studio, Columbia TriStar. Each had volubly blamed the other for its failure. This made Terry, shall we say, terrifying to the studio. And vice versa.

We all looked at each other at the meeting, speechless at the stupefying excitement of the new idea. It was Terry's piece. The enthusiasm for Gilliam turned out to be matched by his own enthusiasm for the script. Jack Rapke called us over the weekend when Terry was halfway through the script. "He's loving it," he teased on the phone. I was delirious. I knew that the script got better and better, that he hadn't yet read the scene that had made me cry, the date between Parry and Lydia. By Monday morning Debra, TriStar executive Steve Randall, and I were on a jet to London to hear Terry's conditions for doing the movie and his "take" (colloquial for point of view). The night with Terry was rapturous. We went back to our rooms at Blakes Hotel and called the writer, Richard LaGravenese. "We've found our captain!" we told him. "We've met our maker." I didn't sleep all night (for a change).

WINNING THE WILD BEAST

Reeling him in, be it the director, star, or studio, is when you actually drag the horse to water, stretch someone's vague interest into devotion. This skill is akin to the lessons women learn in *Cosmo* like "Getting your man to commit." The process resembles aspects of the mating ritual. Directors have fear of commitment too. First, because they have so many pursuers, they don't want to pick too quickly and miss a better script coming down the pike. (Familiar?) Second, because their commitment must be so complete, so utter, so absorbing for the next full year, they can't pick lightly. Last, because they are rated and perpetually rerated by the fate of their last picture, they, more than anyone else, bear the burden of failure or the elation of success.

As with dating, a director has to be "attracted" to the material. It doesn't matter whether it's a visceral or intellectual attraction, as long as he is "intrigued," a word that has come to indicate a specific stage of the game. In one of the rare moments of understatement in all Hollywoodspeak, directors get "intrigued" before they get "interested" (these are degrees), and generally intrigue is hard to come by. Some directors are famous flirts; they get attracted to many more scripts than they get serious about. If a director is intrigued, find out why and pursue it. If it's a lifelong love of airplanes that gets your aviator piece under his skin, send him on a research trip on an aircraft carrier. You're the producer, so you know how to arrange this. (Call the navy.) If he loves the writing, set up a dinner with the writer. If the mystery intrigues, have him meet with a detective. If the science in the thriller thrills him, send him to a lab.

I spent six months trying to woo George Miller *(The Road Warrior, Lorenzo's Oil)*, who, as anyone who knows him will tell you, defies wooing. I sent faxes, books, and *New Yorker* cartoons. He is Australian, brilliant and totally independent. He is so independent he has no agent. It was like sending a message in a bottle. Little did I know that at the time, he was falling in love and dramatically changing his life. I was trying to make a movie. I was determined. I had a great script based on Carl Sagan's bestselling novel *Contact*. But nothing clicked until I flew Carl and his wife, Ann Druyan, to Sydney to meet Miller in person. Muhammad went to the mountain.

As a quintessential tale of development hell, the history of *Contact* is fascinating. I began it, commissioning the treatment on which the novel was based, as my first project with Peter Guber over fifteen years ago. Five years ago Lucy Fisher, then executive vice president at Warner Brothers, brought me back on it after Peter, who had controlled it all these years, left Warners to run Sony. Lucy didn't know I had started the project and advised me to ignore all the prior scripts and return to the original treatment I had developed. Five years, five writers, and two directors later, it is scheduled to start shooting in September 1996.

A final word on wooing your director. It's *Cosmo* time: Be ardent, not desperate. Listen to him talk. Think he's the only one but be willing to live without him. Sensurround your director with the shades and colors he likes about your script but don't be a pest. Directors hate pests. (Who doesn't?) Anyone who calls more than three times in a row doesn't get a return call. Be persistent, but not annoying. Never say die. In the end they will think you have great taste for knowing they were the right directors from the beginning. Make certain that your director believes this about you whether he was your first choice or not. Remember: Once a director commits, he is your first choice. Or forever hold your peace.

Chapter 4

RIDE THE HORSE IN THE DIRECTION IT'S GOING

"True mastery can be gained
by letting things go their own way.
It can't be gained by interfering."

— *Tao Te Ching*

"Read him into the big picture."

— *Harry Cohn*

MOVIEMAKING is a pragmatic art, and Hollywood is the kind of place where this phrase is not an oxymoron. Being a genius involves more than talent here; it involves a shrewd working knowledge of the mechanics and logistics of "the system." "The system," a shadowy orthodoxy that seems to have evolved as early as talkies, is the complex of unwritten rules of how things get done. The educations of agents, directors, writers, and producers depend equally on the mastery of these customs. Getting what you want is dependent on knowing how things work. It is unwise, when trying to get your way, to reinvent the wheel. Get your way *traditionally*, cajoling, hustling, schmoozing, and by generally and genially learning the ropes and climbing.

I had a girlfriend who was a great eccentric, a bohemian, a self-invented vixen. She had a tendency to want to invent jobs, to take unprecedented routes to career places people haven't heard of. She didn't skew naturally to pragmatism. She had connections, wouldn't use them. She had contacts, wouldn't rely on them. One of her well-placed mogul friends uttered this Werner Erhardt–influenced mantra to her, and she repeated it to me. Exasperated, the mogul, a king of pragmatism, advised her sagely upon meeting her, "Sweetheart, please learn to ride the horse in the direction it's going."

This wise remark presumes knowledge of a certain implicit local metaphysics. Energy infuses everything here. Like the medieval substance they called "phlogiston," it takes the form of speed or momentum, a kind of ether through which every event occurs. It contains the pulse of the race, all the races that have been run here, past and future. It is the substance of pace itself, the collective pace of the way things get done, are done, always have been done. You can affect it, you can tap into it, surf and ride it at top speed for a time, but you cannot stop it or reverse its direction. You can use it as if it were a merry-go-round, jumping on and circling for days, as long as you know your place in line. The tragic fate of the lone soldier marching out of step in Hollywood is that he gets stampeded. He'll never be noticed but for the fraction of a moment before he disappears. He's out of sync. Sync rules.

Most Hollywood personalities have no trouble learning to ride the horse in the direction it's going as an instinctive herdlike behavior is dominant among recruits and natives as well (it has naturally selected itself). The Hollywood native is so pathologically heat seeking, he's always riding in the direction of the fastest traffic. By simulating the pace of the horse in front, he too appears to be in motion. This is how he slides into the rhythm of the race.

This rule has a number of common misapplications that make for idea gridlock:

1. They learn the local customs. They blend behaviorally. They submit screenplays of the right length (between 118 and 130 pages, preferably 121) in the right color ink (black). They do things the way they are done.
2. They understand the nuances of power in their region and drift naturally toward its center so they can be bound gravitationally.
3. People read and copy the marketplace, most commonly by studying the grosses and cloning the hits. They prognosticate trends.
4. They eschew originality.

The last conclusion, the most corrupting and banal application of this rule, is responsible for a lot of what we all find so dreary about the work we do. Originality is not required. It's *nice*, but not required. People hybridize and clone last week's hits. Pitch Michelle Pfeiffer as the lead (regardless of the fact that you have no chance of getting her) the week after *Dangerous Minds* opens. Make domestic custody comedies in the wake of *Mrs. Doubtfire*. *The Addams Family* worked? Let's try *The Love Boat*. Sometimes all this cozy following creates a glut in a genre, and most of the handicappers are stunned.

When this occurs, the trendsetters, the ones who read the market by glancing and correctly guessing ahead (the media freaks), breathe a collective sigh of relief. At these moments new currents are stirred in the market and it becomes fluid. When a movie like *The Crying Game,* to note a classic, opens big, it's a wild card and it resets the market. We wander around in a funk for days. "What is it we missed? What should we generalize from this fact?" Weekend box-office results are interpreted with a frightening degree of inaccuracy. People are constantly generalizing from the wrong principles. What did the success of *The Crying Game* mean? America wants cross-dressing movies? People are far too literal minded. But a seasoned handicapper predicts correctly: The market craved freshness, change, unpredictability. Does this mean all unpredictable movies will work? No. If they feature cross-dressers? You guessed it; no. All it really means is that the market has changed a little. A certain open-mindedness that is thrilling to the likes of you and me prevails (for a minute) in the collective sensibility. Suddenly Westerns aren't taboo, and period romances, the farthest outpost of noncommerciality ten years ago, can get made. (For years I dared not even suggest any of my favorite classic novels for fear of exposing my publishing roots — now, *Anna K.*) Our job is to seize this momentary aperture and stuff things through it while we can.

It's important to know a true trendsetter from what is eloquently called a "heat-seeking missile" (a common variety of "golden retriever" exec). In fact, heat-seeking missiles are a subset of golden retrievers — those whose job it is to fetch everything indiscriminately. Heat-seeking missiles are always on top of the hottest breaking stories, scripts, and people, only chasing the hottest momentary impulse of the market.

HSMs are "hipsters." Hipsters all dress the same (down), and the distinction between them and genuine trendsetters is critical. A heat-seeking missile is a hustler in cool clothes who hangs out at the Viper Room on Thursday nights and knows lots of musicians. A trendsetter knew the musicians before they even arrived in L.A.; in fact, he told them to come here and got them into the Viper Room in the first place. (Trendsetters know Johnny Depp.) This is a tricky business. One man's pop-cultural phenomenon is another man's flash in the pan.

Careers can be made in Hollywood by prognosticating, that is, reading the market so well that trends can be spotted. There are some hipsters whose claim to fame is finding the flavor of the month — the musical star, director of the moment, comic strip, whose time in the market is about to pop. When you find these elements early and you're right, as in Michael J. Fox in *Back to the Future* 1, Whitney Houston in *The Bodyguard*, Woody Harrelson in *White Men Can't Jump*, or Sandra Bullock in *Speed*, you hit a mainline. You haven't paid the price for the appeal these players reveal in the box office. You gambled and won. We'll be trying with George Clooney from *ER* on *One Fine Day* — he'll play a single working father who, on the worst day of his life, meets a single working mother, played by Michelle Pfeiffer, on the worst day of her life. Studios gambled on David Caruso, first in *Kiss of Death* and then in *Jade,* and lost. It's a bit of a crapshoot.

Cultivating this talent is an exhausting business best left to the very young. It entails a breathless social life, combing the comedy clubs and making the right parties. More and more it involves watching television constantly and trolling the nightclubs for breaking bands. Not a job for me. Fortunately, I have recently discovered my answer to this dilemma: a kind of familial intergenerational regeneration, if you will. Just when I found myself too tired to watch David Letterman every night and no longer really caring whether or not I knew every song on the Top 40 playlist or the name of the hottest young comic, my teenage son did. He helps me with my homework, and I with his. This is the professional payoff for all of those fights over the car. My seventeen-year-old is unpaid staff. I can stay home and rest up for the next day's battles and rely on my son's impeccable pop-cultural instincts. It's a youth market, and the second-best thing to being a teenager is having one.

My teenage son is my Top 40 expert, and my twenty-something staff prowls the parties. This is a full-time job, one that, thankfully, I have less and less time for. Premieres are by and large a dreary and disappointing lot: publicity free-for-alls. The rule of thumb has emerged that the more money the studio spends on the premiere, the earlier the guests leave.

You can also read the culture by finding the issue of the moment, i.e., Indians, wolves, or feminism, as in *Thelma and Louise*. In these cases, someone tapped into an idea that wanted to be explored in the popular zeitgeist but hadn't yet been touched. When you succeed in mounting a fresh idea, you set the market instead of following it. This is pay dirt you can be proud of. Many more of these trendy ideas bust. Many thousands of development deals lay fallow having chased Madonna or M.C. Hammer or Richard Grieco. This prognosticating is a dangerous business, which is why good hustlers rarely go out on a limb, and when they do there's a surefire desperate buyer in the mix. They're both riding their horses quickly, but they're in the wrong race.

Prognosticating doesn't work when it's the result of guessing and cloning other people's original instincts. Reading the culture — being a culture vulture — is having a nose for issues and fashions when they first emerge off the street. This is first-order awareness: tapping into the state of the "conductive medium" — the state of the collective culture — at a given moment. The talent to read this comes from genuine curiosity — I don't think it can be gleaned cynically — which probes the culture for clues. Engagement in the world, as opposed to just the marketplace, is the sine qua non of real instinct.

The rule "don't reinvent the wheel" (a variation on the theme "ride the horse . . .") works in production too. Last year I took over a movie called *Bad Girls* that had, in production parlance, wrecked. This is the worst thing that can happen to a movie. It shuts down (i.e., stops filming) after shooting has begun, and the director and producers are replaced. But in order to maintain the possibility of proceeding, the studio must keep many people on payroll. *Bad Girls* had four women stars, Madeleine Stowe, Andie MacDowell, Drew Barrymore, and Mary Stuart Masterson, and had been conceived as a women's Western, a traditional Western with a feminist twist. It had been shooting for two weeks. Nine million dollars or so had been spent, and the dailies were an unmitigated disaster. Nothing had worked. It had stopped production with the cast and crew on payroll. The cost of each passing day was enormous — between sixty and one hundred fifty thousand dollars — while nothing was being committed to film. On *Bad Girls* each actress was making close to a hundred thousand dollars a week before the new team resumed filming with a quickly rewritten script.

The studio must make a crucial decision in the case of a wreck: whether to find a way to keep the show going or to cut bait and cut its losses. This is mostly a financial decision, depending on how much money has already been spent, how much more shooting is necessary, and the cost of the committed deals. In some cases, like earthquake, massive fire, or the death of an actor, an insurance claim can cover the losses. But these acts of God are rare: Insurance doesn't pay for your mistakes (or anyone else's). The backers have to bite the bullet. They must stem the hemorrhaging by identifying the probable cause of the disaster, eliminate the mistake, and resume. Sometimes you resume with a part recast, sometimes a new director of photography. In the worst case, as with *Bad Girls*, you start over with a new director and producer.

I think that the picture's collapse was foreshadowed by the fact that each actress was being paid almost ten times more than its neophyte female director, Tamra Davis, who was making her first studio movie. The weight of the "above the line" talent was too great. This refers to the salaries and costs of the producer, director, writer, and cast, which were destructively heavier than the impoverished nonunion "below the line" salaries and costs of the people and equipment it takes to actually make the picture. These days the cost formula for big movies is roughly half above, half below, as was the case with *The Fisher King* and *Sleepless in Seattle*.

Our studio bit the bullet and hired Jonathan Kaplan *(Heart Like a Wheel, The Accused*) to take over the direction of the film. This move was to the studio's credit, as Jonathan was not the easiest choice. In fact he was a perilous choice. Jonathan is a serious director, famous for directing women to Oscar nominations. (Jodie Foster in *The Accused*, Michelle Pfeiffer in *Love Field*.) He was famous for being difficult when pushed, and the studio was in a time crunch. But they wanted a good movie even more than they wanted a cheap movie (the ship sailed on that one when they shut down), so they acquiesced to Jonathan's needs. Within a week he and I had left our lives in Los Angeles to meet our new team on location on a dusty ranch in Northern California. Tamra, who had made smaller independent movies like *Gun Crazy* with Drew Barrymore, had never made a large period movie before. The pressure of being badly produced and inexperienced with major movie stars had toppled the director from the helm of *Bad Girls*.

The whole crew was shaking when Jonathan Kaplan and I arrived on set. Standing receiving line–like, they assembled themselves for inspection. Jonathan was Patton. I was something akin to Lucrezia Borgia. The first bad sign was when the production designer requested to meet us separately from our scheduled location scout, the systematic examination and analysis of the sets and locations of the show with the crew. He had a philosophy about the sets that he wanted to explain before we saw them. I declined the request on principle. This may sound hard-assed, but I was right. Meet us on set, join our scout, and explain the philosophy as we go, I advised him. This made him glum. That it made him glum made me worried. That he thought we wouldn't understand the sets without an explanation was problematic enough. That he wanted us to detour from our tight schedule to meet him at his office was the tail wagging the dog. And his attitude during the scout was the last straw. How helpful could he be in the trenches if he was resisting the very idea of new ideas? We were about to replace him when he quit. The new director had no intention of remaking the past director's failed decisions. A good director cannot put himself into the mind of another director — it is the crew's job to support the new director in merging his personal vision with the show's givens, not to impose old ideas upon him. The crew members who were able to embrace and enjoy the change flourished; those who could not bend with the new prevailing winds were the first to fly home.

These great-looking "bad girls" were supposed to be hookers, so I wanted their costumes to be sexy and fun. The fashion of the moment was heavily influenced by Western motifs, so more than ever the costumes on the first women's Western had to be spectacular. I approached meeting the costume designer, Susie De Santo, with caution and a set of alternative options (read: a list of available costume designers). Susie was not yet well established, having done most of her prior work in low-budget independent films, so I didn't know her work. (Producers tend to be credit snobs because it's easier to evaluate someone on the basis of her hits and flops than it is to actually develop a point of view on her sensibilities. Fancy credits also justify your decision, a posteriori.) But from our very first meeting, at which I encouraged her to watch the classic Westerns for inspiration, I knew I could collaborate with her. She was eager to reconceive the show and she was open to new ideas. Her mind was going a mile a minute. No resistance, no defensiveness, no reluctance. Within three weeks she was turning out the most inspired costumes of her career. She was not precious about any of her past work; her goal was to serve the new team with her best ideas. She was riding the horse in the direction it was going. She is now my costume designer of choice.

This was the operating principle in every department. The old production team — the line producer, unit production manager, and production executive — had to become the new production team, which it could do only by serving its new masters — Jonathan and me — instead of the old budget and its presumptions. This was very difficult, particularly since the studio was sending the same people the opposite signals. These new guys will make their movie with the exact same budget and schedule, the studio instructed. This was clearly impossible. The question put to the old production team was which horse to follow. In the world of a weakened director, the studio exerts the most leverage, but Jonathan and his team were strong.

How did the old production team manage to straddle its conflicting roles? Which horse should they follow now? They had to read the field. They had to decide where the traffic was moving and try to join it. We, the new team, had to spin enough momentum to convince the traumatized crew that the movie would be mounted, and mounted our way. Firing recalcitrant crew members was the necessary and ultimate message, but I like to find less drastic measures as well.

PUNTING

I took inventory of the top-priority problems. The actresses were hanging around a dusty horse ranch with nothing to do; keeping them working was critical. We also needed to be sure that their riding and shooting would make women proud. At the same time we had to address a big potential problem. Our stunt man, the venerable Walter Scott, convinced that *Bad Girls* would never get up and running, was ready to quit when we arrived. He had gotten another offer from Bob Zemeckis and he wanted to go. I couldn't lose Walter; he was critical — for morale for one thing, and because there was no one as good available.

So I created cowboy camp, where the women learned to ride and shoot guns during our short prep, and I put Walter in charge. I made him responsible for turning these gorgeous women into cowgirls, and lo and behold, he was working too. Momentum was generated. The teamsters spread the word: The show would begin again. All through the rest of the show, I teased Walter Scott, "If I tell you a show won't wreck, will you believe me now?"

In general it is good to be wary of an excess of theory in production as experience is the best production guide. It is through experience that we learn that theory is expendable for production realities. The best skill in production is knowing how to punt — find some other way of doing what needs to be done when you discover that it can't be done the way you originally planned. In production terms punting is riding the horse in the direction it's going. Not complaining that things weren't as you had expected but making things work the way they are. Reality crunch; deal with it.

Punting is inimical to theory. On *Bad Girls* the production designer's theories had contributed unwittingly to an unhealthy atmosphere among the cast. Since the sets were to be monochromatic, the only color the camera would see would be from costume. Interesting theory. But no wonder the actresses were in conflict over the one red dress in the wardrobe when I arrived. Solution: a set full of color designed by a brand-new team. And no red dresses. First to go was the production designer, an artist who could not relinquish control to the new director, a talented man who could not ride the horse in the direction it was going.

CHANGING THE DIRECTION OF THE RACE

The key moment in every big career comes when you sense that your influence can change the direction of the race. This is what happened to Quentin Tarantino after the stupendous success of *Pulp Fiction.* He never learned the metaphysics of this place or had to tap into the pulse of the race. He made two movies and became a genre. He can do what he wants. He didn't have time to learn to ride the horse in any particular direction. The race follows him. This is the transcendence of the race, when you can be truly original. This is very rare.

When you are able to change the direction of the race, suddenly you own the track. This happened to Kevin Costner after he made *Dances with Wolves,* and to Steven Spielberg in the wake of his remarkable twin successes *Schindler's List* and *Jurassic Park,* and to Robert Zemeckis after *Forrest Gump.* These guys can do anything they want now. It doesn't matter that you have the same ideas they do; no one listens to breakthrough ideas from a novice.

WHEN A NOVICE TRIES TO CHANGE THE DIRECTION OF THE RACE

Renegades don't succeed easily in Hollywood. Patronizing dilettantes who wing into town wanting to do it their way in their spare time always fail. This is why the West Coast careers of people like *Rolling Stone* magazine founder-owner Jann Wenner, English producer–short-lived studio head David Puttnam, and *New Yorker* critic Pauline Kael wrapped early. They came to town and thought we did things dumb.

David Puttnam was no amateur. He was a great producer, one of the greatest (*Chariots of Fire*), but he tried to buck the system and invent a new way to run a studio when he ran Columbia for a year or so in the mid-eighties. He decided that he would find material anywhere but through the agencies and he pursued foreign directors who had never made an English-speaking movie instead of feeding off the traditional A-list. He had a famous fight with Mike Ovitz when he tried to buck the bottleneck of CAA's control over their movie stars and then decided maybe he didn't need movie stars at all. By that time people were starting to think he was nuts. But when Puttnam decided that Ovitz's terms were too stiff on the package for *Ghostbusters II*, he had taken on a fight he couldn't win, because if he won he lost. Classic cutting-off-your-nose-to-spite-your-face syndrome. Winning was calling Ovitz's bluff and not making the sequel. But by denying his own studio the surefire summer opening picture that every studio's schedule depends on, he committed a boneheaded blunder, one that eventually spelled his doom as a studio head. Dawn Steel, who replaced him, put together the very same package for *Ghostbusters II* as her first deed in office. She rides the horse in the direction it's going. Because he tried to cut CAA and other major agencies out of the mix, many mainstreamers thought Puttnam's behavior the height of absurdity, bordering on the irrational.

Pauline Kael had a deal at Paramount where she worked with Warren Beatty, among others. A fresh mind is dazzling here and wildly feted, particularly one with a pedigree. Her pedigree was the classiest and most richly earned that Hollywood had seen, perhaps since Fitzgerald or Huxley. But apparently (I don't know for sure because I wasn't there) Pauline told execs that they didn't know what a good movie was. She spent a few years developing scripts, meeting with directors and movie stars, I guess, doing it "her way." No movie was ever made. I contend that had she stayed a while and learned the rules, she could have then broken them with the best.

And Jann Wenner, a brilliant magazine mind, thought he could take the town by storm on his off-season as a new hobby. The only movie that came out of his lavish Paramount deal was *Perfect*, the ill-fated health-spa concept romance starring John Travolta and

Jamie Lee Curtis. Teaching the natives is much harder than one would think. There are rules. Hazing rites.

Look at some of the others who fatally rode the horse backward. Former producer Julia Phillips, her career in ruins from drug abuse, ended up trashing her own Rolodex for cash. She couldn't earn fees anymore, and the title of her book *You'll Never Eat Lunch in This Town Again* reflected the swan song that it was. Too many years of riding backward, stoned.

Actress Sean Young couldn't tell the difference between attention and public display of neurosis when she dressed in Catwoman clothes and crashed the Warners gates trying to get an audition with Tim Burton for *Batman*. Chalk squeaking on a blackboard.

Our greatest indigenous genius, Orson Welles, ended his life in dissolute disarray, a victim of terminal exhaustion and fright from years of bucking and fighting. He became less and less effective as the years passed, so he drank more. I was shocked to find so little pity for him in Hollywood when I first arrived. I would stare at him rapt as I had lunch at the old haute haunt Ma Maison restaurant while he sipped glass after glass of red wine and held forth on everything that was wrong with the business. Of course he was right, but one has to learn to live with it. I would watch more seasoned players ignore him with contempt. "What's wrong with him?" they would think. "He could be the top of the A-list if he pulled himself together." But it didn't seem to me that the A-list meant very much to Orson Welles.

You lose if you don't respect the fact that this game has been played in a particular way since its inception. It always has been and it always will be. Only the players change. The custom says if you're not working you should be drying out, at a spa, in rehab, or doing yoga — bending over, getting ready for your next film. There's little patience for artistic self-indulgence. It doesn't fly here. Unless you can open a movie.

READING THE FIELD

Besides mimicking the horse in front of you, how can you identify the direction of the race? You must be able to read the field. In order to interpret it you must be able to see enough of it to determine which way the horses are moving. And why. This takes a while because we are our own distorting lens. It's hard to get perspective when you're being bumped around the field yourself.

Think basketball. Magic Johnson always knew where he was and where every other player on the court was in relation to him, teammate or opponent. He could read the field, see what other players couldn't, know what his teammates were thinking, anticipate the direction of the ball. His global, macro grasp of all the potential dynamics on the floor allowed him to be a beat ahead of the rhythm of the game. When you have this grasp of the whole, instinct becomes a form of telepathy and you can literally make things happen. You understand all the movement around you; you are in balance, filled with grace.

But the reality of entry-level Hollywood is not NBA basketball; it's more like bumper cars. No one can see well enough from the ground level to do anything more than accelerate and crash. There is no vantage point on the ground. Up on the next levels it's like ballooning. People are trying to pop each other's balloons back down to the ground. It's not a pretty picture.

You don't have to behave this way. Just know that the guy you're playing bumper balloons with probably is. The more you rise to a level of competency in the business, the fewer and fewer players there are and the more people are gunning at these high-floating balloons. Those on top have a good view of the field and can therefore make strategic moves. It's an insider's job. An insider is someone who can read the field.

At a certain point you get to float upward. Time, attrition, not being knocked out of the box, untie the sandbags around your legs. Finally you float high enough to be able to see the field. You see where the finish line is. Who's close. You notice a whole level of balloons flying above you, in the stratosphere, so to speak. Like Magic Johnson, these players understand the game so well they set the field.

SETTING THE FIELD

Those players who float many levels above the fray — the Ovitzes, the Geffens, the Murdochs, the Eisners, the Spielbergs — set the field. David Geffen does this brilliantly. For a time — from 1984 to 1986 — I watched a master set the field at close range. As head of development for the Geffen Film Company, I had the extraordinary opportunity to learn at David's feet. Not content to read the field as it is, David is formidable enough to blow certain opponents off the field preemptively with a gruff bluff or shrewd strategy, or even by his mere presence. David is holographic, his advantages multidimensional. He is holding more or better information than his adversary and he is fearless — having owned his own soul all of his career. He is preternaturally instinctive and he is charming: a combination designed to accomplish virtually any objective. He is our Lola in that we have seen over the course of a public, vastly successful career spanning decades that what David wants, David gets.

But what is it like when he doesn't want something? It is harder than a rejection from your average bear of a boss because you so much want his approval. Other bosses can be patronized in private, dismissed as dumb or old or hideously unhip, but David is smart and mentally young and hipper than his staff. He hired us to be entrepreneurs, and so we were, operating on a loose rope that we wanted David to tug at.

Since the beginning of his career discovering breakthrough musical acts in the sixties, seventies, and eighties (Laura Nyro, Cher, Jackson Browne, the Eagles, Nirvana) through his theatrical producing *(Cats, Dreamgirls)*, etc., David has been legendary for his Midas touch. He was the premier arbiter of good taste in pop culture way before he proved his wizardry in the boardroom. He hired people and trusted them to soar, and because he knew everyone and everything, his employees were always pressed to the cutting edge to succeed.

I remember sitting in David's office one afternoon, pitching my heart out about a David Mamet screenplay I was desperate to make. He was reading the newspaper and looking bored. (To repeat: The greater the mogul, the shorter the attention span.) I knew I had only a few minutes to make my case. "He's simply the smartest person I've ever sat in a room with. He mesmerized me. We could make it for — four million. And he'd be ours."

David looked up and stared at me intently. His eyes began to focus on me with great scrutiny. Was he taking me seriously? "You know, Lynda," he said slowly. I leaned in. I thought I had him. "If you got collagen shots, you could be really attractive," he finished. Looking back from the perspective of the Politically Correct nineties, this comment sounds much stranger than it was. David functioned as a kind of personal manager to all of his employees, regardless of gender. There wasn't a vanity tip too personal nor relationship advice too intimate for his never-ending effort to help us on our paths toward perfection in love and work.

I struggled to regain my self-possession. David does nothing without purpose, even if his purpose was my personal improvement. Was this a bluff, a strategy, an insult, or a reasonable beauty tip? I was flummoxed (I wondered if that was his intention). As it turns out, he was way ahead of me. He had already discussed the terms of the movie with Mamet's agent, but who knew? Whatever his intention, his remark had the effect of getting him out of a corner by throwing me off balance. Would I back off, press on, burst into tears, ask for the number of his dermatologist?

Players like Geffen cannot be contained by the size and location of the field. They play on a global field. They are making mega-money at the intersection of entertainment and everything else. Five, six, maybe a dozen other players float here. Tops. Anyone floating above them lives in New York. The sight of anyone floating above these guys is anathema, so they stay here, except in cases like supermogul Barry Diller, who is effectively bicoastal, a testament to his transcendence.

Very few survive the gale winds on the way up. Those who do are the "perennials," as opposed to "dinosaurs," who merely age in fancy cars but are irrelevant. When one of these perennial players makes a move, like when Barry Diller leaves Fox and spends a year mounting a takeover of Paramount or CBS, the field changes for all of us below. Seismic power shifts rock the town. Studios change personnel and personality. It takes a few months for the dust to settle after such a powerquake, and that time is spent assessing the new field through rumor and innuendo. Those who know don't say; those who don't know share everything. At the lowest level of the field, many balloons that might have ascended are deflated. New alliances kill old deals. But many midlevel balloons rise suddenly.

Catch a string. Move with them.

Chapter 5

PUTTING IT ON THE ROOF

"When you can do nothing,
What can you do?"

— *Zen koan*

"We will sell no wine before its time."

— *Ernest and Julio Gallo*

MY ROOM at the Carlyle hotel has been my home away from home in New York. I've been staying there for fifteen years on various studios' dimes, their kind contribution to making me feel like the pampered daughter of a wealthy magnate in prewar Connecticut. With its floral chintz upholstery and floor-to-ceiling windows overlooking the Manhattan skyline, the Carlyle is my New York branch office, where I do my business and watch the city I love and lost.

There I was at the Carlyle about five years ago, preparing to go out with friends, when I was interrupted by a call from my studio head. (I hate when this happens. Just when you thought it was safe to go back in the water or to get on a plane or take a bath or make love or whatever you like doing most in life, you can count on "telephone interruptus.") In the following true horror story the names have been omitted to protect the guilty and the innocent (the director and me).

At this time I was in the latter stages of packaging one of the best movies I have ever made, one that had a brilliant but not necessarily commercial director attached. "I have a great idea!" sayeth the mogul (the worst possible utterance in most circumstances, because in a single sentence you can find your entire agenda — your year — redefined). "You know that director who you think is making your movie?" the studio head went on. "Well, Sydney's movie fell apart and I slipped your script to him." (Sydney Pollack, of course.)

I sat down in my chintz chair, inhaled, and evaluated my situation. If Sydney liked my script, then it would become his for the asking. Now it's not that I didn't think Sydney was great. Even better than great. But I knew that every other studio head in town also knew that Sydney's most recent almost-movie had fallen apart, and he was getting every script. It could take him weeks to make up his mind while he flirted with every go picture in Hollywood. I believed in my director, and he was committed to my project. We had happily dined together only the night before. I could swiftly go from a definite yes to a firm maybe with someone with whom I had no relationship. Before I knew it Sydney would be a glimmer in my imagination and I'd be "loosey-goosey" again, a term that means tumbling with my movie out there in the wind without sufficient gravity to hold us together. Read: I could be back to development hell without a director.

So I said to the mogul, "Fascinating. Why don't you set up a meeting with Sydney next week when Movie Star is back in town?" This would be the movie star that was meeting with my director that week in New York. By delaying the mogul meeting, I'd bought myself a week to firm up my director, his deal, and his relationship with Movie Star. And to see if Sydney's movie would come back together before his sudden availability destroyed mine.

Often what seems like a mogul's commandment is nothing more than a momentary whim. He has twelve of these an hour. If I had mistaken whim for commandment in this case, I would have found myself whimmed right out of my director. Instead, I instinctively knew that time was on my side and if I wanted to affect the outcome I was better off not acting immediately on what the mogul had said — delaying the decision.

By the time I returned to Los Angeles, Sydney's movie had

"resolidified" (read: budget approved), and ipso facto my director and his movie star were happily wed. My studio head had gone on to seed far greener pastures, and I had saved the choice of the captain of the ship, the most important decision a producer makes. I call this delaying tactic "putting it on the roof," and this adage has saved me from many potential major disasters.

In every venture there is a moment when there is no good strategy, when you do not know what to do. When this happens, put the problem on the roof. In other words, postpone resolution until a later date. When the problem is on the roof, it is off the ground, out of play, but still within reach. Rather than make the wrong decision, attenuate the process until you have more information and more of the critical events play out. Rather than now, later is often a better time to make a decision that currently cannot be made well.

As a producer, you will find that people try to provoke your decision, anticipate it, coerce it, force it, through intimidation and persuasion. You must hold a poker face during these times, figuratively fold your arms and take the posture of removed discernment. I call this posture "being from Missouri," the Show Me state. Turn indecision into discernment and you are less likely to be preempted or intimidated. When someone forces your decision or makes it for you, you have given your power away and you become irrelevant in the process, obsolete. The goal is to make your judgment valuable so that people will wait for you to make up your mind. While we were casting a male costar for Michelle Pfeiffer in *One Fine Day*, the agents in the studios who were pitching actors knew that I had strong opinions and would express them to the director. (This was only true because Mike Hoffman, the director, wanted me to. My voice was on loan from him.) My job was to suggest "the fish that goes on the platter," the choices presented to the director. If I had been willing to present everyone unselected, my voice wouldn't have counted. Because my opinion counted, names were thrown at me all day long in the quest to establish the crucial marquee: "Michelle Pfeiffer and So and So in . . ." After the obvious stars that everyone agreed on (Harrison Ford, Kevin Costner, and Tom Cruise) had passed on the project, everyone was up for grabs, from current box-office idols, "How about John Travolta; he's so hot this week," to potential break-out TV star George Clooney, "He's the next Cary Grant!" Hindsight makes geniuses of us all. I wish I could tell you that I jumped as soon as William Morris started pitching George Clooney as Michelle's costar. But movie folk are notoriously TV snobbish, even though we are constantly replenishing our movie-star ranks with each season's break-out TV stars. But I really hadn't watched *ER* (I tried once, but the constant hysteria — the doors swinging open to reveal new, surprising horrors — reminded me too much of work and made me dizzy.)

We had been turned down by the usual suspects — all the big stars who didn't want to be a costar, as it were. (Women never have problems playing the girlfriend, but try getting a big guy to play the boyfriend. . . .) My studio chairman, Peter Chernin, was high on George —Peter had come from TV and knew it well. But Michelle, Michael, Kate (Michelle's partner), and I were all clueless where George was concerned. Then, at an airport, I saw his very handsome face on the cover of *Rolling Stone* and picked up the issue. By the time I'd landed, I was charmed. I called Michael. "I'm very intrigued too," he said. "I want to meet him."

The casting of George seems obvious now, but the tarmac is littered with the carcasses of David Caruso types who didn't fully make the transfer from small to big screen. But the closer we looked, the more George Clooney looked like an old-fashioned movie star. Once he and Michelle met, it was smooth sailing. We closed our deal with him and prayed. Two weeks later, his first feature, Robert Rodriguez's *Dusk till Dawn* opened to $10.5 million. We had to pray no more. We'd picked right, on instinct, and now everyone was chasing him. Before we even started shooting, George was offered the role of Batman. For millions and zillions. I hope we can afford him for the sequel!

The producer awaits new information, or for intuition to strike, or for someone to show his hand or change his mind. If she blows with the wind, that is, accedes too much to the direction the race is going, she can become unnecessary. People can guess what she would say — what everyone else says. This is an easy route to affability, but too much affability and a producer becomes invisible. A producer must hold onto her moments of choice. Own them. Make them hers. Doing this is what gets me in trouble, but it's also what gets things done.

In loosey-goosey moments, if a producer seizes too quickly on the first piece of talent willing to commit to her project, she may sell herself short. Barry Levinson (*Diner, Rain Man, Bugsy*) may have been interested in directing if only she had waited one more week. Timing is everything — for ideas, for implementing strategies, and most of all for decisions.

THE OPTION FACTOR

Moving too quickly is foolhardy, but waiting too long is even more problematic. Losing the moment versus moving on it with perfect timing is the difference between fear of decision making and genuine discernment. Directors postpone decisions because they are always aware that a better option may appear around the bend. They are like people with narcissistic personality disorder — unable to make a commitment to the one they love for the possibility of an even better prospect. The best are masters of indecision. They play it like a violin. The amateurs are paralyzed conductors who can't get the orchestra to play in tune. A producer must know when a director's decision has taken so long it is becoming too expensive, and when "expensive" is worth the cost.

THE FEAR FACTOR

The reason postponing decisions has such a bad reputation in Hollywood is that most of the time we see indecision masking fear. We loathe fear. In any jungle he who gives off the smell of fear dies. Being afraid is the worst reason to postpone a decision because everyone knows you are postponing due to paralyzing confusion, not choice. Paralysis is terrifying in a director and it loses the respect of the crew.

A new director who is being asked thirty questions at once — from what the actor should be wearing to what lens he wants to use to where the camera should be pointing to where the actor should be sitting — is overwhelmed if he's unprepared. He needs preparation to reduce his fear; he needs to be rehearsed; he needs to have thought out every shot and sequence beforehand. He has to have a sense of how he wants to cut the film and what coverage he will require. He needs to sort out the problems before he can find the solutions. He must turn his fear into discernment by asking questions that can serve as the basis for his answers. The producer's job is to help him sort out the right questions to ask and of whom.

So whenever I'm frightened, when my blood starts racing and my head starts pounding and I start smoking a lot, I grapple with ways to break down my fear into components with which I can actually contend. I never put anything in writing, return phone calls, or make decisions until I've sorted out the confusion beneath my fear. The worst time to act is when you're afraid.

That Friday when I knew that Wolfgang Peterson, the director of *Outbreak,* was meeting with Redford in Utah was a very long day (as Fridays always were in "the Zone"). Whom to call first? How to put out the fire? I felt betrayed and confused, inappropriate emotions with which to make phone calls. I had to stabilize the situation with what little information I had and I couldn't stabilize anything if I was out of whack.

I went to Texas that weekend to open my new house. It was February, and the pipes had frozen. I had to fix my water pump and I sliced my finger trying to reach it. Blood gushing from my finger, I heard the phone ringing inside. Susie De Santo, my costume designer from *Bad Girls* who had since become a close friend, answered the phone. "It's Bob Redford," she called to me. I threw a makeshift tourniquet around my finger and ran to the phone.

"How ya doing?" Bob asked.

"I'm bleeding and trying to fix my broken pipes. How's Wolfgang?"

"I'm going to do your movie, Tex."

All the blood rushed from my finger to my head. I thought I would pass out.

"Go fix your pipes, Tex," he said. "We'll get to work on Monday."

Now I could call the chairman of the studio, as soon as I got a butterfly bandage for my finger.

DEFERRAL

Producer and executive types tend to have decisive personalities, if for no other reason than they need to be expedient more often than most other people. Decisive personalities are attracted to power and these personalities tend to err on the side of preemptive decision making, as in: Any decision is better than no decision at all. This edict is only true when cameras are about to roll. Otherwise, maintain your options as long as possible by putting them on the roof, a form of deferral.

A prominent British psychoanalyst, Adam Phillips, in his book *On Kissing, Tickling, and Being Bored,* said that deferral "is an attempt to re-open, re-work the plot . . . a way of flirting, a way of cultivating wishes and playing for time." William James said that deferral is "to go from." When we can't make a good or sound decision, we often need somewhere else *to go from.* You can see how useful a strategy this can be. In certain cases, it is precisely what the doctor ordered.

Over the years I have come to see how slowly and discreetly packets of information emerge, and that the first decision that presents itself is rarely the best because it's never based on complete information. This is not to discount intuition, but intuition tempered with all the critical information by definition results in a far more informed decision. And yet you must make sure that the assembly of all the pertinent information does not take longer than the decision merits. The goal is to wait, not until it is too late, but rather until the last propitious moment to sort all of your crucial data. You know you've waited too long when the decision has already been made by someone else. Or if by the time you decide, all the circumstances have changed.

Putting it on the roof is a tactic. It can be a defensive move, a holding move, or a survival skill, like disappearing. (That's when you put yourself on the roof, which we will cover later in this chapter.) A holding move is a finesse that allows you to delay when everyone around you wants to resolve as quickly as possible. It is short-term parking on the roof. Holding strategies are used for temporarily intractable problems, problems that if brought to a head early will turn out worse, or at least not to your liking. The underlying theory here is that time heals all wounds, or problems are only intractable in a given time slot. Patience, reading the field for a better moment, is optimum. The following is a hypothetical example of the holding move:

A producer has a very hot script. The studio is making up a directors list, figuring out whom it wants most at the helm. The producer gets a call from the hot action director he's been chasing on another project for weeks. His movie just opened to $10 million the first weekend. He is hotter than the producer's script. By far, because he has opened and the script has not. He wants the script for his next picture. The producer is thrilled. Does he say yes? Maybe. Consider the following choices:

1. BIRD IN THE HAND

What is he, nuts? This is a go picture. His studio lives for this. Why is he making it so hard? (Ride the horse . . .) The producer says yes, sets dinner for as soon as the director returns from Tibet (or Sundance or Venice or Berlin). The producer calls the director's agent. Makes nice nice. Calls his studio. Score!

2. LOOKING A GIFT HORSE IN THE MOUTH

The director's movie opened to $10 million, but the producer sees it and hates it. Sure, it's a bird in the hand, but maybe it's a pigeon (or a vulture). This director's interest surely bodes well for the interest of other directors who are more to the producer's liking. He doesn't have to sell himself or his script short or throw a green light out the window (the proverbial baby with the bathwater).

In the second case, the producer puts the bird in the hand on the roof! He puts pressure on his studio by telling them that he has Hot Action Director breathing down his neck. He tells them he has set a meeting for next week and that he can't hold the director in place (shameless overpositioning, but effective) any longer than that. Do they want to come?

It makes no difference to the producer financially which approach is taken, as producers' "net" points are usually worthless anyway. So he might as well shoot the moon. If he goes with a fancy A-list director, he may score a center table at the Golden Globes.

Even if he can't afford the tuxedo. With this in mind, Fancy A-List Director, who is less likely to commit, adds panache to the project just by his interest. And the level of talent he attracts is far higher than that of Hot Action Guy.

So anyway, Fancy Director passes, as the producer knew he would, and Hot Action Director has taken another movie, as he knew he would too, while he was on the roof. No worry; the script is heated up and in play. Everyone knows that if these two guys flirted with the script, it has a shot at being a go movie, and the right director will make himself known. Hot Action Director has been the producer's unwitting ally in precipitating the studio's decision to begin making offers to directors, often the most difficult decision to get them to make. This marks the end of development hell and the beginning of chasing the green light. This result is excellent and devoutly to be wished.

The project is now formally "out to directors." In the producer's intelligence gathering, he will find out who is available and expose the script to the best of them. Maybe he'll hit it big and get Barry Levinson, and when he has his first meeting with him, the producer will be so relieved that he didn't settle on Hot Action Director. This is Hollywood's version of destiny. With a little free will thrown in.

RESTRAINT

"No good can come from this."

> — *Esther Rosen, my grandmother*

"Don't go there."

> — *Ancient Chinese proverb*

If nothing good can come from

1. a conversation
2. a meeting
3. an interview
4. a confrontation

then don't have it.

Don't go there. This may sound like simple common sense. But here in a town filled with raging control freaks, with the hype and hyperbole necessary for survival, restraint is a rare commodity. The tendency is to seek out the fight and join it, to obsess on the problem. As my mother would say, we worry it like a sore tooth. If there's a fire (not literally, a crisis), most Hollywood types don their fire hats and run to the action. They become so attracted to fires they even start them, either to watch them consume their competitors or to heroically put them out (the cheapest way to be a hero). This appetite for war cultivates like cockroaches thick-skinned, asbestos-like personalities that can survive any conflagration. This is strangulation for artistic personalities. And a primary reason for the constant exodus of artists out of town (as soon as they can afford it).

PUTTING YOURSELF ON THE ROOF: LOW-PROFILE TIME

"Got to go disco."

— *Donna Summer*

There are two circumstances when it's time to split (at least that I can think of right now). One is that you messed up royally and no good can come from your presence anywhere. The other is that someone is forcing your hand and you're not ready to move. Avoid the unknown. Not knowing what to do yet does not mean that you are dumb and so you have to guess. It's better to wait than to do something rash, ergo, potentially escalating. Split for the Canyon Ranch. Be on a plane or out of reach in Santa Barbara. Go fly-fishing. Take a yoga class, go to a spa, or get a manicure. Just be out of the office, hard to reach. Just because they're looking for you doesn't mean they have to find you. Actors know this. Directors also know this. We should too. This strategy requires a great staff and a loyal friend or two. Every emergency must be monitored. Particularly in your presumed absence.

Sometimes you have to disappear because there is no other way of avoiding trouble. Becoming scarce is a survival skill. Sometimes you keep a low profile to conserve your energy. By the time you re-alize that you have earned the right not to be everywhere, you are exhausted anyway, so going out every night is as impossible as it is needless.

Disappearing as a strategy rather than a lifestyle choice often comes in the wake of a career debacle. Then it is wise to disappear, preferably to a spa or ashram, to rehabilitate. You emerge tanner and thinner, full of contrition, when someone else is the topic of the month, and you can publicize, à la *People* magazine, your newfound perspective or sobriety or hot deal. Need I say the words Hugh Grant?

When Hugh Grant got himself into a compromising position, so to speak, on Sunset Boulevard, it precipitated the most astonishing collision of high-profile and low-profile strategies I've ever seen. Hugh's strategy was to disappear. If there were ever a time to split, this was it — to nurse his wounds in the country, therapize, and collaborate on a beautifully written magazine profile for three months hence. But this was not to be, because he blew it the week before *Nine Months* had its national release. At the very moment he needed most to lay low, it was his job to sell the movie. Fox's agenda was to open the movie and Hugh was its star. His face was on the cover of every newspaper (tabloid) and magazine in the world. This was an ugly time to fly to L.A. for Hugh.

The stunned and lovely Elizabeth Hurley, Estée Lauder model and ingenue, at that moment the most popular girlfriend in the world, dutifully played her role. She wanted to work in this town again. Fox's only concession to the miserable fact that Hugh had to sell himself in the middle of his debacle was that the company actu-ally sprung for a private jet to fly Hugh and Elizabeth from London to L.A., surprising the entertainment community with a rare show of generosity. But it must have been a glum flight! The two no-tables were greeted by cheering fans and teeming paparazzi yelling, "Elizabeth! Hugh! Did you kiss and make up?" Hollywood is very forgiving, particularly in the face of good copy or hit movies. We love a good comeback.

OTHER GOOD TIMES FOR LOW PROFILE

1. The weekend your movie "doesn't open" — instead it limps through its first weekend miserably and/or gets slammed by the critics.
2. During a secret affair with a movie star (this never happens, as all affairs with public personalities are public).
3. When you get bad press (unless you make the tactical decision that it's high-profile time and you have to press flesh like you're running for office).
4. When someone wants an answer you don't have.
5. When you have the answer but you don't want to be the one to give it.
6. When the answer might be different if you wait a week.

LOW-PROFILE LOCATIONS WHERE NO ONE WILL SEE YOU

Brooklyn
Cleveland
Afghanistan (Unless there is a war.)
Le Dôme at dinnertime

LOCATIONS THAT SEEM LOW PROFILE BUT REALLY AREN'T

Bosnia (You will run into Phil Robinson, director of *Field of Dreams*, with the *Nightline* crew.)
New York (What were you thinking?)
The Viper Club (A *National Enquirer* reporter is there and you're in trouble.)
A gay bar (An ad in *Out*.)

HIGH-PROFILE TIME

There are some moments when a producer, writer, or director simply must be visible, like when she gets a new job or her movie opens to great reviews. Some people must be visible constantly or else they think they don't exist. They vacation where everyone else will

see them and then fret over invitations they don't receive from remote vacation spots they can't get to anyway.

It is possible to make a life (sort of) consisting of traveling with
one's phone sheet and maintaining a high profile year round. There
is a set of appropriate vacation spots for every season: Christmas is
Aspen or Hawaii, preferably the Mauna Kea. Spring, try Sun Valley
or Paradise Valley, or Montana. Summer is Martha's Vineyard or the
Hamptons. (L.A. has no autumn.)

In this version of reality there is somewhere fabulous to be every
night and a person from whom to glean some critical piece of information wherever one goes. So voila! You're always working.
This serves Calvinist and Jewish guilt-stricken personalities who
can't justify leaving town (or the house for that matter) unless they
are working. I find people like this more compulsive than tactical,
although it's clearly tactical when you're young and establishing
your identity. A person who is a decade into his career and is still
out hustling every night, however, cannot make movies on location
because he can't leave town. These are executive types, producer
types, or agents who never meet a single crew member in the whole
moviemaking process but feel responsible for it nonetheless.

I might have been trapped in this syndrome had I not partnered
with Debra Hill on *Adventures in Babysitting, Heartbreak Hotel,*
and *The Fisher King.* Because I didn't want to concede all production issues to her, I got to learn from a great teacher the job of being producer-on-set. This freed me, first from my phone list, which
seemed increasingly irrelevant, then from screenings I didn't really
have to attend, then from my sense of obligation to be at certain
parties. All of this allowed me to see that the face-time, name-
dropping-time, "be there or be square," or worse, "be there or
you're nowhere," Hollywood version of life and work was an impressive illusion. When I was on location, really working, people in
Hollywood were so involved with their own invitations they never
even knew I was gone. This gave me an astonished feeling of freedom, and I grabbed it. Later I came to see that location could save
me from toxic overexposure.

Production on set became an escape route from the horrors and
rigors of development hell and reinforced a lesson I was finding

everywhere: It's the work that matters. It's not the party, not the meeting, not the phone list, not the good table, not the title, not the credit, not the status. Making movies, the actual mechanics of doing the job, is where the action is.

Location living has freed me to come and go as I please. Today my idea of a big time is missing a party. I have found that scarcity helps me maintain some degree of privacy and autonomy. Most of all it gives me freedom from the tyranny of the dominance hierarchy. (I go to Austin, Texas, where no one cares if *Hot Zone* is going or not. For that matter, they don't even know what *Hot Zone* is!)

GOOD TIMES FOR HIGH PROFILE

1. The weekend your movie opens to $10 million or upward.
2. When you are hanging out with a movie star.
3. When your hot English director comes to town.
4. When you get fired. You have to be Okay! Happy! Fine! Mulling over offers!
5. The week any promotion is announced: Watch the friends come out of the woodwork.
6. When the trades announce your new green light. Why not be around for the rare burst of goodwill?

HIGH-PROFILE LOCATIONS OUT OF TOWN WHERE YOU'RE SURE TO RUN INTO YOUR ROLODEX:

The Russian Tea Room when it reopens (You like each other so much better here than at the commissary.)

Herbert Allen's annual retreat in Sun Valley, Idaho (Where powerful men convene to put together deals like the ABC-Disney merger over lunch. How would I know?)

London (At the Groucho Club, international movie watering hole.)

The Lido (The Hôtel du Cap at Cannes festival time.)

Need I say Aspen?

HURRY UP AND WAIT

The pace of business is erratic. Sometimes the pace of change is glacial; at other times bursts of change happen in rapid succession, just like cosmic development. The universe was made in bursts of high energy interrupted by long spells of nothingness. This is my life. The cosmologists call this "punctuated equilibrium." In Hollywood, we call it "hurry up and wait," when nothing happens for what seems like millennia, and then everything happens at once.

In physics, clumps of gas suddenly accrete to become matter, and matter accretes to become massive structures like galaxies. Then for vast amounts of time nothing accretes at all. This is why the universe is irregular. I think it is also why we feel like we're going insane a lot of the time in the movie business. It is a case of punctuated equilibrium too. And highly irregular.

Contact is a prime example of punctuated-equilibrium development. It was the very first project I brought to Peter Guber back in 1979, scientist Carl Sagan's first novel, a big event and a coup for me as a baby executive. Carl's wife and partner, Ann Druyan, was and is my dearest friend. By remarkable coincidence or by destiny, depending on your perspective, Carl, Annie, and I all met on the same night. It was a dinner party at Nora Ephron's house, and as soon as I walked in, she introduced me to Annie, who was then engaged to another dear friend. Talk about fateful encounters.

"You must meet Annie," Nora said. "She loves baseball as much as you do." We've been great friends ever since. Soul sisters. Moments later my soul sister met her soul mate, Carl. And they've been together ever since. We all have.

Carl's novel was about a woman radio astronomer's search for extraterrestrial life, based on the existing S.E.T.I. (search for extraterrestrial intelligence) program, which Carl had been critical in founding against great odds and some formidable scientific opposition. Over four months, we created a treatment that was the beginning of an evolutionary process that would, seventeen years later, result in the movie we are still trying to mount. Like random atoms that, gravitationally bound, become clumps of matter that later combine to form galaxies, the long march to the creation of the universe, or, metaphorically in my case, *Contact,* began with a single burst of energy: the treatment. It was later sold to Simon & Schuster and became a bestseller around the time I left Peter Guber to work for David Geffen.

Ah, but the transition from Guber to Geffen, mentor to mentor, wasn't that easy. It only reads that way in the bio. In truth there was a lost year, my 1984, an important and sad one. I can't remember the exact moment I realized it was time for me to move on from working with Peter. He was running with the projects that I had initiated, and I wasn't willing to abdicate my work just when it was starting to get interesting. Trying to hold on, I looked for a way to cling to my projects with Peter while taking on some baby projects for independence. I was scared and didn't know how to navigate this very thin line. Like Zeus, David Geffen interceded. He took me out for a slice of Ray's pizza and offered me a job with his new film company.

Whenever David and I had a career chat, he'd take me out for his favorite food — a hamburger at L.A.'s famous Apple Pan or a slice of Ray's. Moguls like David are irresistible when they are either courting or coercing you. I was enormously flattered that he saw something in me, but I was ambivalent, a big mistake with David. I asked him if I could stay involved with the projects to which I was contractually bound with Guber, *Flashdance* and *Contact* among them. These projects were the sum total of my last three years in Hollywood, all that I could call my own, and I was loath to leave them. They had become me, and I thought I had become them. If I lost them I feared I'd lose my way.

"No," David said. "You can't have your cake and eat it too." (Sometimes I think only he gets to.) But he was right. He wanted me to give his company my full attention and not split my passion between his projects and mine. I was torn. Was a secure job with a brilliant mentor enough to entice me to give up everything that I had worked on so far?

Scared, I called Barry Diller, a rare use of access I kept in reserve from our time as friends in New York. He knew me *and* David *and* the movie business, so he was the perfect adviser. He suggested that if I wanted to stay involved with my movies, I might consider partnering with Mary Tyler Moore, who had decided to manage her own career in the wake of her recent professional and personal divorce from Grant Tinker.

Mary and I met for lunch at the Café des Artistes in Manhattan and we talked for hours. It was to be the best meeting, in a way the *only* meeting, we ever had. She was exhilarated by the prospect of taking over her own career after years of being mentored by and married to a mogul, Grant Tinker. Her excitement was contagious; we spoke about the movies I would develop for her, the writers we would work with, the directors she wanted to pursue. She wanted to work with the best new writers in town. I knew them. We thought anything was possible. She had no problem with the idea of my staying involved with my babies from my Casablanca marriage.

I was to be the head of her film division at her namesake company, MTM, making movies for her to star in and for us to produce together. In a terrible mistake, I didn't go to work for David. (I didn't strike while the iron was hot.)

Things didn't turn out as either Barry or I (or Mary, I think, for that matter) expected. Her partners at MTM immediately encouraged her to make a movie in New York for three months, the very same months I started. The New York movie was the sepulchral medical melodrama *Six Weeks* (ironically a Peter Guber production). The movie flopped, and her partners changed Mary's phone number. I had to assume that they were not supportive of her desire to develop her own movies, at least not with me. I was put in exile in a small office three blocks away from the studio lot, cut off from any access to Mary. We met only twice more the entire year. I was unable to set up anything through her remaining partners in Los Angeles; they hadn't hired me and seemed to have little interest in whatever movie ideas I could muster. They rejected, among other things, a John Hughes vehicle and many other long-forgotten and misbegotten efforts. Gradually I stopped caring, and agents stopped calling. My momentum ground to a dead halt. Then they fired me. I was out of business, first figuratively, then literally.

I was in despair; I had thought I was a wunderkind, destined to succeed. Since my mentor husband had launched my career, it had been nonstop go, go, go, despite the early, temporary crash at

Casablanca. My husband's work was crashing all around him too, stuck in a political quagmire between the leadership of his company, Simon & Schuster, and its parent company, Paramount. He had staked a claim for Simon & Schuster in the movie business, but his boss, Dick Snyder, was on the East Coast running a publishing house, and the leadership of Paramount had no interest in paving the way for either David *or* its upstart subsidiary. With no mentor to guide his way, David had had to make it all up as he went along. I was frightened for him and tried to give him advice, to share some of the things I had learned from Guber.

But I really had no expertise from which to give such advice. Our marriage was based on the unspoken understanding that he was the daddy and I was the student. It seemed to me that he felt diminished, almost undermined, by my efforts to help. But when my work collapsed, we were back in the trenches together with no other allies, and we leaned on each other for a short while longer. We were broke with a toddler and only our wits to protect us.

Over the hill, *Flashdance* was being made and I was nowhere near it. Tom Hedley had long since been replaced by Joe Eszterhas, who doused the movie with a sleaziness it didn't deserve. But no one cared what I thought; my opinion was not heard, solicited, or considered. My expertise had been used, the baton had been passed, and I was no longer relevant. It was time for the pros. In turning down Geffen I had held out for nothing. Maybe some people can figure out how to have their cake and eat it too. I haven't been able to, so far.

I had a dream around that time that forever changed the way I saw my work. I was a little girl in summer camp, standing in line to do gymnastics. When it was my turn to tumble, the counselor said, "You have to go to the end of the line, Lynda. You can't take your turn." I waited again for my turn and again I was turned back. It happened over and over. Eventually I cried out to the counselor, "All I want to do is take my turn, do my gymnastics!" I woke up with a start and sat up. The dream was about the frustration I had felt at MTM and it told me exactly what work meant to me. It wasn't the money or the glory or the status or the power. It was the incredible opportunity to take my turn.

I was able to return to work with an exhilarating focus I never would have earned if I hadn't faced failure. Now I knew the point of the whole enterprise — my turn at work — and finally I could get good at it.

My time had come; it was my turn to kiss Geffen's ring. "Got to go Geffen" became my mantra. I called David and asked for the job. I told him I'd made a terrible mistake, that he had been right and I had been wrong (David loves this). I told him I had learned the value of this job and that I wanted it and needed it. David saw the precariousness of my position, that he was holding the strings of my career in his hands. My palms were sweaty as he passed the buck. "I'd like to help you out, Lynda, but it's not up to me," he said. "I hired Eric Eisner to run the company."

I was shattered, needlessly. Of course David was in control. I should have known that he was always in control. He was being proper and ceremonial in deference to his effort at hierarchy. But Geffen was the only option in my mind's eye, and I had convinced myself that only with the appropriate groveling would I get my job. Bad timing on my part, I thought. Eric doesn't know me, and I have to start the campaign all over again.

My pride long gone, I called Eric for lunch. One day he called back and I made my pitch, anxious not to sound too — well — anxious. Truthfully, I hadn't any options, at least none that I could see. I had painted myself into a dark corner and I'd lost what small visibility I'd been able to accrue. The campaign was slow and persistent. Over a series of lunches, a ritual courtship, I tried to be helpful to Eric, simulating how I would be to work with. I offered suggestions on material, sharing whatever information I had. I made jokes and swapped gossip. Eventually Eric and I got comfortable together, and David hired me. I accepted a twenty-thousand-dollar pay cut despite the fact that David Obst and I had recently separated, and I had to support my son.

Over the next three years with Geffen Films I had a happy home where I developed scripts and met new writers on David's behalf. The company was in the final throes of postproduction on the final cut on *Risky Business* when I arrived. There were conflicts with the director over the tone of the ending, and David asked for my opinion. I was back in the fray again, the best twenty-thousand-dollar loss I ever took.

In a loftlike perch over a catwalk next to David's office, I took phone calls and worked with writers. My first meeting was with Tom Hedley, whom I brought in to develop a script for Michael Jackson, then in his prime. It wasn't long before the phones were ringing and the scripts were pouring in. I was soaring again, relieved and grateful to be of use.

It was during my first month at work that I attended my first audience test preview, for *Risky Business*. Unbeknownst to me, it was to be the site of a showdown over the ending between the filmmakers and us, the studio. (Whoa, "Us!")

Although *Risky Business* may have been written as a hilarious teen comedy, Paul Brickman, in his directing debut, had shot it lovingly, almost like a French art film. In his first cut, the ending was a bit bitter and sad: The girl, Rebecca De Mornay, rejected the hero, Tom Cruise, who also didn't get into Princeton. David wanted to change the ending and make it more upbeat. The filmmakers were adamantly against it. The test-preview scores were designed to test the effect of the ending and the overall appreciation of the movie. They weren't high enough to secure the ending the director wanted.

I remember the producer coming up to me and saying, "You ought to support the filmmakers. It's your job." I was torn and confused. It seemed to me that it was a comedy, albeit a serious one, and I for one *wanted* Tom Cruise to get into Princeton. We huddled in the lobby and argued and finally reached a decision. We would shoot a new ending, a moderately happy one, and test it. If the scores went up substantially, we would use the new ending. If the difference was negligible, the filmmakers would keep their original ending.

The scores soared. The movie was a hit, though the filmmakers were, sadly, still unconvinced. But I learned all about the power of endings to make a movie work and to take seriously David Geffen's instincts.

For ten long years, including my three years at Geffen Films, *Contact* was no longer in my universe, at least not on my radar screen. Guber had taken it to Warner Brothers, where he had become their premier producer with his partner, Jon Peters. Guber's company developed script after script for *Contact*, each one missing the mark. The movie never left my heart; it was the project I missed most of all as I began my producing career, the one that sprang from the source of my deepest interests. It was a little like giving up a baby for adoption; it haunted me like a phantom limb.

Ten years is a cosmic millennium in the time frame of the movie business. That's how long it took for me to get this project back in my universe, a karmic boomerang. When Peter Guber left Warners in his now notorious move to Sony, the project became free. Lucy Fisher, then executive vice president at Warners (now vice chairman of Sony), who had believed in it and kept it alive all those years, gave it back to me without any memories of my prior involvement. (Of course I would think she's brilliant. But she is!) Suddenly Lucy wanted to accelerate the project. From "wait," I was now in a "hurry-up" offense. For his strong attraction to science and his superior visual skills, I chased Jim Hart, the writer of *Mary Shelley's Frankenstein, Hook,* and *Bram Stoker's Dracula.* After I got him to say yes I had to wait for him to become available. A year later I had a good, solid draft, but not quite good enough yet for a green light. Warner Brothers felt, and I sadly conceded, that although Jim Hart had brought visceral skills to the adaptation and conquered the narrative, he had not drawn the characters' psychological journeys. I had to hurry up and find a new writer whose talents lay in rendering psychological truth to romance. Only then could I generate enough energy that our movie could start to take hold.

In the best of circumstances the writer will not have to be replaced. The original writer of *The Fisher King,* Richard LaGravenese, was both the spiritual and intellectual source of the piece. He was an able professional, capable of adjusting and finely tuning his own work to the evolving needs of the director. But in cases where you must replace the writer, the process of development is bumpier. Sometimes a writer burns out when the project or the process exhausts him to the point of diminishing creative returns. Sometimes you've made the wrong choice of writers in the first place. Other times the needs of the piece gradually change as it gets closer to production — like when an action piece needs a comedy rewrite for Whoopi Goldberg or Jim Carrey (these are expensive), or when a thriller needs a "character polish" to attract Robert Redford or Al Pacino (these are very expensive). Writers whom you can count on to develop go pictures, the ones who have done it time after time, are the most expensive of all. You buy them when you can't take chances — like when a big movie star's commitment is contingent on the script.

After meeting with many writers, expensive and less so, I chose Michael Goldenberg for *Contact*. He has since become a director (*Bed of Roses*, starring Christian Slater and Mary Stuart Masterson), but he wasn't well-known then, nor had he written a go movie, so given the need for momentum he was a risky, though not expensive, choice. (He's expensive now.) But his ideas were so on target, his connection to the piece so profound, his conviction so palpable, I was able to convince Lucy Fisher and her brilliant protégé, Courtney Valenti, that he was our guy. He had an uncanny empathy and insight into the loneliness of our character, Ellie. Up to now, she had been aloof and impenetrable, a radio astronomer with her scanners pointing toward the sky and no connection to us at home. We had no emotional access to her. Michael understood that this was the point, that Ellie looked outward in large part to avoid looking inward. He felt the hole in her soul and made us feel it too. Six weeks after he got hold of the script, a draft arrived while I was shooting on location in Texas. Like the saying goes, I read it and wept. He had licked it.

Physics in the form of energy had been generated. The studio loved the draft and began making offers to directors. Galaxy formation time — when stars can be attracted and movies can get made. It was slipped to Steven Spielberg, the true mark of hot, right after *Schindler's List* came out and although it wasn't for him (for whatever reason), within weeks it had attracted Australian auteur Dr. George Miller. It took a year of hurry up and wait before he fully committed. Then we had eighteen months of three sets of writers racing toward a start date we didn't make. When George Miller eventually left the project, the clock started ticking from scratch. See what I mean about timing?

The secret of almost every deadline (at least any nonproduction deadline) is that it is abstract. You speed to submit a script, pass out trying, and then no one reads it for weeks. Then one weekend the studio reads your script and you commence a new set of rewrites with a new frantic deadline. People are hysterical. They call you day and night to see if you are through. You are through — with them, is what you think. But still you press on, day in and day out, night in and no nights out, until you make your bloody deadline. Then what? You guessed it. No one reads it for weeks (they are onto other emergencies, torturing other writers), and you could die of old age waiting for a response. Then all of a sudden you are awakened from your depressed slumber to confront yet another deadline. That is if you are lucky and you've done everything right up to now. This form of madness is quintessential hurry up and wait. This is true for all professions in Hollywood, except maybe for agents. They can just "hurry up and hurry up" because they make deals, which are always in a hurry. They have no other product (maybe it's their influence that puts the rest of us in such a panic).

We survive this by learning to pace ourselves. (Sort of. We try, anyway.) We have to build pacing into our internal timing and not get exhausted too early. We must learn to discern the difference between a real and a false deadline. Answer: A real deadline costs money if it's missed.

FRONT BURNER/BACK BURNER

There are times when you just have to face facts. Eat the reality sandwich. Despite all of your best efforts, the project you're trying to assemble is not coming together. It will not cohere. Yet.

Because perseverance is such a critical skill, because the ability to go on in the face of constant rejection is our job as producers, it is often hard to tell when it's time to throw in the towel. We are pathologically averse to throwing in the towel. Our job is to keep standing no matter how much force is applied to knock us down.

But there are moments when we must recognize that we are not giving up; we are merely moving on. We are waiting for another day (or lifetime) in which what is now impossible will become possible. We call this moving the project to the back burner, where it doesn't get completely cold but where it is no longer cooking at full boil.

This is a form of putting it on the roof; it's just a very, very big roof. Long-term parking. When you're pushing a project that nobody wants, it gets stale, and all your best efforts are for naught. Alas! It reminds me of what my mother used to say, "Stop knocking your head against the wall." Your brow can get so bloody your vision will be diminished, and it becomes hard to see that all you're doing is wounding yourself and, by extension, the project. Though it's hard to explain to your partners when things are definitively not working, putting a project on the back burner is often the kindest and best thing you can do for everyone.

There are many ways in which the fortune of the project can be enhanced later in a changed market:

1. The genre becomes hot where it was cold. For instance, period pieces are suddenly in. Thank you, *Little Women* and *Sense and Sensibility*.
2. A new, hot director, previously unheard of, is looking for a project just like yours.
3. A new star has broken out of the pack, à la Sandra Bullock, whose special interest coincides with your project. That's one of the reasons *The Net* came together. Sandra was intrigued with the brave new world of the Internet.
4. The studio administration changes, and new people are in power who love your script.
5. You've had intervening good luck (read: a hit picture) and you have leverage and credibility you never had before.

When any of these factors occurs you will take your little pot that's simmering on the back burner and place it on the front burner, full steam ahead. Until then, you have put your project on the roof to take it down another day when the factors have changed. This is critical for the conservation of energy (your own) and for the preservation of your credibility. No one wants a project that has been recently passed on, but people rarely remember the history of the piece when you bring it back to them with new hot elements attached. There is a fine line between perseverance and madness. By the same token, don't give up too soon.

A producer is as good as his inventory, and legendary producers like Ray Stark (*Funny Girl, The Good-bye Girl, The Way We Were,* among others) are playing their inventory for thirty years and more. I think he had *Annie* in development for ten years before he made it. Ray is smart enough to know that the power structure is constantly changing and what was difficult for him to set up one year could become easy the next. (For example, an ex-employee with whom he once developed the project becomes head of a studio. He breeds them.) This takes a profound understanding of leverage, your own status, and the constantly changing status of everyone around you. This is how your inventory stays viable throughout your career. Many of us are still waiting for *The Way We Were* 2, and my guess is that we are not waiting in vain.

If a producer can be described as a dog with a script in its mouth, then a *great* producer owns the kennel with many rare breeds of dogs, each gnawing on a different script. If all fine wines have their time, so do all well-written scripts. A great producer lets go of nothing that was once valuable to him. He builds and works his inventory, keeping it viable, exposing the right script at the right time. Because I lost the race on *Hot Zone* doesn't mean it won't be made. Maybe I just lost the race to mediocrity; so every time I meet a new director who could be right or read a new writer who could save the script, *Hot Zone* moves to the front burner, ready to start cooking. I've been getting rewrites for six years on a property I own called *Above the Fold,* the true story of newspaper editor Bill Kovach and his tumultuous reign at the *Atlanta Constitution.* Recently, Dustin Hoffman joined us in development. A producer's inventory stays visible even when she is not. It is the value of our inventory that keeps us alive during the inevitable ebbs and flows of our personal power.

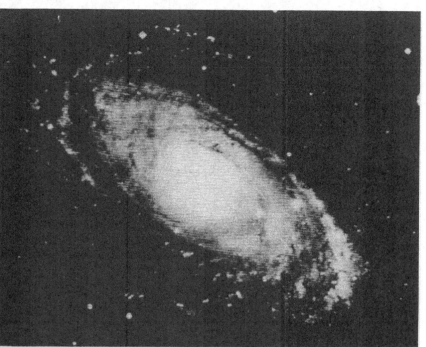

HALE OBSERVATORIES: *Spiral Galaxy in Ursa Major*, 1950

POLYGRAM PICTURES
CONGRATULATES
DR. CARL SAGAN
ON HIS EXTRAORDINARY
13 PART TELEVISION SERIES
COSMOS
DEBUTING SUNDAY,
SEPTEMBER 28TH
ON PBS.

WE ARE PROUD
TO BE ASSOCIATED WITH
CARL SAGAN AND
CARL SAGAN PRODUCTIONS
IN THE MAKING OF
THE FIRST MOTION PICTURE
CONTACT
FOR UNIVERSAL PICTURES
IN 1981.

PolyGram Pictures

Development hell: wrong studio, wrong decade. The only factor that never changed over fifteen years was its author, Carl Sagan.

With Dawn Steel (left): girlfriend, ally, glass-ceiling crasher, bud, and trenchmate.

Elisabeth Shue's first star turn, singing the babysitting blues with the late legendary bluesman Albert Collins in *Adventures in Babysitting*.

Debra Hill, Chris Columbus, and me: A team is born. Our first movie as partners and Chris's first movie as a director was *Adventures in Babysitting*.

Chris Columbus and me at the monitor on the set of *Heartbreak Hotel,* when and where I fell in love with Texas and making movies.

Mother and son on location in Texas: heartbreak time, bonding time.

Right to left: "Bad girls" Drew Barrymore and Mary Stuart Masterson, and *Bad Girls* captain Jonathan Kaplan with teammates Ralf Bode (cinematographer) and me, watching the action on the monitor.

Me with my favorite bad girl in the whole wide world, Drew Barrymore —fellow Texas highways traveler.

Fisher King maestro Terry Gilliam (left) with "Jack," Jeff Bridges.

Meg Ryan searches for Mr. Right, Tom Hanks, in *Sleepless in Seattle*. Good instincts!

"Parry," Robin Williams, dresses up for the date of his life in *The Fisher King*.

At the monitor with Nora Ephron (left), chatting between shots or planning lunch.

Any time a movie star visits you on the set, you take a picture. Sally Field (left) visits Michael Hoffman and me on the set of *One Fine Day*.

My idea of a heroine: Michelle Pfeiffer as the definitive single working mother with her movie son, Alex Linz, in *One Fine Day*.

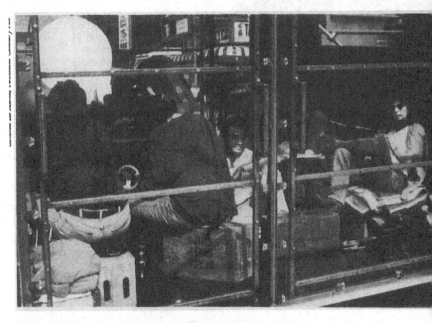

Hard-core production: A grip-designed "lexan" cuts a taxi in half and attaches it to the production crew. Fun! Shooting L.A. for N.Y. on *One Fine Day*.

eing in the loop is getting along with your
rector. Here I am deeply getting along
ith Michael Hoffman on *One Fine Day*.

Chatting with swoony George Clooney
between takes on *One Fine Day*, after which
he was immediately whisked off to the
waiting set of *ER*.

efinitive "Chix in Flix": all the women of *One Fine Day*.
ont row: costumes —Susie De Santo; executive producer—Kate Guinzberg; producer—
e; writer—Ellen Simon; my boss and assistant—Elizabeth Hooper; assistant to the direc-
r—Sarah Goodman; accountant—Barbara Gutman. *Back row:* UPM—Donna Bloom;
producer—Mary McLaglen; assistant accountant—Mo Crutchfield.

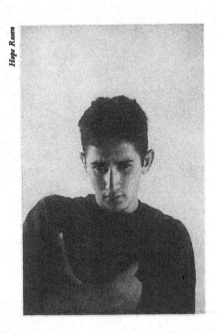

Hope Rosen

Oly Obst at seven-
teen, brooding à la
James Dean.

My true home in
Fredericksburg,
Texas. *Sleepless*
bought it for me,
and there I get to
sleep.

Courtesy of the author

Chapter 6

THE TAO OF POWER

"Those who like to fight
and so exhaust their military
inevitably perish."

— *The Art of War*

"He who comes first will later come last,
as the times they are a changin'."

— *Bob Dylan*

DURING MY DARKEST HOURS in *The Hot Zone*, which extended over eight long months, I developed a monklike routine I was convinced would save me. The basic pattern was to awaken to four phone calls: one from the head of production of the studio, one from Robert Redford's partner Rachel Pfeffer, one from the chairman of the studio, and one wild card, usually from the press. "Is it true Ridley's leaving the picture?" they would ask. "No, of course not," I would answer and then bound off to work to find out if it was true that Ridley Scott, the director of our picture, was in fact out the door.

I would spend the rest of the day trying to hold together all the remaining elements until time was up, seven P.M. With any luck, whoever was left in the picture by then would be held in place at least until the morning, when it would start all over again. At night I would go to yoga, trying to drain the tension from my mind and body. Then I would come home and read *The Art of War* by Sun Tzu (which I later discovered everyone else was reading too) until I dozed off with visions of viruses dancing in my head.

In my borderline state I came to believe that this routine was living and would ultimately spell my victory. That I, exerting my greatest efforts; my well-placed allies; my superior material; and the purity and nobility of my evening pursuits would be sufficient to ensure my success. This defense was all I could muster to protect me from the terror of absolute free fall. It was like living in a nightmare in which everyone watched me try to fly, and the only thing that kept me afloat was the frantic beating of my wings. I constantly felt as if there must be something I could do to keep the impossibly slipping pieces from falling out of the puzzle. I had to keep Redford in the movie at all costs — I believed in him; he had been so honorable to me and was so compelling a personality. My arms flapped faster and faster to stay aboveground. I kept spinning Bob to Ridley and Ridley to Bob. Each would give me his story notes; they rarely jibed. More flapping.

Then there was Jodie, waiting to read the script. Keeping these disparate satellites from crashing was my job and my life. What was I thinking? It seems absurd to me now, or at least hopelessly naive, because like it or not, there was only so much that I in my small corner of influence could accomplish. It was like living in a cancer ward. I felt that everyone wanted to watch me slowly disintegrate. (Paranoid?) I thought my fears were irrational until one day I got a call from a *Los Angeles Times* reporter when Bob fell out after loyally hanging in there for eight grueling, irrational months. For Bob, time had finally run out.

She threatened that if I didn't return her call, I would regret it throughout my entire career. "I don't get this," I said.

She answered, "You were a reporter, Lynda. You understand. We need to feel the heartbreak. You've got to tell me how you feel."

"Am I doing something illegal? Is this the Pentagon Papers? I thought I was just trying to put a movie together.

"Someday," I said, suppressing my indignation, "when I come to understand what actually happened, maybe I'll write about it, but thanks for your concern." I hung up the phone. I had to figure out what had happened and how to proceed. Once again I realized that I couldn't control the outside without an understanding of myself in relation to the tumult. I saw that it had become too personalized for me to gain any objective understanding. I had to figure out what had gone wrong, and my ability to conceptualize would be my tool for cutting through the muck. I had to get back to the eye of the hurricane, to stop being a victim of its catastrophic currents, or I would be overwhelmed. Sadly, I had to remind myself that the situation was merely a work disaster. No one I loved was in danger. It was a movie (or not a movie) — that's all.

The chemistry of the situation had become so combustible and volatile that even the combined control and efforts of my allies and me had profound limits. There were too many factors that put the situation simply beyond anyone's control: a fact that was initially impossible for me to comprehend. This was the moment I came to understand the limits of my power and the limits of power itself. Until I understood what it wasn't, there was no way I could understand what it was.

Power is not a static state. There is no such thing as power in the abstract or Power with a capital P. It is a dynamic noun that behaves like a verb. To power. To take power is the stronger infinitive. The secret that all powerful people know is that no one else gives you power. Someone outside of you can give you authority, but you must take your own power. With power, there is no permission to be granted. Permission must be seized.

TRADITIONAL DEFINITIONS OF POWER

1. The ability to say yes.
2. The ability to say yes and mean it.
3. The ability to fire the people who say yes.
4. The ability not to be seen as the person firing the people who say yes.
5. The ability not to be seen.

POWERQUAKES

The times are always a changin' in Hollywood. Most changes are full of sound and fury and signify nothing. These garden-variety changes are heralded by flashy banner headlines in the trades, but they are merely cosmetic changes — changes in personnel — although that doesn't stop us from obsessing over them. But every so often there is a powerquake so devastating that it actually signifies something. These create fundamental, as opposed to cosmetic, changes.

With cosmetic changes, a regime is replaced and new bosses beget new bosses. They then beget new deals, canceling the old. Often the most noticeable effects of these changes are in decor: Walls come down; carpets are switched (exit Santa Fe, enter chintz). In a cosmetic change the head of production (the person who picks the movies to go into development hell) may be replaced by a peer. Or the chairman (who green-lights those movies) is replaced by someone who is currently running or has recently run a competing studio. This happens all year long, year in, year out.

But genuine institutional change is much less frequent. Hollywood is still reeling in the wake of the most spectacular institutional change I have witnessed in fifteen years here. In July 1995 super-duper-mogul Mike Ovitz, founder of the most powerful talent agency, CAA, first publicly considered leaving his agency to helm MCA/Universal, paralyzing the entire town for a month. Ovitz had sought and achieved hegemony, first over all the other agencies by monopolizing the talent and then over the studios through his agency's bottleneck control of the talent. He did this slowly but surely, unceremoniously and with little fanfare, over two decades by structuring a Japanese-style system inside CAA. Counter to the cult-of-personality, boutique-type agents who thrived as autonomous potentates in the late seventies and early eighties, Ovitz created a system in which no single personality became so powerful as to threaten the good of the whole group. In the drugged-out eighties Ovitz cleaned up by paying close attention to his feature-director clients as their agents slept off the night before. He was the original early bird who captured the worm. His younger generation was trained in prudency, discretion, and sobriety. Under his system teams of young agents would coordinate the day-to-day submissions to their actors under the watchful eye of the senior agents. No one agent was then indispensable to the actor, a form of professional sensurround. Tactical management, in which young agents were given enormous responsibilities and commensurate salaries, ruled, disinclining them to leave. The myth of Ovitz's power perpetuated the bottleneck of control CAA had over major talent. His staff and clients breathed a collective sigh of relief when he declined the top job at MCA to stay in place at CAA. But they had exhaled too soon. In August he made the stunning announcement that he was joining the recently merged ABC/Disney as president, Chairman Michael Eisner's number two and heir apparent.

Everything went haywire once Ovitz removed himself from the foundations of the architecture he himself had helped create. As long as Ovitz was at CAA, the micro–power structure in the industry was stabilized, with the agencies in the dominant position to the studios. CAA was remarkably stable, some agents would say frustratingly so, until Ovitz started his powerquake.

But Ovitz is a visionary. He understood that the stability was only temporary, a local chimera, and that the power of the agencies themselves would be dwarfed by the changes of the oncoming telecommunications revolution. He knew the action was moving and he instinctively led the exodus from an era of stability into the next era of fragmentation and instability, from the local to the global. His departure created an aperture for his number two man, Ron Meyer, to climb through, and soon the entire upper management of CAA had departed to run huge conglomerates or to parts elsewhere.

This has created an upheaval so vast it is utterly transforming the institutional landscape of the industry. Ultimately it will affect hundreds of jobs, the salary scales of all the major stars, and the formation of new agencies, if not studios. All of the competitive talent agencies were destabilized by Ovitz's career change, and powwows are convening as I write as they try to determine how to loot CAA's prestigious client list in the absence of its parent figure.

More than just agencies and actors have been destabilized. Every studio administration is quaking at the immediate prospect of competing with ABC/Disney: their resources, their distribution capabilities, and the unique relationship that Ovitz has with his former clients. To make matters worse, MCA/Universal is now being run by Ovitz's former number two, Ron Meyer (a move that was pre-cipitated by Ovitz's first flirting with the job), so yet another studio is run by the former personal agent of such stars as Sylvester Stal-lone (with whom Meyer made his first $60-million deal), Michael Douglas, Whoopi Goldberg, and Goldie Hawn. How do rank-and-file studio heads compete for talent with the actors' former personal agents?

As the indomitability of CAA appeared to crumble, the compet-ing agencies tried to capitalize (naturally) on the first signs of any vulnerability. You have to remember the source of their unusual (even for agents) glee: CAA had been number one and, as such, vir-tually untouchable for so long. During the era of CAA dominance, agents had been almost paralyzed by the gothic reputation of Ovitz. It was thought that he could do anything: Change a release sched-ule, force casting, stop or start a picture, leap tall buildings in a single bound. The other agencies needed to assume that in his ab-sence the floor would be leveled, the town democratized. And the Wild West–like instability of the first few weeks after Ovitz's depar-ture gave many competitors hope. Rumors flew about the unhappy agents not placed on the newly reigning executive committee. Clients were besieged with destabilizing rumors. Rancor was mag-nified, every defection reported and repeated.

But when the shooting died down, it was clear that the hysteria had been fanned and exaggerated. CAA lost a few clients, but only a trickle of the predicted staff defections actually occurred. (A few big stars abandoned agents altogether and elected to work exclu-sively with their attorneys.) Astonishingly adept damage control went into effect (it's not for nothing that these Turks were trained to be a quietly efficient, mean machine), and within a few months of Ovitz's stunning departure the new CAA was signing new clients at the same rate as the years before.

Certainly the other important agencies — ICM, William Morris, UTA, and the newly established yet already thriving Endeavor (of which my brother Rick Rosen is a partner) — now had more room to move and groove, with no towering figure of mythic proportions to compete against. And a bellicose atmosphere that has come to be called the agent wars, in which gloves have been removed and all clients are up for grabs, has gripped the town. If not democracy, then at least a fierce natural selection now rules. But the governing committee of CAA — Rick Nicita, Lee Gabler, Jack Rapke, Richard Lovett, Bryan Lourd, Kevin Huvane, and David O'Connor — had among themselves long controlled the meat of the CAA client list. Very few stars split. Loyalty — a rarely observed but, when exhibited, deeply earned commodity — reared its local face.

This change at CAA was so huge it almost drowned out the electric buzz still ringing from the announcement of the formation of DreamWorks SKG six months before. DreamWorks is the studio that was formed by Steven Spielberg, David Geffen, and Jeffrey Katzenberg in the wake of Katzenberg's failure to capture the number two slot at Disney, later given to Ovitz. Are you getting the rhythm of this? Usually the more things change, the more they stay the same in Hollywood. But in these kinds of profound realignments of power, actual change occurs, always preceded by months of chaos.

As significant as this institutional change is, it is a symptom of a deeper, more fundamental change, a technological change. Perhaps there have been only three or four such fundamental changes in the history of Hollywood, including the move from silent films to talkies, the birth of television, and the breakup of studio control over distribution. The technology of distribution is now being transformed by the advent of the so-called information superhighway. The proliferation of cable networks, on-line capabilities, the ability to transmit software over telephone lines, Fox's successful fourth network, and the introduction of sky satellite global television are creating literally thousands of new distribution outlets. The telecommunications deregulation bill recently passed by the Republican Congress has forged the way for fundamental corporate realignments among telephone companies, movie studios and cable outlets, and networks.

It is only in the context of fundamental change that we can understand Ovitz's decision to leave CAA, a decision that has left much of Hollywood baffled. The everyday players are so committed to the power firmament — the dominance hierarchy, as they know it — they simply cannot fathom Ovitz's apparent willingness to be seen as a "number two" when he was the definitive "number one" for so long.

This perception, as British philosopher Gilbert Ryle would say, is a "category mistake." Our provincial mistake. We think that who reports to whom determines your power, when real power is the ability to get things done — things that reap billions of corporate dollars. The playing field in which this man is now a number two has global reach and consequences. Still, it seems odd in the little company town called Hollywood.

TIPS ON MOGULS

They Hate	They Love
1. Commercial airlines	1. Private jets
2. Long parties	2. Good gossip
3. Abuse of access	3. Quick phone calls
4. Unsolicited advice	4. Any compliment
5. Good news about enemies	5. Bad news about enemies

CHAIN OF COMMAND

"Who's zooming who?"

— *Aretha Franklin*

To whom one reports is a unit of measure. It measures the exact distance between the player and the center of power. It is the closest we can get to a calibrated answer to the question "How big am I?" More than the size of an executive's office or even his title, which no one remembers anyway, the fewer people between the player and a "yes," the more powerful he is. Inside a corporation the chain of command can become a fine latticework of byzantine complexity. People report laterally, vertically, and sideways, as in head of business affairs reporting to head of production. Sometimes the head of business affairs, the man who makes and structures the deals at a studio, is more powerful than the head of production.

When someone gets a big new job at a studio, everyone wants to know to whom she reports. A few years back, when a former studio head was being courted by a large multimedia corporation to run its film division, the executive ultimately passed on the job, presumably because of reporting issues. Someone else took the job; he had never run a studio, so the specific chain of command was not an issue. Within six months this exec was doing such a bang-up job — kicking butt and taking no prisoners — that he was clearly and dramatically running the ship. There was no discussion of who might be making the decisions. We simply watched them get made. People who care about whom they report to are concerned about their autonomy. But autonomy can't be quantified. It has to be earned. And perceived. I believe that autonomy is as profound an illusion as power itself.

As you can see, there are limits to defining power merely in terms of who reports to whom. A perfect example is Turner Pictures president Amy Pascal. Having to report to Scott Sassa, chairman of Turner Pictures, does not diminish the diminutive, feisty, and talented Pascal one teeny-weeny bit. Over the years, she has shepherded through development and production many hits, including *A League of Their Own, Groundhog Day, Little Women,* and *Sense and Sensibility.* Her taste is so singular and decisive that everyone recognizes her decision making as hers. Her autonomy comes from her sensibility, and this means that her talent is her power base. She can take it with her. It would have been foolish for her to have refused the job on the assumption or fear or possibility that her decisions could be curtailed or controlled. Achievement breeds confidence in those above you. Their confidence in you is the only real autonomy.

In this context perhaps we can try and better understand Mike Ovitz's willingness to report to Michael Eisner. (It's a struggle for many power groupies.) From his new perch at the near helm of this telecommunications giant, Ovitz has a redefined power. He now has a hand in developing a brand-new kind of telecommunications empire (which may someday be his), as opposed to what he left behind: putting together the deals that allowed other superplayers to establish a foothold in this new technological universe. This implies two perspectives: the short view and the long view. Reporting issues define the short-term view; establishing a power base on which you can thrive is the long-term view. Try to keep your eye on the ladder, not on the rung.

The size of the tumult in the wake of the change is a reliable measure of the power of a departee. It matters not if the person was fired or squeezed out, resigned, or was kicked upstairs. The departee becomes bigger than his employer if the ruckus of his departure is disruptive enough. Clearly this is what happened when Katzenberg first left Disney, in a dispute over Katzenberg's not being named to Frank Wells's number two position after his death. The split left Eisner (temporarily) diminished in the eyes of his peers. (Boy, did he get his revenge when he merged with ABC, where DreamWorks had previously made a huge television deal.) Perhaps by the time you are reading this, DreamWorks will have moved its television deal to another network, maybe the one pal Barry Diller began putting together in 1995. Or maybe Katzenberg and Eisner will have buried the hatchet in the name of cosmic capitalism.

During the short period between Katzenberg's leaving Disney and the formation of DreamWorks — the time was described as "mulling offers" — every studio head feared for his job. Out of work, Katzenberg was the most popular guy in town. Who says this town isn't sympathetic? Everyone was betting on Jeffrey. We didn't need a media analyst to explain his prospects. He is a perennial. His power is now personal — larger than any logo. His legend precedes (and may be in danger of exceeding) him. This is real power. When it no longer matters whether a person succeeds or fails on a given project. When his success is, in fact, assured unconditionally by general acclamation.

THE FOUR COMPONENTS OF POWER

1. Usurpation
2. Leverage
3. Information access
4. Perception

Usurpation is the act of seizing power, being in your opponent's face. Think basketball: When members of a defense play "in your face" basketball, they keep their opponents off balance. The more pressure they apply, the more mistakes their opponents make, creating opportunities for their offense to score. To play in someone's face you have to anticipate your opponent's moves: One wrong guess and he's past you. "Robber" barons aren't called that for nothing. They rob. Presumption, entitlement, fearlessness, profound selfishness, are all components of usurpation. In a sumo wrestling match, the winner holds his ground and then gradually, grabbing, pushing, and asserting, invades the space of his opponent by domination. What's his is his; what's his opponent's is his too. When two people vie for control — for the same credit on a movie — the one who successfully usurps is the winner. In Hollywood squeaky wheels get the most grease.

The more Zen application of usurpation is practiced by naturally powerful personalities like Michael Eisner, Jon Dolgen of Paramount, Mike Ovitz, David Geffen, and the talented producer Scott Rudin. They are by nature formidable and intimidating. Their appetite for battle and intrigue make potential rivals exhausted at the outset. These men have nerve, inexhaustible nerve. Their reputations are often so fearsome they truly can be Zen. With very little expenditure of energy they engage in a silent usurpation of other people's power.

Then there are people with great big personalities who can use them at will as a weapon in their work, like legendary action producer Joel Silver (*Lethal Weapons* 1, 2, and 3, *Commando,* and hundreds more). Joel has a personality like one of his action heroes, and when he wants to preempt a big action script that's being auctioned on the market, most producers walk away from the table. It's not worth the tumult and heartburn. If Joel wants the script, it's his. Why bid and lose?

If their rivals didn't cave to their knees in advance, it wouldn't work.

Leverage is the use of superior position for one's advantage. It is the most equal of all forces in an equation, the part of the equation that determines its outcome. It is with leverage that we attempt to control, and, as we know, control is everyone's objective and no one's accomplishment. Leverage is deceptive and relative. No matter how much you have in a given equation, someone can always enter it who has more (Steven Spielberg). This is good if it's on your side, bad if it's on the other side. Leverage is muscle, or the appearance of muscle, which is not an appropriate distinction, as muscle can be defined as the appearance of muscle. Leverage accrues. It is the real brass ring on the tinsel-go-round.

Leverage is good. We like it. It's like "chits" that we use to pay for the stuff that we need to get our work done well. We accumulate these chits mostly with hits. Hits breed chits. People sort of sense how many chits others are holding, and when they assemble the team for a movie, they assemble a poker hand of chits with which they can bluff their way through production.

As the producer working inside the studio, in most cases you have little leverage. So how do you protect your vision? Your sanity? Your baby? You accumulate the leverage of others as you negotiate your way through the process of getting your movie green-lighted. You collaborate (you have to). You become such a worthy collaborator that your more powerful partners (the ones with more chits) actually want you around. This is often complicated by what I call the ownership phenomenon.

When I developed *Flashdance,* I worked for Peter Guber and on my own had no leverage at all — zero chits. But I had found and developed the script and had helped set it up at Paramount. When Dawn Steel took it over as the studio exec, I was stunned to discover that she needed to take it over and make it hers. When Don Simpson came on board to produce, he too had a need to own the movie, to make it his. (The English gracefully call this process "pissing all over something to give it your smell.") The last person Don wanted to talk with was me. He already knew all of my ideas; they were in the script. He wanted to explore his own ideas. And I clung so hard to my ownership of the piece (I feared I'd never find another movie again) that I didn't act like someone the other players wanted to have around.

Rule of thumb: You must never look threatened as the big players come on. The march of the big players is the drumroll that announces the movie will in fact be made. This advice more critically applies to writers, who rarely have any leverage. Not being afraid of the big players is the secret to not being replaced as the process proceeds.

Information access is being on the inside and knowing what no one else knows. Information is currency. The more a producer knows, the better placed he is, the more helpful he is to his team. The ugly secret of corporate power (politics works the same way) is that actually getting something done is absurdly difficult. The decision making process is discreet and piecemeal, and effecting change is cumbersome and slow. But if you have access at least you know why nothing is getting done. With information you are not a mere pawn in someone else's machinations. Well, maybe you are, but you don't feel quite so helpless. When a producer has information, he must never share it, except tactically. Ipso facto, gossips know nothing because they're not trading information for anything useful, unless they are gossip columnists.

A producer or exec shares information tactically by trading it like baseball cards. (No, I don't mean insider trading. I mean protecting allies, guarding flanks, putting your movies back together.) For a producer, the following information would be considered currency:

1. A brand-new writer has just written a smashing comedy that Jim Carrey has committed to, and it's available. This is valuable to someone other than the producer — his studio chief — as the individual producer doesn't have the leverage alone to capture it (with the exception of Scott Rudin or Jim Carrey's manager-turned-producer).
2. Demi Moore's spring slot has just opened and the producer's studio is desperate to work with her this spring.
3. A hot new script is about to come onto the market next week.
4. An agent is leaving to join a studio.
5. A studio executive is leaving to join an agency.
6. Someone critical is in rehab. That person needs to be replaced immediately.
7. Most useful of all, an important cosmetic change has occurred and a new head of a studio is about to be named. The times are again a changin', and this news is currency for all.

At the tippy top information is not only power, it is literally money. With modern-day media moguls like Michael Eisner, Rupert Murdoch, Barry Diller, Sumner Redstone, and David Geffen all vying to power the engine on the oncoming information superhighway, every whisper of new data, any potential technological breakthrough that a rival doesn't yet know about, is vital for hegemony. Power is a place as well as a verb; it is inside the information tent.

One more thing: Although information access is not the most important component of power, it certainly makes you the most popular person at a dinner party and a constant invitee.

The *perception* of power consists of the following:

1. The biggest office (this implies the biggest deal).
2. The best car (this too implies the biggest deal).
3. The most projects (this does not imply the biggest deal; I have a desk full of projects and far from the biggest deal).
4. The most public attention and mention (this means the producer is either hot or in trouble, and I've been both).
5. Being noticed everywhere and being treated deferentially (this implies heat).

These perks are the accoutrements of power that we've come to believe are the sine qua non of big-time success, but they are not really success at all. Rather they are the indicators of "visibility," and visibility is vulnerability. Whatever goes up must come down. Whoever too. So the very status that someone so arduously pursues paradoxically creates insecurity.

My friend Dawn Steel once confided to me that as head of production only, she felt her autonomy clipped. More than anything, she wanted to be the first woman to run a studio: to have all departments — marketing, distribution, and production — reporting to her. Her remarkable eye for the bull's-eye, determination, and perseverance, as well as her brilliant usurpation skills, delivered her this plum in a very short period of time. At her moment of crowning glory, she was chairman of Columbia Pictures with the responsibility of overseeing TriStar as well. She was on the cover of *New*

York magazine to publicize her biography and she was unanimously declared to be Hollywood's most powerful woman. This vortex of publicity marshaled an astonishing degree of almost rivalrous hostility toward her. One magazine put her on the cover calling her "The Queen of Mean." Every week another nasty little item would appear, God knows from where, accusing her of being tough with some secretary or hairdresser. Suddenly she was fair game for every reporter and junior executive in town. People she had never met had an opinion of or an anecdote about her. No day was safe from broadside attacks. She had to wonder at times whether the backlash was worth her immense effort. I think it was, and so does she.

Getting a big title, becoming head of production or even head of a studio, doesn't automatically make you powerful (though it's a great start). Apart from giving the appearance and trappings of power, the title alone doesn't imbue you with the ability to get things done or garner respect. At first it's great tables in restaurants. But many people in positions of power become paralyzed when everyone wants something from them at every moment. This tends to make a normal person feel up against the wall. (It makes a megalomaniac feel great. Ask Newt.) Anyway, when they get there even seasoned players find the corporate ceiling crushing them. There is pressure. Lots of it.

NERVOUS NELLIES

"Out of nothing comes everything."

— *Tao Te Ching*

"Whether you go up the ladder or down it,
    your position is shaky.
When you stand with your two feet on the ground,
    you will always keep your balance."

— *Tao Te Ching*

If there are so many powerful people in Hollywood, why are there so many nervous people at Hollywood parties? Because they're all standing on shaky ground, and the calm ones stay home. As much as the dominance hierarchy seems like a firmament, you can see it is also a playing field that is constantly shifting. Like the tectonic plate it sits upon, Hollywood is subject to seismic jolts and constant tremors. Each season erupts with a new champion, and every so often a genuine earthquake will tear down the apparently secure infrastructure. The fact that everything is relative makes things even shakier.

If you live to get near the top of the heap, eventually you learn that there is no getting there because there is no superheap to be on top of. Witness Eisner, Murdoch, Geffen, Gerald Levin, Ted Turner, Sumner Redstone, all have their fifteen minutes of being number one before a new deal — even more gargantuan in its hegemonic implications — barrels around the technological curve. There's a sort of being on the right heap at the right time. There are glimpses of daylight from the upper tiers, but another body is always climbing up, closing the aperture. Someone can be the most powerful person in the room for seconds, but someone more powerful will always appear. There is no tippy top perch. But the need to believe in hierarchy is so profound in Hollywood that this is tantamount to agnosticism — like saying there is no Prime Mover. There is always a branch of a higher tree looming over your head, and when you climb to the top of that tree, all you can see is how many more trees there are. Then you try and buy up all the other trees, if the branch you're hanging from doesn't break along the way.

The problem is you can't buy all of the trees because even if you had that much money, new ones keep sprouting up. You can have *some* power, but for power freaks some is not enough. It is not *all* of the power. There is no such thing as all of the power, no matter how mighty you are. Ultimate Power is the elusive golden ball that everyone thinks everyone else is holding. But no one is. Knowing this should give some relief to those of us with sleeping problems, but no such luck.

No matter how much I learn, whether I'm winning or losing, having an up week or a down week, being crowned the Queen of the May or being scraped off the bottom of somebody's shoe, I still can't sleep. I know three A.M. all too well. I call it the hour of the wolf, when my mind suddenly jolts awake with an exaggerated list of mistakes I might have made the day before. I talk myself down. I remember colleagues who have confided that they too are awake at three in the morning, mulling over errors that I would consider inconsequential. Should I call them? No. Still, I can't sleep. Is Mike Ovitz awake? I wonder. Rupert Murdoch? How about Peter Chernin? Sherry Lansing? I like to think that there comes a time when you can sleep through the night, but I doubt it. Nervousness and anxiety are the fuels that feed the process. Insomnia is the cost of our ambition.

BULLIES

One night during the shooting of *This Is My Life*, Nora Ephron's directing debut about the effect of success on the relationship between a single mother and her two daughters, I called a guy producer friend for advice. The movie starred Julie Kavner, Samantha Mathis, Gaby Hoffmann, and Dan Aykroyd. By and large, things were going well on this production; we were like a family. But sadly, that night I had had to replace the cinematographer, who had been working for three weeks, as he wasn't properly lighting the picture. I had to replace him quickly to minimize damage to our production schedule and crew morale. When the producer heard the note of strain in my voice, he said cheerfully: "Don't feel bad. This is great for you! The first thing I always do when I arrive on my set is fire someone. They know who's boss after that! And everyone gets right in line."

I was stunned. The idea that firing someone could be regarded as either fun or strategic had never occurred to me. (I always thought about their families.) Since I don't go to such extreme measures, I wondered, do my crews think I'm a wuss? Absolutely not. Do they know who's boss? Absolutely. Somehow, although I am a short female who does not fire people the first week without cause, my crews *still* know that I am the boss because I make it my business to know what they're doing. And my reputation, for better or for worse, precedes me. This need to scream, berate, fire a lowly employee, demonize, or terrorize is fake power. It indicates deep-seated insecurity. The more beloved you are by your troops, the more devoted is their service to you in battle. (Witness the success of the Vietcong and Ho Chi Minh.) Petty tyrants are pathetic. I've seen well-known bullies go berserk when their planes are delayed, as though shrieking and threatening will make the weather change. Bullies are famous for being constitutionally incapable of waiting for a table in a restaurant, as though the very act of standing were an exercise in withering public humiliation. Bullies berate those who support them the most, as though the familial nature of work allows for truly abusive and demeaning conduct. Bullies have been sued for forcing their secretaries into everything from sex to drugs to fraud, and no bully has ever admitted to making a mistake. They often eviscerate their underlings in front of others in a public display of the casting off of blame. This is very unattractive, not to mention pathological. Many of us have fearsome reputations and are thought to be bullies whether or not we truly are. Personality plus power equals fear. *Buzz* magazine backhanded a bunch of us this year and pegged us as bullies. I was listed in the company of notables like Joel Silver, ex–Paramount chairman and producer Stanley Jaffe, current Paramount chairman Jonathan Dolgen, megaproducer Scott Rudin, and actress-diva Whoopi Goldberg.

Bullying personalities get away with murder in Hollywood and mistake their behavior for power, but *we* should not. (I certainly seem to get away with nothing.) It is hot air only, exhausting and debilitating. You will not see Mike Ovitz berate anyone in public. It's more than "noblesse oblige." It's conservation of energy. And loss of control is the true face of fear.

True power is invisible and impeccable, like good taste. It is never clumsy or artless. Powerful people whisper, suggest, seduce, in order to coerce. They only use volume for effect. This is how you can tell a blowhard from a mogul. We have our share of screamer-moguls here — some quite notorious — but I contend that they explode with less frequency as they rise up the ladder because they feel less thwarted (read: there are fewer people above them). The implied threat of their temper gradually frees them from having to use it. Most powerful people don't need to coerce; their mere presence is coercive.

It took me a long time to learn this, and just this month the chickens came home to roost when the *Buzz* issue appeared. I was awakened early one morning by a phone call from my "d" girl announcing, "You have been named one of the ten biggest bullies in Hollywood!" I was in the company of some of the most powerful, wealthy, legendary screamers in the business. If I was going to get a whiplash from an angry ex-employee and had to take a hit, I grumbled, at least I wanted to be paid as much as the rest of them. (Whoopi was on the list and she gets $10 million a picture. That would work for me.)

I was hurt and angered by what I thought was a mischaracterization. In fact, the whole thing made me so furious that I finally had to see from the scale of my reaction that it must, in some important ways, be true. Anyway, I guess it meant that I'd become successful enough to become a target, the small consolation that many of my friends (and my son) offered.

But coming from a background in journalism as I do, I've always found it hard to reconcile my idealistic roots at the *Times* with the way that entertainment journalism is practiced. I've often been in the position of defending the whole idea of a free press to many of my friends. Because what passes as journalism here is too often not journalism at all. It is the dyspeptic reporting of poorly sourced gossip, directed at targets who are often the object of a reporter's jealousy. Often journalism in Hollywood is sourced by a particular vendetta — the unexamined premise of the tip is, why is the person divulging it at all?

The personalities who are attracted to entertainment journalism are the kind that are attracted to celebrity but ambivalent about power. They tend to have a need to inflate and deflate their subjects almost at whim, and it reflects badly on the press as a whole. In Hollywood the stars and moguls who are the press's momentary obsessions often rightly cannot distinguish between the aims of real journalism and the tabloids because both are staked outside their homes. In their isolation they have come to question the very power of the First Amendment, a sad state of affairs. At this moment of my first bad press, I almost understood.

As it turned out, *Buzz* was a few years late with its scoop about my temper. Since I had a major insight on location five years ago, I've prided myself on my newfound ability to find my "Zen" center, which keeps me grounded in the face of daily horror. (I remember when Nora and I first got our green light on *This Is My Life*, she kept saying to me, "Let's stay Zen, Lynda. Stay Zen.") More important, since that time, when I began to release the illusion of my ability to control anything in my life, I have had no true reason to lose my temper. (Usually. People screwing up royally and lying about it still gets to me, big time.) Reaction and resistance are inevitable. I learned that anger is the reaction to a thwarted expectation of control — and I know there isn't any control, really. Here's how I learned this. I will never forget this moment.

I was on location with Nora in Toronto shooting *This Is My Life* and I needed to work out. The physical exhaustion of making the movie, compulsively wanting to be there for Nora at every second, our tight budget and cinematographer problems, were making me pretty tense. I always have a hard time sleeping, especially when I don't work out, so on a recommendation I tracked down a famous Yogi living in the woods behind the King Ranch. He was known for his gymnastic brand of yoga, for which I pursued him, but his class began with a half hour of breathing, which bored me witless (I like the jock stuff). "Breathe in ten, breathe out twelve. Breathe in ten, breathe out twelve," droned the Yogi. My mind was racing. This is the most ridiculous thing I've ever heard, I groused to myself. "Breathe in ten, breathe out twelve." Gradually I decided to try to breathe in to the count of ten. As I surrendered to the breathing, I suddenly realized that breathing in to the count of ten and breathing out to the count of twelve was one of the hardest things I had ever tried to do. And that if I couldn't control my own breath, what on earth made me think that I could control anything or anyone else? Maybe all that I could ever hope to control was myself. Things have been a lot more peaceful ever since.

THE SAD TRUTH ABOUT CONTROL

There is none. This is the fact that confounds the most effective of moguls: Power does not breed total control. In fact it breeds the illusion of control, which can be dangerous if you don't understand the distinction. Control freaks who believe their own press are constantly disappointed to discover that their power has limits. They live in continuous struggle with the borders of their control, in conflict with everything and everyone. Every losing bout is a bruising humiliation. This degree of illusion is exhausting and tends to extinguish the life force of everyone but the most pathological, raging control freak.

Artistic control is another piece of the illusion. Successful auteurs, wunderkind or otherwise, have a high degree of autonomy only if their movies make money. Woody Allen's autonomy has survived years of breaking even or worse because his movies cost so little. Control is a function of money. (Surprise!) If you are an independent filmmaker and you make a movie for five thousand dollars that you raised yourself, à la *El Mariachi,* you have control. But as Robert Rodriguez, the maker of that film, inevitably will learn, the more successful he gets, the larger the budget, the more numerous the collaborators, the less control he will have. Unless or until he finally becomes Steven Spielberg. (Maybe that's why nobody else has any artistic control, because Steven has it all.)

So who else besides Steven has control? Creatively, megadirectors like Robert Zemeckis, George Lucas, Sydney Pollack, and Rob Reiner have control. Otherwise it is by and large the financiers who have control. If you are making a movie with a director whose last movie was a blockbuster, his studio doesn't want to alienate him, which gives him operational leverage. The degree to which the studio is willing to bend to maintain and sustain the relationship with the director or star, or even you, for that matter, is a function of leverage. The same request made by Clint Eastwood and gladly acceded to by the studio (budget issues, number of cameras and editors, postproduction time) will be flatly denied to most others.

THE USE OF NONPOWER

My lesson about the Zen use of nonpower came from the unwitting assistance of the late mogul-producer Don Simpson *(Dangerous Minds, Crimson Tide, Top Gun, Days of Thunder)* in the so-called *Naked Hollywood* flap. In this BBC/PBS miniseries, all facets of Hollywood were investigated: the studios, the agents, the directors. The episode on producers featured Simpson/Bruckheimer making *Days of Thunder* and Debra Hill and me on the making of *The Fisher King*. Don and Jerry were at the crest of their high-flying testosterone era — it was a race-car movie, after all — swaggering in black leather and black Porsches. It was an image they had gladly cultivated, but under the scrutiny of the BBC it looked *très* eighties. The era of antiopulence was dawning, so we girls, adorned in jeans and ensconced in funky *Fisher King* production offices with cork bulletin boards, trying to cut a wardrobe budget, read, in contrast, better for the times. So they (the guys) hated their segment and, being the effective producers that they were, tried to kill it. They called all the newspapers. Got Paramount to withhold footage. It was set to air around the time of *Fisher King*'s national release, so the prospect of our segment not being aired was a large drag. I tried to contact my friends in the press, but everyone I reached had already talked with Don. I was paralyzed.

Then an ironic thing happened. So much energy had been exerted trying to kill the piece that it sparked a buzz. People started talking about the producers segment. If it was the only piece not to air, it was, of course, the only one everyone wanted to see. A bootleg copy was passed around Hollywood. Finally PBS, the American network set to air the series, was embarrassed into airing a version of the segment. Only our half was broadcast on our release date. As a result of the minicontroversy, it was the most widely watched segment in the series. Simpson/Bruckheimer's efforts had helped us. My inability to do anything retaliatory turned out to be an advantage. And a great lesson. I learned the publicity version of "from nothing comes everything." I manifested power by doing nothing, standing tall like a reed (as the *I Ching* would say) and not being blown over by the hostile winds.

THE HOLLYWOOD CATEGORICAL IMPERATIVE

Immediately upon the trade announcement of your promotion, you must manifest your new power by hiring, firing, doling out perks and deals, making tumult in the service of friends and to the detriment of enemies. Taking care of your friends (in moderation) when you can is the Hollywood Categorical Imperative. Do unto your friends so they will do unto you. After you've taken care of your friends, then engage in conspicuous consumption, the other cardinal rule of all new regimes. Go on a public shopping expedition. Buy hot scripts, books, and packages off the marketplace preemptively. Show your new muscle to the sellers by being their top buyer. This creates a wonderful wake of happy, newly perked, contented fans behind you, singing your praises.

A corollary of the Hollywood Categorical Imperative is Never Dump a Friend When He's Down; Never Desert an Ally After a Flop; Never Refuse a Lunch with a Recently Fired Exec. It's not just cynical base covering. Everything that goes down doesn't necessarily go up, but a lot does. Talented people and allies need to be supported in their isolation. In karmic terms the gesture is rewarded a thousandfold. True Hollywood compassion is self-referential: always knowing that *you* could be the one who's down and at one point will be. Real empathy for being in the boots of the other is the only antidote to the chilling and pervasive local *schadenfreude*, the rooting for others to fail as a way of life.

The Hollywood Categorical Imperative has worked for me. That is why I obey it. I take care of my friends so that eventually they can and will take care of me. This is the burden of power. I became a producer through the largesse of the Hollywood Categorical Imperative. When Dawn Steel became head of production at Paramount, I was still at Geffen, three years in. The bloom had begun to fade off the Geffen rose, though I hadn't quite realized it yet. The early years had been so exciting and family-like it took me a long time to realize I wasn't getting anything done. Activity, not action. I had developed a number of scripts, though none of them excited David. It's clear to me now that they weren't that exciting. But I was passionate about them nonetheless, and David was tepid.

David believed in heat; he lived at the center of the universe, where everything was very hot, and often that made me feel as if I lived in the chilly suburbs of the galaxy. My kind of development took a long time — young, inexperienced writers who hadn't had a picture made were my specialty then. So even when I found something hot from my outpost, David had reason to be skeptical.

So when I had something that turned out to be as hot as an exploding star, to punish the metaphor, he didn't blink. Through an old friend from high school in San Francisco, I got hold of an early draft of Zemeckis and Gale's *Back to the Future*, but David didn't respond. (I told him then that Spielberg believed in Zemeckis, who at that time had only made the marginal *Used Cars*. David said, "Lynda, if Steven liked this so much, *he'd* produce it." He did.)

I confided to the newly empowered Dawn during a dinner that I was beginning to feel paralyzed around David and couldn't tell anymore if my scripts were ready or not. I added that I needed to begin to please myself, since for me, David was so difficult to please. Dawn listened carefully.

"What do you see yourself doing a year from now?" she asked.

"I want to be a major producer at a major studio," I answered.

"Well, the only part you don't know is production," she said. "Why don't you team up with Debra Hill, who is making *Clue* for me right now — and you partner up as producers for Paramount." It was a brilliant idea. I could find and develop the scripts and Debra, having come up through production, could make them.

I called Debra, with whom I had developed *Clue* while working for Peter Guber. She had impressed me with her superior production skills: a kind of elevated common sense meets problem-solving genius. She had the right stuff. "What do you see yourself doing in a year?" I asked her.

"I'd like to be a major producer on a major lot," she answered. It was a marriage made in heaven.

HOLLYWOOD'S CATEGORICAL IMPERATIVE STRIKES HOME

Partnering with Debra and going to work for Dawn was the beginning of my true freedom and ability to find my own voice in my quest for movies that expressed my particular sensibilities. It's hard to do that when you're being paid specifically to please someone else and to anticipate *his* sensibilities. (Or his view of the box office.) In retrospect I am profoundly grateful to David Geffen for having been, for me, so hard to please. At the same time, he gave me something he was uniquely qualified to give: the highest standards. I never felt in any given moment I worked for him that I was living up to his expectations. Had he been easy for me to please, had I seen him as the approving father, I might have stayed there forever, locked into the powerful hook of perfect daddy and performing-seal daughter. But I was afraid that there were no tricks I could perform for David that would make him flip. In the end the withholding father I turned him into turned out to be better for me — he helped push me out of the nest. Otherwise I would have been afraid to fly.

My beginning to soar had serious consequences in my personal life as well. Like the single thread that unravels the sweater, my need to be free extended to my marriage, where things had been getting increasingly testy. Our careers were never in sync, and I began to feel that my husband disapproved of my independence. I started feeling guilty — an inferior mother for working so hard, a dilettante for going out on business dinners. As I had begun to rise under the stewardship of mentors Guber and Geffen, my husband had been working alone in a vacuum as the head of Simon & Schuster Productions, with no mentor at all. As I was thriving, he was flailing. The fabric of our intimacy was tearing, weakened by our career struggles in Hollywood.

I became angry. If my husband resented my soaring, I thought I could soar without him. But I was young and didn't know what coldness lay ahead. We had a five-year-old child who loved us both dearly, but my courage to change was a kind of anesthesia to my future problems. When I won my freedom I found myself truly alone. I had no husband, responsibility for raising a young child, and a brand-new job.

At first I took to being an independent producer and a woman alone like the proverbial duck to water. I tightened my budget, moved to a smaller house, hired a great nanny, and derived enormous strength from my teamwork with Debra. No one was there to resent my evening work or social life. I loved being single; I could flirt and date and play for the first time in ten years. There was no boss to criticize the script that excited me; there were no fetters slowing me down but for the care of my son, which was turning out to be easier alone anyway. Being fully responsible for him built up my confidence as a mother, and as our bond grew stronger it accelerated my drive to achieve a comfortable lifestyle for him in the marketplace of Hollywood. I did not want my son to have to suffer an iota for my choices.

Soon Debra and I were partners and ensconced in a trailer we redecorated on the Paramount lot. We were happy peas in the Paramount pod. We hired the talented Stacey Sher as our assistant and started cracking. Writers by the half dozen moved into the trailer to finish or start scripts. There they remained, late into the evenings, sipping Johnnie Walker and helping each other out — the ubiquitous (in my life) Tom Hedley, Bill Lancaster, comedian Merrill Markoe, actioner Greg Pruss. A couple of them lived there for a while, our homeless writers. It was a hobo version of Hollywood in the thirties. We bustled and thrived. Soon every producer wanted a trailer of her own.

From here we began our climb to somewhere. Debra and I were great partners but never best friends; the professional nature of our partnership is part of what made it work. At first I loved the fact that I developed the scripts and Debra made them. But then I got hooked on the set — on actually making the movies — and I no longer wanted to relinquish all the production work to Debra. She was such a good teacher that I learned to love production, and suddenly we were both doing one thing instead of two different things. Since I wasn't off full time developing scripts, our volume suffered, and hence we had to split a single fee for half the intended amount of work. After four great years together we were outgrowing the terms of our partnership. We decided to sever it so each of us could earn her entire fee, still partnering on all the movies in our inventory. It is fitting that our last movie together, *The Fisher King*, which we bought as our partnership was dissolving, was our best.

COMBAT

Combat is inevitable. The goal is to subdue it into conflict and re-solve disputes rationally. But sometimes this is not possible, so fighting is unavoidable. Here are a few of the forms of combat I have seen in the trenches.

HAND-TO-HAND

By far the most unpleasant. Two people or studios duking it out on the phones where the success of one requires the death of the other. (Metaphorical death will suffice.) With any luck the need for this form of combat diminishes with experience (and powerful allies). It is seen most regularly in start-up careers, when people are willing to sandbag their best friends for a deal (and no one can afford a lawyer).

As in: "There's not enough room for two of you. Would you mind dumping your partner?"

"Certainly, may I help?"

Best remedy? Get everything in writing and turn it over to a lawyer. Or "Next." There are always more deals. Few if any are worth dying over.

SECONDS, AS IN A DUEL

1. Assistant-to-assistant: As in, "Her assistant was mean to my assistant." I've seen relationships played out through secre-taries. How exhausting for the staff! But the exec's nails stay clean using plausible denial, i.e., "I never canceled lunch! Your secretary canceled twice on me."
2. Lawyer-to-lawyer: As in, "My lawyer is tougher than your lawyer," where your ability to pay high fees secures you the alpha-bulldog position on the hierarchical ladder of barking dogs.

WAR OF WORDS

In the trades, in the mags, this is high-level sumo wrestling. To actually say something mean on the record is a major touché — as in Geffen's famous swipe at Michael Eisner in *The New Yorker:* "As tall as he is, he's a little guy." (Now they may have to work together at ABC.) The reason a producer never goes on the record is that even when he believes that he'll never work with a person again, even when he's absolutely sure, he's likely to be wrong eventually and find himself on the same side of the table with his onetime permanent adversary. When you trash someone on the record, you will pay. Libel lawyers will get rich.

WAR OF ATTRITION

A common form of combat featuring a battle that has gone on for so long the participants no longer know what they are fighting about. Iran and Iraq in Hollywood, it drains both of the warring parties' credibility and resources. Battles of attrition can kill their warriors, but rivalries can also be invigorating. The point is to last. An old Hindu saying comes to mind: "If you sit by the river long enough, the body of your enemy will float by."

A COUPLE OF ARBITRARY RULES ABOUT COMBAT

1. Don't be afraid of it. If a producer shirks battle she will be stampeded.
2. Don't be a psycho and seek it out. Try to avoid feuds. Pick battles carefully, because enemies proliferate without effort if one is effective.
3. A person is as powerful as his worst enemy. (This is an effective mantra when a very powerful person is on the attack.)
4. Don't work overtime on the fight. He who saves his energy has time left for work.
5. Don't nurse old wounds. Healing is good.

Finally, if you are in a war where the damage is beginning to exceed any possible gains, surrender, Dorothy. You will be astonished to learn how little you have lost, because no one will even remember what the spoils of the original war were supposed to be.

NERVE

Unfortunately, nerve, not talent, is the one necessary and sufficient trait for success. (Wouldn't it be ideal if it were talent? But talent with no nerve is like the sound of one hand clapping.) Nerve is critical for usurpation. It is necessary in the accumulation of leverage. It helps you gather information and it is how people identify a player or a player-to-be. Nerve is not desperation. Desperation negates and has a scent that is abhorrent to all players.

Nerve most commonly comes from having nothing to lose. Otherwise it is a heroic virtue that derives from confidence or conviction. That means you're either so low it looks like up to you, so rich you can sustain a loss, or believe in something so strongly you don't care what anyone thinks. It's easy to be nervy when your livelihood is not at stake. This has, sadly, never been an option for me, but it is how the game is most effectively played. As in all high-stakes gambling, you should never roll the dice with dinner money. You must play baccarat as if you were an aristocrat so you are not devastated by any likely subversion. Always remember the famous adage about the movie business: You can't make a living, you can only get rich. So I have to play like I'm a high roller whether I have the cushion or not. When Monday morning comes and I've rightly walked away from a bad deal, it only feels good when I have money in the bank. Low overhead can be a great protection, one that I've never afforded myself.

One of the most winning power strategies is the ability to walk away from a deal. People want you when you don't need them and it stuns them that you're willing to split — it implies that you are fine without them. Then they wonder how they will be fine without you. When Laura Ziskin was asked to run a new division at Fox, she took months to decide. Her ambivalence raised the ante — certainly her salary — for the studio. As noted above, the ability to take this position implies options or money or both. No one cares where the money comes from, either: arms merchants, beauty salons, money launderers, mafiosi (kind of charming, in fact), shopping centers. Money talks; nobody walks. The tragedy is that talent with no nerve equals failure, whereas there are many careers that attest to the power of nerve alone. Harry Cohn, crass former garment executive who founded Columbia, is the paradigm. Scores of others have followed in his image.

A director can have nerve and no talent with a good producer and crew. If she has talent and no nerve and no producer with nerve, no movie. Someone in the mix has to have nerve, and most nervy people have bad manners. Nerve mixed with style, of course, is the ultimate. Many elegant people are embarrassed at the show of nerve, moxie, or unbridled aggression. They try to cultivate stylish ways to be in your face, but in the end being in your face is being rude and not being in your face is being absent. Subtlety doesn't work here because no one is looking long enough to see it. Modesty prior to success is too authentic for Hollywood. It makes everyone uncomfortable. Anyway, too much modesty inhibits nerve. Modesty postsuccess is what passes for grace.

A FEW CLOSING WORDS ON POWER

Power is not a hat you wear or a state, like nirvana, you can achieve. It is the functional ability to get things done in some version of, as Frank Sinatra would say, "my way." This year for the first time I have begun to feel an inkling of my power, and it is different and far more discreet than I ever imagined. When I fall in love with a screenplay, it's easier for me to buy it, because financiers are now willing to bet on the fact that I can make the script work and get it made. I used to get depressed when I read studios' notes — analyses — on the scripts I developed. Now they no longer have the power to upset me. I know how to undo them.

For the first time, leading actors request meetings with me and not just the director. Marketing departments change their advertising campaigns when I feel that they're not up to par. Things have gotten easier, so it's now possible for me to directly affect the quality of my own work. I am no longer at the mercy of the "gatekeepers," so whenever necessary, I can protect my writer and my director and the integrity of the work. In those cases, I am responsible for the work that appears on the screen, and if you don't like it you can blame me and the team I picked. That is my power.

Chapter 7

MY NEW BEST FRIEND

"Teach us to care and not to care."

— *T. S. Eliot*

"Make new friends
But keep the old.
One is silver
And the other gold."

— *Janet E. Tobitt, Ditty Bag*
(Girl Scouts of America)

ONLY NOW am I beginning to untangle the complex strands of conflicting self-interest and need that confuse friendships in Hollywood, both local and imported: those you make at work and those you bring to work. I have lost friends to other friends, watched friends become rivals and rivals become enemies. I have lost partners, writers, and boyfriends. I have made every mistake in the book. I even invented some new ones. I've found that in order to survive with some degree of my humanity intact, I had to learn the subtle differences between alliances and friendships. The intermingling of the two can poison them both. My true friendships that have survived the decades of work are of two sorts.

First there are the pure ones not generated from or by work — think of them as the friends you started with: pals from childhood, college, early, funky jobs, those you weaved your dreams with. These friendships are purposeless — they exist for their own sake. Then there are work alliances that have transcended commerce altogether and blossomed into genuine friendships. These alliances have passed the test of time from logo to logo, and loyalty has grown out of the process of trustworthy work.

Alliances are conscious relationships in which each person actually cares about the priorities of the other and will exert effort to see them through. But no one is a saint in Hollywood (are you surprised?), and we must remember that there can and will come a time when the essential self-interest of one ally conflicts with that of the other. This is how friendships are damaged. The pressure to sandbag can reach critical mass in any alliance, no matter how strong. The goal is to contain the damage so the alliance can survive. The public display of effort helps.

In a one-company town so tyrannically ruled by its dominance hierarchy, work-dominated friendships are too often a function of movement up or down the ladder. You would think that friendship would be a respite from the unceasing competition, the dull siren of extraordinary expectations — some form of emotional reparation from battles with the forces of nature and ego. Sometimes, thankfully, it is. But too often, because friendships that thrive inside a work network are subject to these forces, there *is* no consolation. Being at the table and being able to play is supposed to be consolation enough. If you try to build a genuine friendship you find an unending series of challenges to that relationship when either of you has something important to gain or lose. At every juncture Mephistopheles is offering deals with increasing allure to sell out your friendship.

Sociologically and genetically, men are accustomed to mixing their friendships with competition, whether in sport or in pursuit of their means of survival. Women are accustomed mainly to competing for men, the means-to-a-means for survival. Men are trained to relish the Darwinian nature of their ambitions, and alliance building is natural to men as a component of empire building. That doesn't mean that they are uninjured by betrayal or that losing a job to a best friend doesn't sting as badly. It's just that rebound-revenge is a preprogrammed instinct, and because the cuts are less surprising they heal faster.

During *Flashdance* Dawn Steel and I learned how debilitating competition to metaphorical death can be. When she, as vice president of Paramount, in the natural flow of the hierarchy took over managing the project that I had developed for three years, our fledgling friendship, which then was only a tenuous alliance, collapsed. For a time we literally hated each other, as though each of us was inimical to the success of the other. When more success followed in her wake — she made *Footloose* with no input from me — I realized she had real talent. But would her success spell my failure? My boss, David Geffen, ever the painful lesson giver, offered Dawn a job, senior to me, and invited her everywhere. I was livid. He ignored me, expecting me to be a pro. Then one day he called me into his office. "Lynda, get it," he said in his impatient declarative. "This fight is doing you no good. Call Dawn. Congratulate her. Rise above it." (Hollywood specializes in acts of grace that are good for your career.)

Rise above the person who took credit for the movie for which I felt responsible? Rise above the person who was swiftly rising above me? Did I have this in me? Timidly I reached for the phone and called Paramount. Dawn took my call immediately.

"I just want to congratulate you," I said, voice quavering. "With *Footloose* and all your other hits, I see clearly that you are remarkable."

Dawn was amazed. Overwhelmed. "Will you be my guest for the Women in Film luncheon next week?" she asked. "I'd love to sit with you."

The phone call left me feeling high, as if I had transcended the rivalry. Suddenly the fact that we *both* could be good became clear. Now her power was unthreatening: Not only was it not bad for me, it was good for me. We could support, enhance, and complement one another.

The Crystal Awards luncheon to which Dawn had invited me (and at which Barbra Streisand was both recipient and guest speaker) was an experience neither of us had ever had with a true peer. During it we plotted our next ten years and whispered our secret ambitions. "Next year I'm going to be head of a studio and be married," she confided. I thought she was nuts, but I supported her anyway. I had never met a woman who could be so bald about her ambition. It charged and delighted me. It allowed me to consider equally towering intentions. Why not? Why should I crave a less powerful role for myself because it was socially more reasonable?

Lo and behold, the next year came, and Dawn was the president of Paramount and married to producer Chuck Roven (and pregnant too). And my first deal as a producer, my partnership with Debra Hill, my very autonomy, were assured under Dawn's Paramount umbrella. She empowered me.

An alliance was born. A fledgling girls' network. Moreover, a real friendship was born then too, one that has since tackled innumerable hurdles. For the past ten years our plans have been shared and have overlapped. I was maid of honor at Dawn's wedding, and when it was time for Debra Hill and me to sadly end our partnership, it was Dawn who made a deal for me as a solo producer, the first she brought to Columbia when she was made president. I learned that what's good for the goose can also be good for the gander — the basic tenet of alliances — or, in this more complicated case, that what's good for the goose can also be good for the other goose.

BRICK BY BRICK

The same year that I met Debra and we had drinks at Le Dôme to discuss *Clue*, Dawn and I first dined at Port's (a now defunct restaurant) to discuss *Flashdance* strategies, back when I still hoped to have a strategy on *Flashdance*. Brick by brick, the people with whom I would build my career were beginning to assemble. I must have had five hundred business meals that year (I think of it as a semester), out of which four or five long-term alliances have developed. (And maybe one genuine friendship, to give you a sense of the ratio.) In the early years you hone your instincts by finding teammates and playmates, making good bets and bad bets on the nascent talent you have access to: what baby writer has a fresh voice, which young actor is a flash in the pan, who's the flavor of the month and who's the real thing. These instincts will turn out to be your most powerful tool for picking and making movies: They help hone your point of view, without which you are indistinguishable from the hustler trying to elbow you off your tiny stool near the table.

A producer develops alliances by requesting breakfast dates (with buyers, of course) because requesting lunch blind (as in date) is presumptuous. If the producer is particularly charming and pitches something that the buyer likes and his boss eventually buys, then he becomes a strategic ally. (If the picture gets made and is a hit, they're best friends for life. A flop, they've never met.) The producer then maintains that alliance over the next seventy-five years, sending flowers and champagne on the occasion of every promotion, marriage, or birth. Interestingly, the most critical moment in the maintenance of that alliance is if (when) the buyer gets fired. (This is inevitable.) Other people will delete him from their Rolodexes and phone lists. The ones who hang in there are mensches, friends, human beings. (This policy is now so ethically correct that it has become almost commonplace to find that unemployed movie executives are often too busy to lunch or breakfast with middle-level sellers, at least in the first two months.)

SOME RULES FOR GROWING FRIENDSHIPS IN A CONTAMINATED PETRI DISH

1. A producer never picks over the cadavers of his friends. If a friend's movie falls apart, he is not the first to call its director or cast.
2. He does not gloat about (or in any way feel good about) his friends' failures.
3. Anyone who hurts his best friend has hurt him too.
4. He revels in his friends' successes.
5. He is always in town or else he ostentatiously flies in for their big moments in the spotlight — premieres, showers, weddings, big birthday parties, and obviously the Oscars (although this could be interpreted as self-interest).
6. He calls them the minute he sees their names in the paper.
7. He tells them it's not as bad as they think, as long as their names are spelled right — and the reporter is obviously jealous of their success.

8. He doesn't raid or hire his friends' employees. If he must, he *asks* them first.
9. He shares any information or gossip that is crucial to his friends' career.
10. If someone offers a producer money to sell out a friend, he doesn't. (And he doesn't then regret it.)
11. He defends his friends eloquently when they are gossiped about.
12. He loves them more when they are down. No one else will.

FAUX FRIENDSHIP: MY NEW BEST FRIEND (NBF)

Notice in conversation that people never just *know* each other in Hollywood. They're always each other's "new best friends." As in, "Johnny Depp. He's my NBF. I love him. He's so great. He's so cool." This means that you might have spent Saturday night in the same room with Johnny Depp, or have sat next to him at breakfast Sunday at Swingers Restaurant on Beverly Drive.

The concept of the New Best Friend is based on social mobility. The fact that it is new and suddenly intimate means that it is propitious, opportunistic. There is a lot of tactical cultivation of NBFs. A particular job requires a particular brand of hot friends. Hot friends are chits. They are to be bandied about at meetings, and parties, in phone calls. They are almost leverage. The following would be each job's perfect New Best Friend.

If she is a

1. Studio exec: her perfect NBF would be a hot writer or a breaking stand-up comedian.
2. Writer: director
3. Director: star
4. Star: another star
5. Gigantic star: chairman of a studio (I thought that Debra Winger and Barry Diller looked particularly fabulous palling around together in the eighties.)
6. Agent: studio exec, hot writer, director, star
7. Gigantic agent: gigantic star, chairman of a studio, super-duper investment banker–guru Herbert Allen

Alliances are cultivated in Hollywood like gardens. They are tended, nurtured, fertilized (bullshitted?), picked, and displayed. This is how work grows. Work is building relationships, brick by brick. This takes effort, money, style, and phones. This is why florists do so well in Hollywood. (Hollywood equation: demonstrable love equals big flowers.)

A good career move is to reunite with a former enemy. I am reminded of the tearful reconciliation of Dean Martin and Jerry Lewis on the latter's telethon. And the drumbeatlike updates on the status of the relationship between Eisner and Katzenberg. If Michael Eisner and David Geffen dined right now, it would probably make the front page of a national newspaper. Best friends make big news when it's the reunion of former enemies. The energy released from the implosion of an adversarial relationship into an alliance creates a ton of matter in the form of new deals.

FAUX FRIENDS VS. STRATEGIC ALLIES

Faux friends are temporal, contingent on the vagaries of time, place, and logo. Strategic allies have weathered the test of time — they have transferred from logo to logo, regime to regime. A strategic ally is a long-term commitment, which around these parts is pretty short term, memory being a tactical thing. Many people believe that if you have lunched with the same person in three different jobs he is a strategic ally. A true friend doesn't care where you hang your hat, as long as you're getting to hang it.

HOW TO TELL AN OPPORTUNISTIC, FAKE QUASI FRIEND FROM A STRATEGIC ALLY

1. Beware of all people campaigning for your friendship. Especially if you're hot that week. Too much obvious effort is suspicious.
2. Beware of obsequious human beings. Everyone here has a strong, healthy ego. (Natural selection requires it.) The most dangerous wolves are in sheep's clothing.
3. Beware if someone courting you has too much to gain. Study the gain/loss ratio.

4. Beware of inappropriate personal revelations — these are often part of a campaign.
5. Beware of people whose entire group of friends is recently celebrated: It's better when their friends have been long celebrated or are likely to be celebrated in the future.

SUDDEN SUCCESS: BREAKING OUT OF THE PACK

The implications of sudden success are like the commutative principle of mathematics. You and your friend start out equal. If she is now a success, then, Q.E.D., you are now a success. This translates into the tradition of "carrying your friends." All your dreams, all the plans you made together at the Olive restaurant over martinis, had a common theme: Whoever gets there first reaches out and pulls the others to the table.

When Shane Black, writer of *Lethal Weapon,* made his first million, he wanted to carry all his roommates with him into the highest ranks of Hollywood writers. (So he wouldn't be the only one punished with a huge check.) Because all his roommates were also writers and they had lived together since film school days at UCLA, it sort of worked. Those guys (the self-named "Pad-o'-Guys") fortunately were talented writers, and for a few seasons in the late eighties, they shared Shane's heat, though none of them ever met his price tag. Three or four real careers were spawned by Shane's loyalty, part of which must have been attributable to his simple desire for good company during good times.

More commonly you see suddenly successful writers attaching family members (wives, uncles, sisters-in-law, brothers) to their new deals. The consequences ultimately define the reasonableness of the gesture. Did the attachment carry his weight? Did he deliver? His failure will always be considered the fault of the powerful friend, ipso facto, no more friendship. (This is related to the age-old adage that no good deed goes unpunished.) It becomes increasingly hard to carry friends who don't cut the mustard without diminishing one's credibility. Sainthood is irrational, unnecessary, and potentially self-destructive.

YOUR BIG NIGHT(MARE)

The following is an account of a writer's premiere, the kind of event where all his family and friends are corralled to celebrate. They are celebrating the writer's new perch on the lowest rung of Hollywood's ruling elite.

EXT. ACADEMY OF MOTION PICTURES ARTS AND SCIENCES, WILSHIRE BLVD. — WEEKDAY NIGHT

PAN THE CROWD swarming outside the double doors. A PUBLICITY TYPE guards the entrance, armed with a list. Rushing in are invited guests and recruited teenagers. The guests are slightly older and, as always, pretentiously underdressed.

CUT TO: *The WRITER, twenty-five, cute, sensitive, anxious as hell. Tonight his first produced screenplay debuts to the industry. He is accompanied by his PARENTS, who have flown in from Pittsburgh for this auspicious evening. They slip past the PUBLICITY TYPE, nodding a greeting.*

CUT TO: *INT. LOBBY. A buzz permeates the room. Agents, executives, and other assorted naysayers coagulate into small exclusive groupings. Photographers snap pictures of the various celebrities present, who have no connection whatsoever to the film.*

CUT TO: *E.C.U. (extreme close-up) of the WRITER, his eyes darting around the room, searching for recognition. He gets none.*

WRITER Come on, Mom, Dad . . . let's go upstairs and sit down. I'm sure they've reserved some seats for us.

They make their way upstairs, away from the madding crowd.

CUT TO: *INT. SCREENING ROOM. The roped-off section is empty except for some members of the press. Rowdy teenagers fill the rest of the seats. The WRITER and his PARENTS duck under the rope and are immediately accosted.*

PUBLICITY TYPE I'm sorry, these seats are taken.

WRITER But I'm the Writer, and these are my parents. They've flown all the way from Pittsburgh. I'm sure it's okay.

PUBLICITY TYPE Oh! I love your work![1] Your last movie was fabulous. Please, sit right down.

Unruffled by the PUBLICITY TYPE's mistake, the WRITER and his PARENTS take their seats and await the credit sequence. Finally the lights go down and a rumble of applause begins to erupt from the bleachers.

CUT TO: *producer's credit. Applause.*

CUT TO: *writer's credit. No applause.*

SMASH CUT TO: *The WRITER's face. Despairing.*

This is the last thing the WRITER remembers until the lights go up ninety minutes later.

TIME DISSOLVE: *Ninety minutes later.*

Crowd streaming out of the screening room, muffled conversation. The WRITER and his PARENTS wend their way to the catered party downstairs.

CUT TO: *A FOXY JUNIOR EXECUTIVE. She spots the WRITER and makes a beeline.*

FOXY *(flirting)* You must be pretty good.

WRITER Gee, thanks. That must mean you like the movie.

FOXY Oh, it was beautiful. I loved the cinematography.[2]

---

1. Love as Covering Your Back End: This is a very common form of love in Hollywood. You never know who is about to become indispensable to your career, so you must play it safe, just in case. Today's waitress is tomorrow's hyphenate (writer-director, writer-producer, producer-director, etc.). Arrogance is very expensive and must be doled out carefully, with considerable forethought.

2. Love as Mild Indifference: At a screening, Hollywood etiquette prevails. That is, if you absolutely abhor a picture and you cannot bring yourself to lie, you must find socially acceptable compliments. "I loved the cinematography" implies that you didn't like the movie, but covers your derriere (see footnote number 1). Other handy phrases include: "It's all up there on the screen," "Only you could have done this," "It's gonna be huge," etc.

CUT TO: *The WRITER's face. A complex circuit of exposed nerves. Suddenly he is surrounded by well-wishers, including two AGENTS and a PRODUCER.*

AGENT #1 One hundred million. Nothing less.[3]

AGENT #2 And foreign. *Forget* foreign and videocassette. You're a rich man.

WRITER Really? You really think so?

PRODUCER I'll have no problem setting up that first screenplay you wrote now. Who knew you were brilliant before? Anyone? Tell these putzes. *Me*, right? Am I right?

AGENT #1 Early? You want to talk early? Tell him who your first meeting was with.

CUT TO: *The WRITER's face. Incredulous. The AGENT has clearly forgotten that he canceled the meeting.*

The WRITER, feeling trapped, sees ANOTHER WRITER shyly approaching him for cover.

OTHER WRITER You must be depressed.

WRITER *(alarmed)* Why? What happened?

OTHER WRITER The way they butchered your script. I loved the first draft.[3]

WRITER You read the first draft? I can hardly remember it.

OTHER WRITER The director asked me to rewrite it. But I thought it was just fine, so I turned him down.

The WRITER does not know what to say. This information is staggering. He doesn't know whether to thank the OTHER WRITER or burst into tears. He decides to be discreet.

---

3. Love as Unrestrained Envy: Mildly disguised hostility packaged in a backhanded compliment is, oddly, a real compliment. It means you may actually have achieved something, if only the envy of your peers. (In Hollywood, as on Wall Street, envy itself is an achievement.) The least likely people — your friends, as in this case — are unhappy with your success, and perfect strangers delight in it. Lovely, isn't it?

WRITER How's your Barbra Streisand piece?

OTHER WRITER Passed. I'm rewriting it for Whoopi Goldberg.

WRITER Hope you get out of development hell. . . .

OTHER WRITER Thanks. And good luck on your picture — hope it doesn't get lost in the holiday crunch.

The WRITER strides purposefully through the room — without a purpose. He sees his OLD GIRLFRIEND. Home base.

OLD GIRLFRIEND Sweetheart! I'm so proud of you. Did you hear I just got a development job at Queens Road? I really miss you.[4]

WRITER I find that hard to believe, but if you say so. Did you like the movie?

OLD GIRLFRIEND Sweetheart, I want you to meet my boss, Harry. Harry, this is my great love, the writer I was telling you about.

The WRITER is history. He's outta there.

WRITER I gotta go. Gotta find my parents. They're missing.

She turns to her boss and breaks out in giggles.

OLD GIRLFRIEND You brought your parents? How quaint. Kiss, kiss . . .

The WRITER is feeling murderous. He wants to grab his PARENTS and leave. But he cannot because he sees . . . MUSIC UP . . . The STUDIO HEAD. The WRITER slows his gait and saunters past as though he didn't see him, just in case he isn't recognized.

WRITER *(tentative, choked)* Larry? Hi! I'm — the Writer? You remember? We went out on your boat when we closed my deal?

---

4. Love as Currency: One person's beat is another's career boost. Casual dalliances are suddenly and vigorously renewed in anticipation of your success. Beware: No relationships in Hollywood are innocent. Yesterday's one-night stand is today's development executive.

The STUDIO HEAD looks at him blankly. He knows millions of writers. Which writer could this possibly be?

STUDIO HEAD Of course. Terrific to see you. What's new?

C.U. OF THE WRITER'S FACE. *Confused. What's new? His goddamn movie is opening, what more could be new?*

WRITER Do you think we're gonna open?

The STUDIO HEAD, relieved, now knows who this writer is.

STUDIO HEAD It'll open all right. . . . Whether anyone will be there or not is another question.

He guffaws. He thinks this is hilarious. Needless to say, so does everyone around him. A studio head never laughs alone. The WRITER, looking mortified, tries to laugh.

WRITER *(catching on)* Well. I just want you to know that I really enjoyed working with you. Every minute of it.

STUDIO HEAD I know. We're really happening, aren't we? Everybody loves working with us because we're the best. I've put together the best team in town. Creative, production. . . . And don't worry about opening, because I have the most enormous distribution apparatus.[5]

The STUDIO HEAD turns away. Conversation dismissed. The WRITER gets the picture and resumes the pretense of looking for his PARENTS.

CUT TO: *A GORGEOUS BABE with large eyes concentrated on the WRITER's conversation with the STUDIO HEAD. She loves writers in a big way and collects them, like vases. She steps into his path.*

---

5. Love as Self-Love: It is simply mind-boggling the degree to which affection is self-reflexive in Hollywood, the American capital of narcissistic personality disorder. Hollywood players see images of themselves wrapped around everyone else's triumphs. It is not the director's brilliance, nor the depth of the characters created by the writer, nor the actors' perfect performances; if the picture is a hit, it is the studio head's enormous distribution apparatus that is responsible (the only metaphors in Tinsel Town are sexual ones). Conversely, if the picture flops, it is because of the director's lack of talent, the writer's mindlessness, the actors' shallowness, etc. Self-love knows no impediment.

GORGEOUS BABE Hi. You must be the Writer. I just had to tell
you that I cried when I read your script. The execution was as
strong as the concept. I felt like you were writing to me.[6]

E.C.U. OF THE WRITER'S FACE. *Enthralled. Finally his expectations are being fulfilled.*

WRITER What's your name? What's your phone number? Who
represents you? I want to take you home.

*GORGEOUS BABE takes out her Filofax and hands him her card. It
reads "Gorgeous Babe Development." The WRITER puts the card in
his jean jacket pocket, next to his heart. She walks away; he is dazed.*

CUT TO: *The DIRECTOR. English, natty, working-class, snotty,
surrounded by well-wishers. Laughing and shouting he motions to the
WRITER, about whom he is now making jokes. He loves to laugh
about writers. He thinks they are the slowest class of people on the
planet.*

DIRECTOR Shakespeare! C'mere! Come meet some powerful
people!

He turns to his friends.

DIRECTOR *(explaining)* Writers love powerful people.[7] That's
how they get work. We had quite a few bouts on the script,
didn't we, Shakespeare?

WRITER Well, we had a disagreement or two . . . but all in all . . .

DIRECTOR *(interrupting)* I asked Shakespeare to rewrite a short
scene we were about to shoot and he handed me thirteen pages.

WRITER It was a pivotal scene.

---

6. Love with the Proper Stranger: As Jim Morrison sang, "People are strange." Even in the
era of AIDS, a groupie's admiration is still the ultimate accoutrement of public success. Old
friends are old business because you already know what they have to offer. Everything that is
new is fabulous, because you haven't been disappointed by it yet. In modern Hollywood the
mark of a hot writer is the beautiful girl on his arm. Very modern. But beware: Yesterday's
M.A.W. (model, actress, whatever) is also today's development executive.
7. Love as Never Having to Say You're Sorry: Directors never have to say they're sorry. If
they insult you, they know that for the right price the studio can get you back, and if it can't,
there are thousands more of you out there dying for the job. So you hold onto it, and they
become monsters. But don't forget — you're the lout; they're the geniuses. If your picture
is a hit it's their success. If your picture is a flop it's your failure.

DIRECTOR To writers every scene is pivotal. But you gotta love Shakespeare. Who else could I spend six hours with debating the motivations of a pimp?

WRITER *(teeth clenched)* He was not a pimp. He was a door-to-door salesman.

The AGENTS crack up. They know who gets them the biggest commission.

AGENT #1 I think you did wonders with his script.

The WRITER glares at AGENT #1 (who had been fawning over him only moments before). When he becomes a writer-director he won't sign with any of them. Then he remembers . . .

WRITER My parents! I've completely lost them!

DIRECTOR *(laughing too loudly as usual)* How sweet of Shakespeare to have brought parents. Are they excited about your big night, Shakespeare?

For the thousandth time the WRITER restrains the urge to punch him. One day he will sink the DIRECTOR in his Bloody Mary.

CUT TO: *The WRITER, weaving through the crowd. As they say in Hollywood, hatred hangs from the rafters. Many smile or wave. But the only people he wants to see are the ones he saw at birth. A commodious embrace encircles him.*

CUT TO: *His MOM, thrilled, tears in her eyes.*

MOM I never would have dreamed when you were just a baby . . .

WRITER *(relaxing)* Oh, Mom, don't get corny. . . .

MOM But honey, you've made me so proud.[8]

---

8. Genuine Love: If you are lucky, eventually, in the midst of all the horrible and exquisite hype, you will learn who really loves you. They are not very many, and the circle only gets smaller. Your wife, if she married you before your success, loves you. Your siblings probably love you, if they're not thwarted — and envious — themselves. And most of all, your parents love you. Back home, your triumph is their triumph. Or, on second thought, is this just another example of mutual self-interest, the most common form of love in Hollywood? No. It only seems that way because in the midst of accelerated hype everyone's motives are temporarily suspect. Two weeks after your movie opens you will finally realize that you have a coterie of people who truly are rooting for you. Root for them in return. You will discover that this is not mutual self-interest but a much sweeter thing: genuine love.

WRITER *(beaming)* Thanks, Mom.

MOM This is the happiest night of my life.

WRITER *(preening)* Really, Mom?

MOM Oh, yes, darling. Tonight I saw Joan Collins! At my own son's party!

ENTOURAGING

Another concomitant of sudden success is the growth of an entourage, like a limb. Eddie Murphy is the most famous example of this, traveling with no fewer than twenty high school buddies at all times. (This was before he was married. Marriage is the most common destroyer of excessive entourages.) It seems that few feel success can be endured without a lot of company. Triumph is a lonely business, and the newly triumphant one feels guilty and isolated leaving his struggling pals in his wake. The entourage inures you to the slings and arrows of New Best Friends, hustlers you will meet who are out to use you. Much better to be used by those you already know.

An entourage is a friendship empire. When I was first breaking out of the pack (*Flashdance* had given me some sort of credibility), I found myself traveling with a bunch of people everywhere I went. I checked in with these same people every day and planned my social schedule with them (screenings, dinners, workouts, parties). Safety in numbers. Each of them knew every detail of my life — my crushes, defeats, semivictories. But they were not my friends. If I had been invited nowhere, they would have been elsewhere.

When I moved into production and had to exert all my energy all the time, I suddenly craved privacy in what little spare time I had. I stopped returning their phone calls and starting skipping parties. When I looked back on the year before from my solo vantage point, I saw that something vampiric had happened to me. Each member of my entourage seemed like a parasitic organism that had been living off of my energy and my small victories. There wasn't enough left of me to go around.

Entourages, although fun and distracting for a while, end up being exhausting. They give you the impression of friendship without providing any because they lack real intimacy. It is having a friendship with a group in general as opposed to having one in particular.

WHEN FRIENDS BECOME ENEMIES

"Keep your friends close and your enemies closer."

— *Don Corleone*

There are two reasons that I've grown to loathe midweek Hollywood parties. One is because as I get older I resent extending my workday indefinitely, and two, because of the kind of thing that happened the other night. I ran into someone I didn't mean to and surprise: drama ambush! Who needs this after a bruising day on the phone?

French actress Irene Jacob was being feted by her Los Angeles managers on the occasion of the premiere of her role as Desdemona in *Othello*. I wasn't planning to attend, but a woman I needed to interview for a position at my company was going, the managers, Nick Wechsler and Keith Addis, are my pals and particularly charming hosts . . . and oh, what the heck, I was in a good mood. My week had ended well, which was astonishing considering how badly it had begun: Sandra Bullock had taken another movie instead of mine for spring, but by Friday we were finally making progress casting Michelle Pfeiffer's costar in *One Fine Day*. (You'd think this was the definitive no-brainer, but no — the usual suspects don't want to costar in *her* movie. Read: Her part would always be equal to or slightly more prominent than theirs.)

Anyway, I sort of swept into the party and bussed cheeks with the best of them. Suddenly I felt what I can best describe as a disturbance in the field and I looked up. A wave of revulsion was aimed my way. (This is what I imagine being hit by a gravitational wave from a local black hole might feel like.) Someone was hating me at close range, and I knew who and why.

Surrounded by a group of admirers was an ex-employee/ex-friend of long standing. When I met her gaze she looked away. I reached for Loretta Young deep inside and waved and smiled. Hesitantly, she lifted her arm. Acknowledging my presence seemed to make her go concave. No amount of surrounding admiration resuscitated her posture. At that moment my feeling for her changed from apprehension to sympathy. Just seeing me had taken all her power away; she had hurled it away as though the mere sight of me were the negation of her existence. I tried to make eye contact, but all night long she eluded my gaze. I felt myself morphing from Loretta Young into some strange version of the Dalai Lama. I once loved this girl; I had mentored her from a baby, and she had thrived. Why now would the mere sight of me be so undermining? Months ago I had called her for drinks. It had been five years since we had worked together, and I felt it was time to clean up the confusing emotional mess that had spread between us. So far I hadn't heard back.

I've found that former friends — false friends — make the worst enemies. First of all, they know everything about you. This is no small thing. Second of all, you've mixed them with your other friends and, as in divorce, the untangling of loyalties is ugly. Intimacy is a dangerous past for a bitter present.

Hollywood is the capital of Splitsville because self-interest rules. Inside self-interest lurk greed, ego, and the struggle for survival. Hollywood attracts people with a need to create a larger-than-life identity, people looking to invent themselves. They do this through their relationships. Sadly, conflict invariably erupts in a relationship and often exposes the neurotic wiring, the underbelly of an emotional connection. Underneath the facade of smiling alliances is a complex of unfulfilled needs and longings whose sources are primal. What looks like an employer-employee, producer-director, writer-producer relationship is really the recreation of father-son, mother-daughter, sister-brother in the unconscious struggle for family survival.

In the mentor-protégé relationship, a particularly loaded one, the *All About Eve* syndrome is common. Gratefulness creates resentment; idolizing a mentor is the preamble to being disappointed by her or wanting to *be* her. With women this is even more dangerous as we haven't yet fully unwoven ourselves from the entangled shroud of our mother-daughter issues, the old bondage paradigms. I created mothers out of both Dawn Steel and Nora Ephron and then had to work hard to see through the myopic lens this put on both friendships. The latent energy that makes imploding friendships so dangerous is the fact that they are the playlets of this familial struggle, now acted out on the treacherous stage of work.

My early mistake was to become dependent upon the kindness of my employees. Literary agent Erica Spellman once chastised me by saying, "Lynda, you're very popular. You don't have to make your employees your friends." But for many reasons — wanting company on my rise, guilt for my success, the placating desire to spread my good fortune around, mistaking my office for my family and my life for work — I gave myself away to my protégés. Mother taking care of daughter, daughter taking care of mother, was a familiar and powerful dynamic for me — and it subverted these relationships.

The colliding dynamic of the protégé's part is equally as powerful as any operating on the mentor: Protégés must overthrow their mentors. As night follows day, the growth of the protégé becomes inhibited by the existence of the mentor. How can there be two of them? One has to go. This is dangerous. Hegel called this collision the Master/Slave dialectic: The master becomes dependent upon the slave and therefore must cut the umbilical cord for the survival of each of them. In the case of my first protégé, the woman at the hot party, it was time for her to stop being me and start becoming herself. I had helped her find a new job where she thrived impressively, but the damage of the separation has been hemorrhaging for years regardless. I seem to be unable to stem it. It will have to heal over time, if at all. This is why we need the coziness of our unconditional friendships. They are incalculably precious. There is so little safe turf on which to land here, smiling faces give us no comfort. With our popularity a ranging number like the daily Dow Jones average, our few true friends protect and nurture us. They are the source of our fuel.

LOVE IN HOLLYWOOD, SO TO SPEAK

If true friendship is a remarkable thing, imagine the likelihood of true love! (Does sex simplify or complicate the deal? You guess.) I have always believed, based on random samples, that the best marriages in Hollywood are the oldest: those couples who married in their youth before they came to town (although the remains of marriages poisoned by fame are strewn everywhere), before anything else laid claim to their souls. These unconditional old-fashioned marriages can be bulwarks against the pervasive emotional alienation of Hollywood. Those who can nestle inside these cozy partnerships are indeed blessed.

True love comes prior to success. If you fall in love when you are famous, rich, or already a success, that trait is part of the deal — part of the original attraction. It cannot be subtracted, particularly as so many lives in this town are motivated by the dream of grandeur. Success is a distorting lens for both sides; it implies an advantage to the more accomplished ones who expect some kind of trade-off (control) in the transaction. On the other side, the less accomplished ones also have motives attached to their attraction: To fall in love with certain people is an undeniably cool career move. But great career moves do not great loves make. Relationships are constantly torn asunder on the sharp rocks of seasonal failure, and the unsightly remains of broken relationships are strewn everywhere. And everywhere we find former friends picking over the carrion if the newly unattached party has something special (read: prestige) to offer. This kind of love is conditional by definition, too mixed with greed to survive in a pure state. Remember: Like the color black, business mixed with anything turns to business. And when business goes sour, you switch businesses.

If you do fall in love at work anyway, against all of my best advice, a few tips:

1. No trades in bed.
2. No more than two business engagements a week apart.
3. No more than two business engagements a week together.
4. No talking about business on the weekend (unless one of you is in extremis).
5. Take vacations where your Rolodex isn't. This excludes Aspen, Easthampton, Martha's Vineyard, and, even though it's very big, large parts of Montana.
6. Celebrate the other's success. Don't compete. (Try not to.)

7. Be outrageously romantic and don't be the only one not to send flowers on a promotion, even if you're a woman.

8. Be a good wife. Both of you.

9. Spend lots of time emulating traditional families: Visit in-laws frequently (unless it's absolutely intolerable); attend children's plays, PTA meetings, each other's school reunions; go hiking or camping. (The latter if ethnically possible. Jews are exempted for genetic reasons.) See France by bicycle. Pretend you have no money.

MARRIAGE AS STRATEGIC ALLIANCE

The best other marriages — the ones that begin and yet thrive in Hollywood — are strategic alliances. When both spouses are (in the industry parlance) "pros," they work together, they compete, or on the rare occasion that their jobs are unrelated, they work side by side, their agendas never colliding. When two equal partners compete in one fabulous unit, like megaproducer Kathleen Kennedy and Frank Marshall, her husband-partner, or Laurie MacDonald and Walter Parks, who run DreamWorks together, a couple holds a single unit of increased leverage that is more than the sum of both members' chits. More and more married couples are partnering in business, finding that they give so much of their time to work, any other less committed spouses would shrivel up and die from neglect. Teaming up doubles the commitment to the team and to the town.

When a couple is on two separate tracks but with complementary careers, one of the two is always on the "in," protecting the exposed flank of the other. (With a well-liked and successful couple like Lucy Fisher, now vice chairman at Sony, and her husband, Columbia producer Doug Wick, neither one is ever on the out.) As emotional armor to protect you from the constant barrage of negativity and gloom, having one person always rooting for you is no small advantage. When one spouse is a nonpro, he or she is definitely the wife, whatever the gender. Doctor-husbands of lady agents are routinely ignored at dinner parties (unless they are plastic surgeons), and the nonpro spouse gradually misses more and more industry events. Who can blame him?

STRATEGIC DATING

In adapting our work lives to our love lives we have to learn when and how to date strategically. Otherwise one is always working, and this leads to Hollywood's version of alienated work: All work, no play makes Jill a dull girl. And Jack the dullest of boys.

At an industry screening, a producer is working, so he must bring someone good for work (read: someone in the business, preferably a notch higher than he on the dominance hierarchy, but the same notch is fine). If he brings a civilian no one will talk to her, and they will have a fight on the way home. He will try to convince his date that he hates Hollywood values and the incessant trade talk as much as she does, but she will not believe him. And she is right, because he will take a hot writer to the next industry screening.

DATING A CIVILIAN: THE ADVANTAGES AND DISADVANTAGES

Upside	*Downside*
1. No trades in bed.	1. He never knows what you are talking about.
2. Fewer business engagements.	2. Business dinners are stag, to avoid mutual humiliation.
3. Learn new things about, say, botany.	3. Nobody listens or cares.
4. Offspring are less likely to become William Morris agents.	4. They grow up to be agents anyway, and it's your fault.
5. He still loves you when your luck is bad and tells you everything is cyclical.	5. You hate yourself and act horribly to him and accuse him of not understanding the business.

THE REAL THING

Love and friendship, two of life's abiding rewards, are endangered species in Hollywood. People crave both, mistaking alliance for friendship, lust for love, and ambition for both. If pure, undiluted friendship cannot find a place to thrive inside one's life, work grows like a kudzu vine into every crevice of existence. Friendship can degrade into currency and disappear as long as it is subject to status accounting. If you can trade up, trade in, or trade off a relationship, these interactions are ruled by commerce. And commerce is ruled by human interactions. So on we go building alliances, breakfast meetings tumbling into lunch meetings, lunches transforming into dinner parties. All is work and work is all.

But how many breakfast meetings can we tolerate? Here is the paradox. We fear that to stay human, we may lose our edge. Keep the edge, lose perspective. The trick is: Render unto Caesar what is Caesar's. Give everything to work when working. But do not render everything else to Caesar too. In other words, to survive we must keep private portions of our lives for ourselves, and these are our precious friendships, our life-sustaining relationships, unadulterated by any ulterior motive. The real thing.

Chapter 8

THE MIXED NEWS ON CHIX IN FLIX

"If this is the best of possible worlds,
what then are the others?"

— *Voltaire, Candide*

"Funny business, a woman's career: the things you drop on your
way up the ladder, so you can move faster, you forget you'll
need them again when you go back to being a woman."

— *Margot Channing, All About Eve*

WAS sitting in a production meeting recently, intently trying to find potential budget cuts to present to the director of *One Fine Day*, when I was struck afresh by a scene that had become commonplace: Every person in the room was a woman. There was me, the executive producer; Kate Guinzburg, Michelle Pfeiffer's partner; the writer, Ellen Simon; the co-producer, Mary McLaglen; the unit production manager; and the accountant: all women. (It later turned out that even the best boy on this movie was a girl.) It was a bottom-line-type meeting, which made it all the more extraordinary in its contemporary ordinariness, in that we were charged with cutting a half million dollars from our budget by that afternoon. I froze the frame in my mind for a moment and beheld what I can only describe as a classic we've-come-a-long-way-baby moment, realizing how impossible this sight would have been fifteen years ago, when I first arrived in Hollywood. Among the many misconceptions that dogged and stigmatized women in the late seventies and early eighties were the beliefs that a woman couldn't command the respect of the crew, that she couldn't be responsible for a large budget, and that a woman's talents were primarily behind a desk, preferably behind a book or a script, preparing notes for her boss. That women could ultimately succeed in leading a crew and in protecting the bottom line is a testament to how untested the prevailing wisdom had been.

My generation and the one just before me have triumphed in Hollywood beyond anyone's expectations, even our own. Sherry Lansing, our patron saint, has gone from studio executive to major producer to studio head, consistently succeeding in all jobs. Dawn Steel went from merchandising to developing scripts to head of production and chairman in front of my very eyes. Barbra Streisand gave license to other stars to take control of their careers. And over the course of their careers producers like Paula Weinstein *(Fearless, Flesh and Bone)*, Kathleen Kennedy *(Jurassic Park, Congo, Raiders of the Lost Ark)*, Laura Ziskin *(Pretty Woman, To Die For, What About Bob?)*, Polly Platt *(Terms of Endearment, Say Anything, Evening Star)*, Denise DeNovi *(Little Women, Batman, Edward Scissorhands)*, and Lindsay Doran *(Sense and Sensibility, Sabrina)* have built a body of work so solid no one can doubt their endurance. And there are many, many more, in fact an astonishing and ever-growing array of first-rate women producers.

Women have proven to be good in all the essential areas: people handling, development, and physical production. Not one has crumbled under her heavy load. Bloody but unbowed the lot of us, over time we have pleased the powers that be and proven ourselves. We have made a ladder for the up-and-coming generations of new female moviemakers. I don't know the exact male/female ratio in Hollywood, but I believe that the quantity of women has quadrupled since I began. There seems to be no real glass ceiling anymore, except at the highest regions of corporate ownership. This is a far cry from what it was like when I began as a "d" girl for Peter Guber.

At that time an unofficial quota of one woman at each studio or production company prevailed. It was the woman's job to read the scripts, prepare her boss's notes, dress well, and help the crucial small talk at the meeting, acting much like a gracious wife. In the last decade women have become powerful executives, joined the directors A-list, become major producers, and achieved parity — in numbers if not in pay — at all levels of the studio system.

What we've learned is that as the workplace has become more equal in numbers (though as yet it is far from equal), our salaries haven't. What does this mean? With the exception of one or two women who have become studio heads and whose deals involve stock options, golden parachutes, and huge fees on the scale of the old boys' network, most successful women do not make two thirds of what their male counterparts make. Most successful male producers make between $750,000 and $1 million per movie; their successful female counterparts make between $500,000 and $750,000. This salary discrepancy has a psychological as well as an economic dimension. Women start with lower base deals based on the archaic supposition that we are not supporting families. If we are, we are more needy and dependent on a deal. This is a vicious cycle.

For producers, new deals are generally based on prior deals. This is because unless you have tremendous leverage, like a giant hit at the time of your renegotiation or multiple parties seeking your services, the studio's business affairs department insists that any new deal be merely a small increment over your prior fees. They do this for reasons of precedent, otherwise anyone could ask them for anything at any time, and there would be no rhyme or reason to their decision making. The process sustains the status quo.

Women do not trade upward as easily as men, particularly if they have families to support, and this is the psychological component. If you're needy you take fewer chances and have no leverage. Women do not fail upward like their male counterparts, either. We haven't been around long enough to have earned the privilege. As with all minorities, we know that our successes have to keep mounting because there is no infrastructure of support if we fail. I could live happily for the rest of my life on the deal Frank Price reportedly made when he left as head of Columbia.

In the rare examples of Sherry Lansing and Dawn Steel, who fractured the glass ceiling, their exit deals were commensurate with their jobs. Mostly, however, it seems that even successful women are unable to fully capitalize on their successes. But there's more:

When an aging "d" girl is out there without a job, it's a cold town. I hate to think it's true, but people would rather give a tryout to a new "d" girl than be seen working with someone who's been around the block too many times. The women's network has to become compassionate enough to take care of its own. Perhaps we're still too grateful to be doing it at all to go out on any limbs for one another. To this extent, scarcity consciousness still thrives.

Over the past years, however, we have begun to develop alliances with one another. This was hard. The atmosphere when I arrived among the dozen or so token women was close to scathing. Any failure of one woman was a failure for the entire gender. When a woman got a big job, it meant another woman had one less opportunity. We were trained to compete with one another, not with men. At long last we have come to see that our competitors are *all* other producers, not just women producers.

THE STATE OF AFFAIRS

I had a romantic adventure recently with a hot action writer (this means he's really macho and knows how to order a martini) and before I knew it, the romantic adventure I thought I was having turned into a romantic adventure I was to produce. I was sitting in a darkly lit hotel bar on Sunset Boulevard staring into his piercing blue eyes, listening to a story point. "Why does this feel like work?" I thought to myself, almost batting my eyelashes. Because it *is* work, it dawned on me as a steady stream of action set pieces rolled off his tongue.

During my early exciting dates with him I used to wonder, "Is he flirting with me to work or is he working with me to flirt?" It was the first one. Remember, it's always work, whether you mean for it to be or not. All those dinners and martinis birthed a movie idea, nothing more. When he went on to another project, I suffered not from unrequited love but from unrequited work. This is where we live, we women in Hollywood, on the precipice of glamorous exhilaration and the Zen slap of humiliation.

Though there's plenty to lament about, this misses both the

point and the opportunity. This is a place for women to study business and learn to enjoy power; fill your emotional needs elsewhere. There is enormous and unprecedented opportunity in Hollywood for women. At current writing, there are no fewer than five women heads of production and one studio head. Cable and television are woman rich. Oscar broadcasts have been dedicated to us; reporters all over the world cover us. But the emotional backlash to this new-found abundance is extreme.

Men have responded dramatically to this shift in the dominance hierarchy, first through punishment and withdrawal, and ultimately by making it work for them (by hiring women). In other words, it's turned out great for work and lousy for romance. So if it's power a woman is seeking, there is probably no better place for her to strike it rich. If it's love she is looking for, I advise her to look elsewhere.

The cost of all this gender bending has been enormous. The everyday social fabric of Hollywood has come unraveled: It seemed for a time that people had stopped dating. Men are exhausted and enervated, while women are doing hundreds of military push-ups in aerobics classes all over town. What's up?

The first thing you notice about women in Hollywood, besides their low percentage of body fat, is how few are married. And the number of great-looking, successful single women without a social life is staggering. There are many reasons for this. The most glaring misconception about Hollywood is that it is the romance capital of the world. My advice to women with conventional dreams who are planning a career in Hollywood is (a) Marry young, and (b) Stay married. If this sounds drearily suburban, it's because underneath all the pseudodecadence Hollywood is really a very conventional place. Its daring pioneers, role models to many, those aggressive women in control of their careers, are largely at home at night, in bed with a script, lamenting their loss of a picket fence. No matter how successful the woman, and often the more successful the woman, her dreams of a nuclear family die hard.

These days, sleeping one's way to oblivion is more likely than sleeping one's way upward. Marry them — or date out of town. Here are some useful guidelines for women so they can tell whether they've been asked out on a date or a meeting:

1. If it's lunch it's a meeting.
2. If it's dinner it might be a date or a meeting or both.
3. If he orders a drink it's a date.
4. If he doesn't it's a meeting (or else he's in AA).

As we dress for our date/meeting, we must always keep in mind that our success makes us a little scary to them because (surprise!) many men haven't yet fully developed the ability to deal with a powerful and intelligent woman on her own terms. Most men don't know exactly what they have to offer us if we already have what they have, and they don't know if they've been asked out on a date or to a meeting either.

The fact that I know little or less about the man's point of view in Hollywood doesn't stop me from theorizing about it endlessly with my girlfriends. This is because all of us secretly fear that we have become the men we wanted to marry and that if we *were* men, we'd be chased around the block by hordes of fabulous women. Male execs are treated to a full dance card immediately and continuously. We all fantasize about what the life of "Guy Movie Riley" must be like, lounging at your pool, receiving phone calls from new bimbo/postteen recruits straight off the ferry from Vancouver.

Men can date down, laterally, and up. (They rarely choose the latter, but there are notable exceptions: the brave husbands of powerful women, whose friends speculate privately about how these men can sustain the ego damage.) Women are allowed to date laterally and up, but they usually date down (more to choose from). I haven't figured out if this is good or bad. Ambitious younger men, or for that matter ambitious older men down on their luck, rarely strategically grab the coattails of powerful women. The male ego usually cannot bear the public display of inferiority. The successes, deals, or advantages that can be gleaned from such a woman are publicly tainted, whereas the spoils gained by an ambitious woman from her powerful male lover are much less so. It stinks, social Darwinism. But it's better to face the truth than long for a reality that doesn't exist.

The hideous truth is that this is still the bimbo capital of the world, and men have lots to offer bimbos: great tables in restaurants that you can get yourself. All-access passes at the Forum, which you can have too. Screening passes for the next Oliver Stone movie. But you have your own. He can bring a bimbo and get away with it. You can't. The competition is so staggering and all encompassing that no one wants to maintain it under covers. When it's so dog-eat-dog, it's hard for dog to love dog.

FLIRTING AS A JOB SKILL

Flirting is an essential tool for surviving the gender gap. Not serious, provocative flirting, Lord knows. Despite a recent martini trend, there is practically no liquor here (think health, think body, think control — the Christian Coalition would like it more than they think); virtually everything is tactical (no sloppy mistakes), including flirting. The key to tactical flirting is not unfamiliar: With eyes focused on her prey, she makes the other the most interesting person in the world, as though the person were a real date. His interests interest her. His past movies are among her favorites. And she listens to his daily feats of epic deal making with appreciative expressions of support. The point is to make him see that she is fun to work with because she *likes* him and that she's not looking to find fault or to judge him. If he thinks she likes him, he's less likely to wound her — overtly, anyway. Tactical flirting is walking the line between virtual and actual seduction. No clothing is ever removed — actual sex is not even an afterthought.

Let's face it: Arnold Rifkin, president of the William Morris agency, sort of flirts with his most important client, Bruce Willis. As does/did Ron Meyer with his guy, Sylvester Stallone. And when Elaine Goldsmith spends hours on the phone talking about boys with her client Julia Roberts, aren't they sort of flirting too? It's all sort of flirting — a world greased by charm and seduction — because nobody really fucks. I've been flirting with my agent, Jim Wiatt, the enormously popular, boyish, and handsome president of ICM, for a decade now. We've never seen each other socially during the entire time he's been in charge of my career. But a call about my deal never closes without my telling him I love him, and I giggle at the opening, "Hiii, Jimmy," like a high school cheerleader cooing at the captain of the football team. Maybe unconsciously I need to feel I'm his favorite (like a shrink); maybe I think he'll pay more attention to me if he knows how much he means to me; maybe it's my residual dad thing, seeing as how an agent is as close to a pater-protector a girl producer gets in this cold town; or maybe I'm attracted. Who knows? My guess? All of the above.

Flirting helps grease the wheels of business. Men are afraid that with women down in the trenches watching them they will be exposed — caught vulnerable: A woman might witness a moment of weakness he otherwise might have hidden. But flirting breaks down that initial mistrust and allows a man to realize that the woman doesn't care if he shows weakness. Who wouldn't under this kind of pressure? It shows that she still likes him and thinks he's a neat guy, and that she's normal (i.e., the girl next door, from home, not the Marina), and allows him to relax. I think the key to being a successful woman executive is making the men around you relax. Try as I may, I still make most men jumpy. My "flirting" skills obviously need improvement. This is probably one reason that I'm a producer, not a studio head.

TYPES OF HOLLYWOOD MEN THAT HOLLYWOOD WOMEN SHOULD AVOID (LIKE THE PLAGUE)

1. Men who read the trades in bed.
2. Men who say they are looking for a smart, real woman and then pick their dates from the *Academy Ingenue Guide*.
3. Men whose Christmas card lists are longer than CAA's.
4. Men who work on Sundays or after eleven P.M.
5. Men who take their portable phones into the movies.
6. Men who know too many maître d's at too many of the town's trendier haunts.
7. Men who sit in the first booth at the Monkey Bar.
8. Men whose job description starts with "used to be manager of . . ."
9. Men straight out of rehab.
10. Men who have been married more than three times.

11. Sixty-year-old moguls with baby seats in their Rolls-Royces.
12. Any man who goes on industry-based male-bonding rafting trips.

This leaves Harrison Ford. And he's already married.

SURVIVAL SHILLS FOR GIRLS

We are the first wave of powerful women in the movie industry. Not that Mary Pickford and Ida Lupino didn't pave the way for us, but it was almost forty years between Ida Lupino and the first great onslaught of women working in the film business. Because we are the trailblazers, we are constantly confronting situations with which we are completely unfamiliar. We have neither a reference point as women here nor historical antecedents for the behavior expected of us. We are wearing a gender lens through which everything can become distorted. Let's take it off.

Everyday, run-of-the-mill business junk in Hollywood — like simple lying — astonishes women, leaves us speechless, and we take it personally. "Hello, he lied" defines the local ethos. A simple declarative statement, like "Fox has offered two hundred thousand dollars for the screenplay," is taken literally by us — silly things that we are. Our male counterparts take this sentence with a grain of salt. To them it means maybe Fox is interested. When someone says, "Demi Moore is attached to my movie," lo and behold! We'll repeat it to our bosses. Our male counterparts will say to their bosses, "Her agent claims Demi Moore is attached." They are right again. We must learn this quickly. And we do, we have, we had to — watch that gender lens!

Lying turns the wheels in Hollywood, and we women must develop ears to hear it for what it is, or else we can be bluffed hourly. Men know how to hold a poker face, an essential part of every man's — and woman's — survival skills. People can read on *my* face every single thing I'm thinking. I was once mad at Nora Ephron and tried to hide it when I ran into her at a party. She found me later in another part of the room and teased me, "Lynda. Skip subtlety. It's not in your repertoire." Believe me, no one could read on

Mike Ovitz's face when he planned his big move to Disney. But I'm learning.

Women tend to feel guilty when they lie and angry when they are lied to. These emotions do not belong in the workplace. Bluffing skills are needed for all high-rolling activities: script and book auctions, negotiations with actors, all deal making on our own behalf.

SITUATIONAL ETHICS

Very early on I realized that the sandbagging and bluffing and lying all around me were demoralizing. There were no role models for the ethical behavior I was used to (locally, at best a vague concept), and after three years at the *New York Times*, where having your tab picked up at a restaurant was considered unethical, I was at sea. But I am also a survivor and a pragmatist; I couldn't just throw up my hands in despair. If this was how business was done, I thought, I'll just have to make up my own personal ethics. They evolved while working with Henry Winkler, one of the true sweethearts of the motion picture business.

My boss at that time, now a major producer, had a deal with Henry; we got to be partners with him on his ABC network commitment in return for our developing movie scripts for him to make the switch from television into film. It was my job to develop these scripts. I grew to adore Henry while he and the writer and I worked together week after week on the first script. Finally, when the script was ready, I brought it to my boss. "It's done. It's marvelous!" I said. He was noncommittal and looked at me oddly. "That's nice," he said. "Maybe we should do another rewrite." I got it. In the vulgar terms of the movie business, Henry was being jerked around. The deal we had made with him was a sandbag so that we could piggyback on his television deal — permanently, or as long as possible at least.

My heart started pounding and I felt a little sick. What should I do? How could I not tell Henry that he was being manipulated when he was such a doll? But I couldn't betray my boss either. I was enough of a pro to know that. I stewed all night (the beginning of a trend) until I figured it out. First thing in the morning I called Henry. "You know, maybe you should slip your script to Paramount," I said. "They're looking for a comedy just like this." I think Henry understood. If not, he simply took my hint and asked for the script in turnaround. This was fine with my boss; he could be gracious in giving it back to Henry to set up elsewhere. My relationship with both my boss and Henry remained intact, as did theirs. Skating the fine line requires little white lies, bluffing skills, and tactical withholding of information. As girls we didn't have an opportunity to practice this sleight of mind and mouth. But as women in the workplace we now have the need to learn and practice. It's a new kind of athleticism. Today the jock in me rules.

OUR CAREERS, OUR SELVES

Another thing that doesn't come naturally to most women is fighting on our own behalf. This is because historically we are the conflict defusers. I know that there are equally conflict-phobic men and plenty of ego-driven women, but I still maintain this theory even at the risk of perpetuating a banal generality.

When a woman is in a fractious deal dispute, I see she often fights harder for the interests of her writer or director than for herself. This feels anthropologically related to raising children. When we fight on behalf of our children, we are ennobled. So we can muster up a lot of nerve on behalf of another, the surrogate child: the weaker writer, our noble director — or even for an abstract principle. Remember *The Player*, when the development girl, alone in fighting for the integrity of her movie, broke her heel running across the lot trying to find her boss to save the picture, while he and the director sat in the editing room happily trashing the movie they'd all dreamed of by changing the ending and selling out for commercial success?

But ask us to fight on our own behalf and the skill doesn't come naturally. Our problem is that we are so eternally grateful for being at the table at all, we don't feel entitled to ask for more than a seat. So in negotiations we are fearful of alienating our superiors. We are afraid of appearing shrill, demanding, selfish, not a team player. In placating others we camouflage our strength. We demur and in so doing we defer our own interests. We have to learn what we should reasonably expect for our services and ask for it, not with guilt or apprehension but rather with full self-awareness of the compensation — in all areas — that we deserve. If we do not get it we must walk away from the table, even if we can barely afford to — the rent, the rent, the rent. They will not hate us for it as we fear. In fact, they will grudgingly come to respect us for it.

I think that a real psychological advantage for younger women today is in watching their mentors finally be rewarded. ("We'd like to thank Barbra, Dawn, Sherry, Nora, for not backing down in the face of success. . . .") When the new recruits see it happen, they naturally feel entitled to be rewarded for *their* work. Nobody killed us, they think. Little do they know how hard people have tried. I don't know a female veteran of Hollywood who does not feel like a warrior. But the goal is to become a warrior who recognizes the discrete reality of the situation and creates her own ethical behavior — a warrior to respect and admire. And who can support herself and the integrity of the movies she chooses to make.

SPORTSTHINK FOR GIRLS

"The overemphasis on protecting girls from strain or injury and underemphasis on developing skills and experiencing teamwork fits neatly into the pattern of the second sex."

— *a gymnastics coach*

We are in boot camp. No doubt about it; this is a marathon, and women have to learn the athletic skills that men bring to the game. Luckily for me I was a jock. A tomboy. Without a doubt, this was better preparation for my work than anything I learned in college. I rough-and-tumbled with my brothers as a kid in suburban Westchester County, New York, and consistently got selected by the neighborhood boys for first base in our local pickup baseball game. I learned how to work with my teammates to execute a double play and I learned what winning felt like. And losing too. But at ten years old I had to stop playing baseball. When all the boys in my pickup team went on to Little League, I was supposed to make the transition to dolls. No Little League for girls. I hated dolls. Had I been allowed to compete on this larger playing field, my training would have been closer to that of most men. But my sports education was thwarted (woe is me), and my tomboy went dormant.

Today I watch my male friends playing basketball — killing each other, kneeing, swiping, swearing, genuinely loathing each other as they risk mutual injury to win. Then the game is over, and they're out for a brewski, backslapping one another as they review the game blow by blow. What I know is that we women still personalize "combat," which makes getting through the day more painful and draining. After a bruising game like that, we would retire to an Epsom-salt bath to nurse our wounds, wondering if any of the other players were really mad at us. How can we concentrate on winning while worrying about everybody's feelings?

Winning is not a traditional female instinct and it is not a particularly attractive trait to men in women. We are not sure that winning is becoming to *us* either. (It is to me now, and to most successful women I know.) But for the masses, five thousand years of hardwiring fights the image. We fear that if we win it's at someone else's expense. Someone has lost, and we feel bad for them.

Male bosses are afraid, often rightly, that our emotional reactions will lead them into bad deals. (Their worst fear is that they will be emotionally manipulated — literally whined and dragged into a deal they otherwise wouldn't have made.) Women (and many men) have to learn the macho principle of deal making: If you win by overpaying, you lose. (This is probably why Barry Diller walked away from the Paramount deal. He lost his studio because the price was too high but maintained his credibility on Wall Street for another day. Next!) It feels good not to be snookered. Men actually get charged up from it. Women become more credible players when they are hard-nosed, skilled negotiators, and here modeling male behavior is not wrong. (There are finally female models for this behavior: Robyn Russell, until recently head of business affairs at Sony, and Helene Hahn at DreamWorks.) It is reassuring to men when women understand how to stay firm and not be fooled or "agented," i.e., taken in by an agent. And to cultivate this often alien skill, women must be able to walk away from a deal, or at least appear to. This is how you learn to win.

I had an epiphany once watching a game of playground Red Rover with my nephews and nieces. In the game two teams holding hands face each other. One person calls out, "Red Rover, Red Rover, let Jennifer come over!" and Jennifer runs across and tries to bash through the other team's line. If she succeeds she picks a person from that line to join her team. If she fails she must stay on the other side. Whenever it was a girl's turn she picked her best friend. Whenever it was a boy's choice he picked the strongest boy on the other team. Men play to win. We like to tie. (Men in Hollywood do not believe this. They think we're out to beat them.) We need to get used to the idea of winning. The feeling of winning. It has to be normal to be female and win.

Basketball is the perfect spectator sport for the study of the mechanics of team playing and winning. That's why men are so glued to their televisions during a tournament like the Final Four. All forms of combat, gamesmanship, bluffing, intimidation, perseverance, and teamwork are on virtuosic display. I'm hooked. I watch the graceful athletes move the ball around the court, constantly conscious of the positions of their opponents. We women need to get used to the fast pace of our game and we too (metaphorically, of course) need to practice passing the ball. We don't know how to pass — make a play without going for the basket ourselves. The most driven of women are likely to be solo players — "lone rangers," as some of the most talented women producers are called. No one helped us; no one passed the ball to us. Historically we are afraid, for good reason, that if we pass the ball the male who catches it will get the credit. Or that someone will drop it and we will fail. But it's impossible to build a team if we can't learn to pass and play. Our ability to rise farther up the ladder will be hampered by our need to control, our difficulty with delegating authority. Like the big sister who made everything okay for the entire dysfunctional family, many women rose through the ranks by doing everything for their bosses. They've done everything by themselves for so long they can't stop. These women cannot gain the perspective necessary for executive balance. We must become basketball players and mentally play guard, not center. We don't have to go to the basket, but if there's a clear shot we should.

While shooting *One Fine Day* I discovered another, less theoretical, reason for women to embrace basketball. Lunch on our set was a freewheeling, one-on-one basketball match between swoony jock-star George Clooney and shorter but wiry (and very jocky) director Michael Hoffman. Apart from the stress-relieving sweat they both enjoyed, the court was a battle of wits as well as bodies and roused them both to new heights on the court and the set.

The male-bonding sessions reached such a testosterone high that at one lunch on the set of a high school gym, the grips and electric team challenged Michael and George to a game. Everyone watched and cheered as the above-the-line team astonishingly managed to beat the cowboys of below-the-line. But no sooner had I started organizing cheers and color analysis than suddenly the God of Production Caution seemed to intervene.

A very large grip elbowed George in the eye. Despite the efforts of a Florence Nightingale–like eye-repair team, George's eye closed up and he couldn't shoot the rest of the day. We had to return George to the set of *ER* — which he was still finishing up — with a closed and black eye. Oops. Potential producer's jail for me. "You let George Clooney play *basketball*??? *For real*???" The studio was aghast. "Boys will be boys," I explained.

NATURAL ADVANTAGES OF WOMEN: YES, THERE ARE MANY!

1. The maternal instinct is extremely helpful in the nurturing end of the business: producing.
2. Intuition keeps women more in tune with the market.
3. Women have an overwhelming and overweening sense of responsibility. (Who else could you call after midnight to track down a FedEx package?)
4. They believe in monogamy. Maybe they make more loyal employees. Maybe not.
5. Their passion increases their perseverance during the impossible development process. They believe in things when

everyone tells them they're nuts. (I was trained by sixties rock lyrics. To wit, "He's a Rebel": "Just because he doesn't do what everybody else does, that's no reason why I can't give him all my love.") We will be seeing more and more women at the podium accepting those Academy Awards won after twelve years of strife. Women stick with their projects until they leave home.

6. They have patience. Even an impatient woman like me is more naturally patient than your typical type-A male exec. Programmed biologically to endure nine months of hell for a lifetime of responsibility, a woman's ability to wait until the proper moment to make a move is superior.

7. Women have flexibility and agility. No one promised us a rose garden or a straight path to glory. Since busted by Ibsen in *A Doll's House,* women's remarkable ability to end-run oppression and outthink and outmaneuver stronger adversaries with subtle moves has been the stuff of lore.

8. We have an innate sense of fashion, so we look good at those endless meetings.

We do things differently, with our own homegrown brand of common sense. I recently had an extraordinary conversation about this with Laura Ziskin, who runs Fox 2000, one of the two feature-film production divisions of my studio. Laura is a stunningly astute player of the movie business game, the only head of production I've ever worked with who can read the fine print of a budget. (Good news and bad news. Bad news: She knows all your little secrets; you get away with nothing. Good news: She understands the context of all your production problems and is a valuable and sympathetic partner.) Having been a great producer, she is gifted and proactive as an executive, herding movies into production like a lioness guarding her den. We were in the middle of very tense negotiations with Michelle Pfeiffer for *One Fine Day.* The negotiations had been dragging out for what felt like weeks, and nerves and tempers were frayed on both sides. I was Henry Kissinger doing shuttle diplomacy between Ed Limato, Michelle's agent at ICM, and Laura. She had been explaining to me why Ed had to call Fox business affairs to counter their last offer, and Ed had just told me why Fox business affairs had to call him first to counter *his* offer. It was a Mexican standoff. Ed wouldn't call Fox, Fox wouldn't call Ed, and meanwhile everyone was in a panic about not closing the deal. It seemed completely absurd to me.

Laura said to me, "Can I be confidential with you? Is this a guy thing, this 'I can't call him until he calls me'?" Hearing Laura mouth my secret musings thrilled me. I said, "I always call. I'll call three times if I have to. It means nothing to me. I'll do anything to close the deal so I can sleep at night." It's a guy thing, we concluded. Granted, there is a certain formality to a studio-agent negotiation. Offer, counteroffer, counter-counteroffer, counter-counter-counteroffer, etc. However, in this case the madness was derived from the fact that each party claimed to have made the last phone call. Finally both genders working together resolved the deadlock. With Laura's quiet encouragement, I went to see Peter Chernin, Fox's chairman, to ask for his help. He is too powerful to care about protocol. (This is one of the great things about Peter: He doesn't stand on ceremony; he's a closer. He'll bend a sympathetic ear to all sides and *then* get what he wants.) He got in his car, drove to see Ed Limato, and the deal was closed that day.

BEGINNING THE LONG TREK TO UNEQUAL EQUALITY

Whenever I speak to women starting out in the business, they invariably ask me the same question. How do you get taken seriously? I always give them the same answer. Take yourself seriously. Assert yourself with the conviction that what you have to say is at least as interesting as anything else being said and then take your shot saying something genuinely interesting. If you can't, wait. Don't talk to hear yourself speak but rather to express a point of view that is uniquely your own. Listen carefully. Men like women who listen. Women like women who listen. Women these days can draw from more traditional female qualities to fuel their work. A ladylike and feminine persona is pleasing to many male employers. It is the "Father, may I?" model. But the paradox is that this image works best as a protective coloration. We can't really be asking permission for everything we do or we won't get anything done. We must acquire the skills necessary to become a tough negotiator and an able adversary, a subtle technician and a worthy teammate, without scaring the bejesus out of our superiors. The goal is to be able to think in the way that men have learned to think without becoming one. This is not masculine behavior we are learning; it is professional behavior.

GIRL STYLE PARADIGMS: FUZZY VS. CRISP

The "d" girl — remember, *d* is for development (there are "d" boys and they dress well too) — is the cherished junior exec job for women in Hollywood. It is probably the best entry-level job for a college grad in America. And yet it is a treacherous trek, as the road is littered with Eve Harringtons and their victims. A woman with talent, however, can find a fast track. Or at least a track. I've noticed that there are two major styles of female executives in Hollywood: fuzzy and crisp.

The fuzzy girl is artistic; her hair is wilder (rarely blow-dried); she wears secondhand dresses. Often the fuzzy girl is more talented, more compatible with writers, but there is an inborn impediment to fuzzy girls in climbing the ladder: their bosses. To the extent that the patriarchy still exists, it reinforces the crisp, good-daughter paradigm in a town where style says everything about taste.

A fuzzy girl can get caught in her persona because she is expected to get too emotionally involved and not be able to maintain appropriate distance. She is expected to whine, beg, and plead for projects because she *cares* and gets attached to things. Producers, because their status is totally dependent upon the success of their current season, are allowed some style eccentricities, particularly in the wake of hits. (People are very forgiving of producers who have just had babies too, because it makes them appear normal for a moment.) The fuzzy model is always acceptable, of course, in writers. This is also true for men. Being kind of distracted, artistic, vague, sensitive — these are all excellent traits for writers. They bring out the maternal in the woman executive, the paternal in the male executive, and this is how talent gets embraced by its protectors: the agents who have to mediate between it and the exploitative buyers.

It should be noted that the elevation of brainy, artsy Amy Pascal, fuzzy girl extraordinaire, to the presidency of Turner Pictures after at least one crisp girl turned it down was a triumph for fuzzy girls everywhere. So was the bonding moment between quintessential fuzzy-girl producer Lindsay Doran and her best pal, star-writer-intellectual Emma Thompson, when congratulating each other on their best picture award for *Sense and Sensibility,* at the Golden Globes in 1996. Lindsay, true to her fuzzy-girl roots, wore a vintage dress and no makeup. (This is almost saintly lack of pretension, for which Lindsay is legend.) I nearly burst into tears at the sight of such good intentions connecting with big-time reality.

The crisp girl suggests the Smith/Wellesley girl: one who always returns phone calls and dresses for success. She can and often does rise to the top by innocent flirting, preferably while married. The crisp girl (an Ann Taylor crisp before she can afford Armani) maintains a professional demeanor without appearing (dreaded word) "tough." Crisp girls can be ruthless without anyone noticing.

Style for women is a vital component of success. It's equally important for men too, which is why (I think) Barney's is cleaning up in L.A. (at least this week). If you can afford it, Armani is the rule for crisp girls on the move. It's expensive to succeed (in fact, it's expensive to even try to succeed), and on weekends in Beverly Hills the Armani boutique is like a commissary. There are other good reasons to dress well. Hollywood must be the only place in the world where hardworking women who do the same bone-crunching work as men compete with the most beautiful women in the world — in fact they are competing for men with women whose *job* is to be beautiful. (And who have all day to devote to it. I think it's tax-deductible for them too, a true injustice.)

The glamour services that flourish here all foment the dream machine, and who is more susceptible than the women who manufacture those dreams for a living? The most glamorous women in the world, the most ambitious, the starlet wanna-bes, the shrewd beauties with their eyes on fortunes, the greatest call girls and courtesans in the world, come here and try to win husbands. Young college graduates hell-bent for success soon find themselves competing for men with the literal objects men have long fantasized about: starlets, cover girls, pop stars. This comes as a shocking realization to everyone. The guys who were formerly fat high school rejects you never would have considered dating are suddenly attractive to cover girls. The girls who rejected these guys in high school and college can no longer hope to catch one. Here all women are one. Working women behind the camera, in front of the camera, the haves, the have-nots, the husband-haves, the husband-have-nots. We all go to the same facialist or manicurist. We know where the best collagen shots are. And that's before we even get to work.

But no matter how we pull off our look, with effort or none, in the end it is the work that counts. Style counts, but it doesn't pay. Finding and hitting the bull's-eye pays. Once enough men finally believe in our ability to find great projects and get them made, we begin to break out of the pack. There is a pantheon of female moguls today: the ones written about, gossiped about, emulated, ripped off, adored, and reviled. They do not ask permission and they have the same expectations as men. But when, God forbid, they show their ambition, well, the old insecurities rear their ugly heads, and successful women are called ball-busters and worse. In the words of Barbra Streisand, the first and foremost woman pioneer of our generation, in her now well-known Crystal Awards speech at the Women in Film luncheon in 1986:

> A man is commanding — a woman is demanding.
> A man is forceful — a woman is pushy.
> A man is uncompromising — a woman is a ball-breaker.
> A man is a perfectionist — a woman's a pain in the ass.
> He's assertive — she's aggressive.
> He strategizes — she manipulates.
> He shows leadership — she's controlling.
> He's committed — she's obsessed.
> He's persevering — she's relentless.
> He sticks to his guns — she's stubborn.
> If a man wants to get it right, he's looked up to and respected.

If a woman wants to get it right, she's difficult and impossible.

Enough cannot be said about the degree to which Barbra trailblazed for the rest of us. For years she was the only bankable female star, during which time she used her power to extend her creative voice through directing and producing projects that she, above all, believed in. Her famous perfectionism, alluded to in her speech, has created the impression that she is hard to please, but Barbra is harder on no one than she is on herself. Throughout her career she has paid dearly for her power, her personality, her convictions. But she is unstoppable, a natural — compelled to communicate. She is a living symbol of a woman with ideals and the wherewithal to pursue them. She is scary to men in the power elite as well as in the reactionary backwaters. There is not an ounce of "Father, may I?" in her.

THE TEN COMMANDMENTS FOR CHIX IN FLIX

1. THOU SHALT NOT CRY AT WORK

Ever. One of men's most legitimate fears about us is that in a moment of crisis or argument, we will break down and resort to tears. They simply don't know how to react to strong emotion in a professional context. When we cry they feel an unfair advantage is being taken, as they suddenly see a previously tough colleague as their own emotional wife, daughter, or, worse, mother wanting something from them. If I get distraught or want to cry, I take off. I disappear in my car to cool down, while my assistant screens my calls. Tears don't belong in the office. You must gather your thoughts, then subtract inappropriate emotion from the equation and behave like a pro.

2. THOU SHALT NOT HAVE AN AFFAIR WITH THY BOSS

(I personally don't know why you would want to. Talk about a busman's holiday! No relief.) It's a truly terrible idea to sleep with your boss. First, it's the shortest route to getting fired. (Never underestimate the wife.) Second, even if a woman does wonderfully well and buys a thousand great scripts under his tenure, her success will forever be attributed to her special relationship. *Don't think no one will know. Everyone will know.* Remember *The Player:* "All rumors are true." If a woman must have an affair at the office, she should try a peer.

3. THOU SHALT SUBDUE THY SEXUALITY

Only actresses are allowed to be overtly seductive; it's their job. Like in high school, women must guard their reputations, and come-on is uncool. But they must also take flirtatious pleasure in male company. Men will be so relieved to be noticed. Big sister works for me. Little sister is even more effective.

4. THOU SHALT NOT DISH OTHER WOMEN

Year of the woman or not, about this we all try to be politically correct. There are plenty of men around to bash us. Competing with women is passé. Compete with everyone.

5. THOU SHALT UNDERSTAND THINE OWN PERSONAL STYLE

A woman must know what she looks best in, define her personal style. She must wear it well, keep it clean, and get great haircuts. She must have a great facialist, nutritionist, manicurist, and, most important, colorist. No one goes gray in Hollywood, and style always, always matters. It says you know who you are. (Or who you want to look like, at least.)

6. THOU SHALT ENTERTAIN

Entertaining always enhances a woman's profile, though there's nothing quite as dreary as an industry dinner. She must pretend she doesn't mind, and reinvent the dinner party with a fascinating mix of breaking writers, English directors, and handsome Young Turks.

7. THOU SHALT KEEP THY MIND AND BODY WELL TUNED

Keep reading books. Not just for work. Work will not sustain intellectual curiosity. Be terrified if it does. But books do. And be peripherally active. It's the only good thing about Southern California. I find it helpful to think I'm in training. I use sports metaphors and give myself motivational pep talks. Be your own coach about everything.

8. THOU SHALT RETURN ALL THY PHONE CALLS

The Sherry Lansing secret to success. Damnit, be polite. No one can bear the arrogance of a woman who doesn't return her calls. How dare she? Isn't she grateful? Anyway, we know better.

9. THOU SHALT NOT APPEAR TOUGH

Only men are allowed to be tough. Why is this? Angry women remind everyone of their mothers and their potential wrath is more painful. We must be conscious of this disparity, fair or not. The trick is to be tough-skinned without seeming to be tough at all. It is best to display softness as a velvet glove over a firm hand. (Think Liddy Dole.) This requires avoiding power struggles for their own sake. Screaming at anyone is a mistake, even in private. (This includes all service-related screaming at hairdressers, messengers, assistants.) A team can't be run like this. Everyone is waiting for powerful women to become dragon ladies: It makes good copy. Don't play into ugly expectations. Be smarter.

10. THOU SHALT BE A PRO AT ALL TIMES

Taking disappointment in stride, being graceful in the face of rejection, keeping perspective on the true scale of a problem, are all large parts of being a pro. Feuds must be avoided because anyone with whom a woman is feuding is likely to show up in a crucial role in her next project. Composure is the key. No one wants to work with a nut, no matter how talented. People must feel they can count on you. And when they can, you're a pro.

THE BOYS' CLUB: ARE WE IT?

You can argue that being a member of the studio-head club makes you a member of the old boys' club, but Dawn Steel would tell you differently. A woman can rise to the top of the corporate hierarchy here, but the boys' club remains just that: the Boys' Club. I've concluded after many years of hoping otherwise that it is intractable. Impenetrable. The Afrikaaner Resistance Movement of Hollywood, it is a bunch of privileged veterans tenaciously holding on to the last bastion of their exclusive power. They won't give it up. It's all they have left, so why should they? (It is quite liberal in its internal policies, however: Gay men are welcome, and felons.)

Like any guerrilla movement, the boys' club thrives underground in innocuous-sounding outings like Katzenberg's annual river rafting expedition, Herbert Allen's Sun Valley, Idaho, corporate retreat, cross-country jaunts in Warner's or Sony's or Geffen's jets, trips to Saint Bart's with CAA's Young Turks. I've never been on one, though I've longed to be invited. Dawn Steel made sure that the Katzenberg rafting-bonding trip was degenderized when she sent a female blow-up doll to accompany the guys. My image of gentleman ranchers cutting cattle and making deals is way off. On Herbie Allen's Sun Valley retreat, apparently, Wild West or not, the moguls stay in condos and meet on the golf course to conglomerate. Michael Eisner's Disney married Tom Murphy's Cap Cities/ ABC on a recent links outing. These are the real corridors of power, and there are no girls here.

This new generation of men, true to the venerable, honor-bound tradition, adheres steadfastly to the old. The old initiates the new. As Stark chose Guber and Guber chose Melnick, and later Canton chose Josephson, so it goes.* The young aristocrats preen with their selection. They are the hottest guys in town. Everyone knows who they are. Neat guys like CAA's Jay Maloney, Columbia's Barry Josephson, or Warner's Lorenzo di Bonaventura are bonded in their weekends — at Guber's humongous Aspen ranch, at private retreats in the Caribbean, on jaunts to San Francisco or Austin — as well as in their work. One generation of players, as a

---

*The patrilineage goes like this: Seminal Columbia mogul Ray Stark handpicked Peter Guber to run his studio. Dan Melnick became a producer under Peter Guber and later, as head of production, approved Peter Guber's movies when he became a producer. Or something like that. Then Peter Guber became a giant producer at Warners and helped elevate his ally and protégé Mark Canton from executive VP to president. When Guber went to Sony, Canton soon followed, and there his closest male protégé became the popular Barry Josephson, who is now president of Columbia. *La ronde masculin* continues.

fraternal right, reaches down and seemingly hand selects its progeny.

The boys' club continues and thrives. There is nothing to be done about it. You can try to marry into it, you can ignore it, revile it, admire it. But you cannot join it. So there.

I have a fantasy, a little extreme but not altogether far-fetched. Maybe it is a clue to why the storm between the sexes seems to be subsiding, for the moment. See, we have our network, and they have theirs. Then one day, in our utter isolation (except at meetings), someone (an eternal optimist) will get the great idea that we should have mixers, like in college. The boys' network and ours, see. And we'll even spike the punch and loosen up a little. And at first they'll be on one side and we'll stand (not as wallflowers, though) on the other, then some brave soul will ask someone to dance. (Probably a boy will ask a boy and break the ice. We can count on our gay friends to remind us how to party.) The next thing you know, we'll all start dating again (not strategically, either). It will definitely be good for business, as well as the soul.

Meanwhile, things are looking up on the love front as the decade draws to a close. This season no fewer than four powerful lady moguls, long single and picky, met their dream mates, truly, and have plans to or have already taken the hike down the aisle. Picket-fence dreams intact, careers under control, we're starting to feel like we can have it all. The tragedy of the career women, as ingrained in our brains by forties melodramas, is finally becoming a lie. Bette Davis would have been so proud. We're doing it in part for her legacy and that of our thwarted mothers, as well as for our daughters, strapped to our backs on the set, watching us take command.

Chapter 9

WHEN ON LOCATION THERE'S ALWAYS TEMPTATION

"I can't go on. You must go on. I'll go on."

— *Samuel Beckett*

"This show's gonna wreck."

— *teamster captain, Bad Girls*

MY FIRST GENUINE production emergency erupted immediately upon my arrival in Austin, Texas, in 1987, three days prior to commencement of photography on *Heartbreak Hotel*. It was a romantic fantasy, set in the early seventies, about a young boy's effort to introduce his lonely mother to Elvis Presley, starring Charlie Schlatter, Tuesday Weld, and David Keith as Elvis. To be directed by Chris Columbus and produced by my partner, Debra Hill, and me, the movie had been prepped in Los Angeles by a production manager without my involvement. I didn't know from prep. This was my second movie as producer and on my first, *Adventures in Babysitting*, I had happily ceded all preparation and production issues to Debra. I had thought I could wing in from the coast and oversee opening day festivities, kind of like the baseball commissioner. I was in the zone, like most producers, delegating the little details like crew deals and scheduling the movie to underlings. Debra, the physical production expert of the two of us, was still in Los Angeles doing postproduction on her movie *Clue*. Little did either of us know that I would be ambushed on my arrival with the ominous news that there was to be a "parking-lot meeting" (read: crew mutiny) on the day we were scheduled to commence. I had never heard of a parking-lot meeting, but I knew this was not good.

Complicating it infinitely further were some urgent personal problems. My ex-husband had remarried a very difficult woman, a symphony orchestra conductor. David sued me for custody of our child, Oliver, then nine, arguing that I was leaving Los Angeles to go on location and could not adequately care for him. I suspected that David's new wife had encouraged him to sue. Meanwhile, she and David had moved to West Virginia, where she was conducting, so the broadside was launched from across the country to my production trailer in Texas. I was dumbstruck, having devoted my life to my son, who was living with me and going to school in Los Angeles. The possibility of losing him was devastating. I was served papers at precisely the same moment I heard news of the parking-lot meeting on my film. I was struck with simultaneous blows below the belt. But I had to proceed; there was no one else in charge. I had to create a home for my son on location. There was no time to freak out or fall apart. Oliver's need for security and stability gave me mine. The personal attack armed me for struggle and made me determined to be present for both my son and my crew. I took Oly out of private school, flew him to Texas, and hired him a tutor and me a lawyer.

For the parking-lot meeting, the reporter in me went to work. Who was leading this revolt and what were the issues? I was mapless, clueless, without allies on the set or even the knowledge of where to find any. I now know that the teamsters know everything and I avoid ambushes by getting the scoop from the driver on the way in from the airport. Over the years, on various projects, I learned things like the actress is screwing the cinematographer; the construction coordinator is a drunk; the art director is padding receipts; the production manager is an idiot; the key grip is screwing the wardrobe department; and hair and makeup are at war among themselves. A normal day on set.

Fortunately, this time the crew leader turned out to be a very attractive key grip. Very. I sought him out, and we took a long walk along Lake Austin on the day prior to the proposed walkout. The crucial issue was that the production manager at the studio had neglected to secure the "legal turnaround" for the crew, he explained patiently. I didn't know from turnaround either, but my grandfather had been a labor organizer, so I was all ears.

The crew's turnaround was the guaranteed eighteen hours of rest they would get between a late Saturday night and an early start on Monday. The unclosed deals, as they were written, allowed for no guaranteed rest time for the crew whatsoever. I told the key grip, Tony Marra, that I would "get into it" immediately and to prepare his crew to go to work in the morning with the understanding that the parking-lot meeting would take place if the turnaround could not be secured. Then I got on the phone with Disney and whipped them into a frenzy. That evening two Disney production suits flew by private jet to the set. The crew knew they had been heard, and I became their producer. When in doubt, get on the phone and yell. Someone's bound to listen, particularly when production is about to be derailed. That means money — physical production is the business part of show business. And, in its own way, it's the show part too.

Sometimes we forget that the point of the entire Hollywood adventure is actually to make a movie — that is, commit a screenplay to celluloid. We get so consumed with the deal, the scene, the who's-on-first of it all, that we lose sight of the point of the enterprise. This reaches its most absurd conclusion in some people's resistance to leaving town — going on location — based on an unfounded fear, I think, that in their absence they will literally disappear. Many studio head and agent types never leave town. For them location is an out-of-the-way place that you have to take two planes to get to, then you eat dinner, watch a few boring shots that take endlessly long to shoot, and take two planes home.

This is sheer madness. Being on location has saved my life more than once. During *Heartbreak*, it helped me forge an even stronger relationship with my son. Oly (his nickname; he *hates* the name Oliver) was schooled with the kids in the movie in the mornings and fished with the teamsters in the afternoons. He saw me work, and saw that I took time for him without the two colliding. It turned out to be the best thing that ever happened to us. Oly came to understand what I do and was proud to watch me do it. He learned that as important as my work was to me, he was more important. My work was no longer apart from him but a part of him. By the wrap party, Oly sang lead with the band. This was my critical test as a working mother, my baptism by fire, integrating the two most important elements of my life. My son and I became a team and we've been one since. A year or two (and much too much money) later, the custody suit was finally dropped. Oly's relationship with his father improved dramatically. David and his second wife divorced, and she moved on to marry an unsuspecting governor. Hurray!

THE SHOW IS MADE IN PREP

On a normal show a producer's job is basically done during pre-production, or "prep," the six to eight weeks that precede shooting. It is important to note that in production, we always call a movie a show and we call preproduction prep. We call the fun part (hiring the new team) crewing up. Your use of this terminology is how other key crew members know you've done this before. Crewing up is when you turn into the CEO of a minicorporation, staffing from scratch. Santa Claus time.

Prep is a good news–bad news joke. The good news: You've got a green light. The bad news: You can't make your movie for the budget. (It was once said of Paramount in an earlier incarnation that it gave you a green light and then dared you to make the movie.) Presumably prep is the process of planning the shoot and then arriving at an approved budget, determining the amount of money it will take to prepare, shoot, and complete your movie. This includes the number of days you need to shoot, crew salaries, star fees, and critical assumptions about production realities: weather, effects, stunts, extras. Then, commonsensically, we defend these numbers and assumptions to the powers that be.

The ritual is a little different now. In today's world each movie's budget is pre-figured by the studio before the producer really knows what she needs. The studio models the genre and cast of the movie and tries to predict its profitability. It then addresses the few glaring budget assumptions that the script entails. The number the studio has in its collective brain is a function of that reasoning. They don't tell the producer the real number (duh!) for the same reason I don't tell the costume designer her whole budget. The number we get, the number they tell us we cannot exceed for fear of a fate worse than death, is usually a large fraction of the real one. (What is that fate worse than death? I call it producers jail.) Then you quibble and posture and bluff and play brinkmanship.

"We're not going to make the movie at that price. Forget it."

"Fine. Put it in turnaround. I can get it made for this price across the street."

You cannot cave now, as you are fighting for the lifeblood of the show: the salaries of its most important crew members — the cinematographer, production designer, costumer; the possibility of distant locations; the principal cast; the time it will take to shoot; the look of the show. All this is what makes prep the crucible for the producer.

I was scouting locations for *The Fisher King* in New York with Terry Gilliam, my coproducer, Debra Hill, the writer, Richard LaGravenese, and the cinematographer, Roger Pratt. Scouting with Terry was extraordinary because he is so brilliant visually and what he is imagining is so physically demanding, either because it is too high up to see or too high up to access. He is always looking up; my neck was constantly craning, which was aggravated by the fact that I was on crutches from a gymnastics injury during the entire scout. Suddenly Terry would stop in front of what appeared to be nothing. He'd seen a beautiful piece of stone cornice-work, forty feet up the building in front of us. I saw nothing; he saw a textured background for an expositional scene. This is why he was the director and I was the producer. His job was to find stimulating visuals, mine to get the crane it would take to shoot them.

One day we were scouting Grand Central Station for a scripted scene to take place there. It was a memorable moment for me; I had virtually grown up at this station since my dad commuted through it his entire adult life. But it looked brand-new through Terry's eyes. He got us to the tippy top of the station. We had to take a rickety elevator and climb the last few flights. The perspective was amazing. Terry looked down, quiet for a long time, watching the rush-hour traffic, just as Parry, the homeless person Robin Williams was to play, would have. "They look like ants down there, don't they?" he said. "What if they all started waltzing at once?"

To understand just how spectacular this idea was you have to understand the scripted scene that this visual would replace. It was written as a long dialogue and musical number in which Jack (Jeff Bridges), the tortured, down-and-out ex–shock jock, finally starts to see the special wisdom with which the demented but inspired Parry sees the world. It is also the moment Parry comes closest to meeting his secret love, Lydia (Amanda Plummer), on her daily jaunt to Grand Central Station. Ultimately Jack redeems himself of his dissipated past by arranging a date between Parry and Lydia. In this scene he understands how much Parry's Dulcinea means to him. In one stroke Terry replaced the need for words with an unforgettable set piece, one that would come to signify the romantic and fantastical style of the film.

But it would take a thousand extras and an additional day and night of shooting. Each day in New York cost $125,000, so that was the minimum budget increase before we even approached the logistical problems. Debra and I put our heads together, literally, as if we were in a huddle. There was not a moment when either of us considered saying no. We both knew that the idea was masterful and if we didn't give Terry these moments of his own true gifts, why had we hired him? And yet we couldn't stretch our budget. TriStar was all over us: two women producers joining forces with the notorious Terry Gilliam. (TriStar had released the doomed $70-million *Adventures of Baron Munchausen* and believed they had reason to panic.)

Then Debra figured out that by replacing a big set built in New York with a model, we could move the scene to a stage in L.A., where shooting costs are about half the $125,000 a day budget. It would take three days to shoot, and the upward of $150,000 savings we could put directly into extras and equipment for Grand Central. We would borrow from Peter to pay Paul. We moved the money around and gave Terry his waltz scene without ever having to beg or even ask the studio.

PRODUCTION: IT'S NEVER AS GOOD AS THE DAILIES OR AS BAD AS THE FIRST CUT

Once shooting starts, the department heads hired by the producer and the director run their departments. If you've done a good job in prep, you as the producer are the watchful observer during shooting. You put out the occasional fire, assert authority, reassure everyone. I have a Florence Nightingale kind of approach on the set and my most important function is often as medic. I know the physical state of every actor and crew member on my show: who has a sore throat, whose back gave out, who has a migraine, who has a special diet. Any emergency is my responsibility. When a stunt-woman was thrown from her horse during a high jump over a wall in *Bad Girls*, I ran from video village to her side. I held her hand and shouted to the AD to call for an ambulance over the walkie-talkie. I comforted her and checked whatever vitals I understood until the ambulance came, calming her and the crew. I couldn't leave the set so I sent a PA with a portable phone and her best friend to accompany her to the hospital. The PA called in to me with updates, and I informed the crew that she had bruised her shoulder and suffered a slight concussion. There were no serious fractures, and she wanted to come back to work. I made her take a day off, and she returned triumphant. This is how a movie crew, functioning like a single organism, lumbers from setback to success.

Sleepless in Seattle was a well-prepped show. In fact it had begun prep before Nora asked the studio to bring me on as executive producer. I had an excellent line-producing partner in Pat Crowley. A line producer is the person hired by the creative team and the studio to be fiscally in charge of the movie. He approves the crew deals, oversees the production manager, and is responsible to the studio for the physical production of the show. This show was producer rich. Gary Foster had developed the script at TriStar and, with Pat, had begun prep before I arrived. Our biggest challenge in production was getting rain in Seattle during a drought-ridden summer, an unexpected problem given Seattle's reputation. That and figuring out while shooting in Baltimore how to find the sixty or so café lattés every four hours that we'd all gotten addicted to in Seattle. The show came in on time, on budget, and was a huge hit. Sometimes it works like that. Don't count on it.

A show falls behind when decisions aren't made on time. A show in trouble in prep has critical casting still open in the last few weeks and some of its locations not locked in. If a movie falls behind in prep, it will stay behind and is likely never to recover.

If you, the producer, are too busy during production, you've got problems. It means you're handling issues that your department heads should be handling. Such was the experience in reconstructing the collapsed *Bad Girls*, which I came to think of as my punishment for how easy *Sleepless* had been.

BIGGEST ISSUES ON AN EASY (WELL-RUN) SHOW

1. Where to live (this takes up most of our time).
2. What food to serve at dailies.
3. When to break out the brew.
4. Where to hold the wrap party.
5. What to wear.

On *Sleepless in Seattle* I wore a *Fisher King* jacket and was teased by Tom Hanks, who informed me with his signature curly, ironic smile that he never allowed producers to wear jackets of movies that he hadn't been in. I teased him back, reminding him that he had rejected a role in *Fisher King* and telling him that frankly I felt that he was adding insult to injury. He didn't approve of my Birkenstocks either. Come to think of it, Mr. Hanks turned out to be a serious critic of set wear. Actually, everybody is a critic of set wear, each in his or her own way. Everyone is a secret costume designer on the set. People are judged by how they dress on set. Just like in high school, lasting impressions are made on the first day.

SET WEAR

If it's hot, wear Gap shorts, preferably khaki, and a cute T-shirt. People assiduously read your T-shirts for telltale personality info, so be aware — and wary. Dressing down is the rule; grunge was invented for set wear. If it's cold, Eddie Bauer, of course. Uniform. Never wear fancy clothes unless you're Nora Ephron in Armani. It works on her. I don't know why. But I still like her best when she's wearing sweatshirts and baseball caps.

With the possible exception of female directors, people overdressed on the set look as if they have escaped from an English crew, where gaffers wear jackets and ties. Another thing: What is it about directors and baseball hats? Directors always wear baseball caps; it's de rigueur. I think Steven Spielberg is responsible for this.

The rules on wearing your crew jacket with the logo from another movie are: (a) If it's a really recent movie that hasn't come out yet, you can wear it, and (b) If the movie has been released for over a month, it's over, and the jacket shouldn't be worn. Except in extreme bad weather if the picture is or was about extreme weather conditions. Then it's thematic. I wore my *Fisher King* jacket proudly and inappropriately everywhere until Tom Hanks busted me.

HOW TO BE COOL ON SET

1. Wear the right clothes.
2. Feel comfortable on a grip truck.
3. Have a friend in video village (the little power tent where the video monitor records the scene under the watchful eyes of the inner-core shooting crew: the director, the cinematographer, the producer, the assistant director in charge of the set, hair and makeup, and often the prop and costume department heads).
4. Know the names of the teamsters (very important). Many producers make the mistake of not appreciating the teamsters. Sure, they cost a lot of money and they eat a lot of doughnuts, but they can be great allies too. The teamsters drive the hair and makeup trailers, and the grip, camera, and

electrical trucks, the sum total of what it takes to move a shooting crew from place to place. They get up the earliest to set up base camp and then rest (and gossip and eat) until it's time for a company move. Other teamsters drive the actors, director, and producer to set and they hear everything, which is why they are an invaluable font of production intelligence. On *Heartbreak* the teamsters and my son and I became such pals that I was made an honorary teamster for the Austin Local. (So if I never win a Crystal Award I can still die happy.)

PRODUCTION DON'TS

Being on location is more fun than a barrel of monkeys, more fun than any grown-up should be allowed to have. It is summer camp for adults, a temporary life where art and commerce truly meet. Once you try it, you're hooked for life.

When you're a newcomer, these are the dumbest things you can do and say in production:

1. Don't park your car in the middle of a shot. That is the single worst thing you can do in production. The entire shoot has to stop while a PA figures out whose car can be seen by the camera that wasn't there in the last take. (It won't match.) Then, as you repark your car in front of an impatient audience, you think you hear a collective mutter, "What a jerk." (You do.)

2. Don't cough out loud during a take (while filming). The fear of doing this is so mortifying on set that people have been known to risk an unnecessary Heimlich maneuver to avoid being caught coughing and ruining a shot.

3. Don't ask a really stupid question in the wrong place at the wrong time. It's always the wrong time. And stay away from the video monitor unless the director wants you there. Instead, wander around trying to appear purposeful. The best information can be gleaned from people at the remotest distance from the monitor. The importance of people on the set is inversely proportional to their distance from you.

4. Don't show up unexpectedly where a meeting might be assembling. Avoid all huddles. Unless it's one you're supposed to be in.

5. Don't let your portable phone or pager ring on a set. This is the most common horror for a novice: forgetting to turn the power off his portable phone. It is just about the tackiest thing a producer can do. The crew looks to the sky.

By the way, visitors to the set are great. Everyone loves to get visitors to the set — as long as they don't park in the shot.

There are only two kinds of shows: hard shows and easy shows (see above). You know when you're on a hard show every hour of the day. On a hard show everything is hard. Even the easy parts.

BIGGEST ISSUES ON A HARD SHOW

1. Can we survive the stress of the next hour?
2. Can we make the day?
3. Will this movie ever wrap?
4. Will the plug be pulled?

Actually this list is endless. You know how happy families are happy in the same way and unhappy families are unhappy in different ways? Well, hard shows are unhappy in a thousand new and original ways every day, and happy shows are happy in the same way — they just work. They run, autopilot-like, with good parties and great catering.

Each movie has a Morse code of crisis management — imagine it in binary form — so that *B* is for a big problem, and *S* is for a small problem. The rhythm for most movies goes something like this: BSSSSSBSSSSBSSSSSSB (wrapping).

Presumably, on a well-run, organized show the problems get smaller as the shooting goes on because the biggest ones are in the beginning when the studio hurdles exist, when the personality hurdles are the most extreme, and when the logistic hurdles are the most difficult. And, more important, when "they" can still pull the plug.

Sleepless had an easy shoot, though you wouldn't have been able to predict that during prep. We had BBSSB up through prep: This was the Morse code of production. Tom wasn't fully committed for a couple of weeks (Big problem, as Big as it gets). We couldn't find a kid we were happy with (Big). We were fighting with the studio over budget (standard Big but not too bad, as we never were forced to kill one of our four locations, the movie's jewels).

One Big problem during shooting was a potential crisis. The boy we had finally cast was adorable but terrified. On the first day of shooting he froze beside Tom Hanks. We had flown out an acting coach to support him during rehearsals, but her prognosis was negative. We had to replace the boy. The two-part schedule of *Sleepless* turned this potentially gigantic problem, which might have shut down production, into a manageable emergency. We rescheduled Meg Ryan's scenes, all of which were without Tom or the boy, for the first two weeks of shooting, while I organized a massive search for a replacement. A casting director flew in boys to read around the clock.

Then Nora had a brainstorm. There was a boy she had loved during auditions but couldn't get because he was in a TriStar TV series, which was scheduled to start midseason. We would call Tri-Star TV and beg. The boy, Ross Malinger, would be of greater value to his series after a movie with Tom Hanks, we argued. This time we chose right. Ross was letter-perfect from day one.

Once shooting was under way with Ross, it was SSS all the way. Our only big problem during shooting was, as I mentioned, rain. The lack thereof. We were shooting in Seattle in summer, the only two months of the year when it doesn't rain. But half the jokes in the movie were about how it rains all the time in Seattle, and we needed rain for most of our exteriors. Usually this would be easily solved with a rain machine, but Seattle was in the middle of the worst drought in its history, so sprinklers were legislated for only one hour a day, and citizens were measuring their showers. In the greenest city in America we couldn't waste water without risking the ire of the entire population.

PUNTING

Ultimately, one of the great rules of production prevailed: Necessity is the mother of invention, or what I call punting. We found an ecological consultant who devised a recyclable-rain machine that drained all of the water from the rain tower back into a tank that re-supplied it.

Punting is changing tactics with equanimity. Without panic or hysteria, we punt when we must reconceive an entire scene, stunt, or setup to conform with newly discovered production realities. In each department the mark of a pro is his skill in punting. Prop masters, who have to contend hourly with reality on set, need to be great punters. Directors, who may have planned an entire scene in one direction only to discover a fire truck that cannot be moved in the shot (one of a billion trivial examples), also must be great punters. Costume designers, who wake up in the morning to find that the scene previously scheduled to be shot that day has been changed and they have incomplete wardrobe for the scene now planned, must punt. Everyone has to punt, but most of all, the producer must punt. It's her job.

On *The Fisher King* our biggest production problem was rain as well. But this time we had too much. It rained and rained through our short New York schedule. It put us behind schedule, as we were shooting on the streets of New York and there was only so much material we could shoot in the rain. We weren't allowed to have many interior sets in New York because shooting there was so expensive; it had been mainly approved for exteriors. Finally it poured so hard we had to take an interior scene that had been scheduled for L.A. and move it to New York. It was to take place in a Chinese restaurant, but we had enormous problems scouting the right restaurant in New York. You'd think New York would be teeming with Chinese restaurants eager to be used in a movie and to be paid for it. But no. The ones we liked would not stay on call and were prohibitively expensive. Our location scout found one available on the day we needed it, but we had no time to see it until it was time to shoot.

This was a Thursday night, when we were supposed to be shooting the "cloud-busting" scene in Central Park, where Jeff and

Robin lie on the grass of Sheep Meadow, looking upward, and mentally disperse the clouds in the sky. About eight o'clock the heavens opened up, and we decided to go to "cover." By the time we loaded all the equipment and moved from Central Park to Chinatown, it was about midnight, and we had a four-page scene with a musical number to shoot in one night. Good luck. It was insane. The director and most of the crew had never seen the location, and we were about to shoot the most romantic scene in the movie, in which Jeff's character, Jack, begins to realize that he loves Anne (Mercedes Ruehl). Finally, on this night all her imperfections are acceptable to him.

By midnight we were just beginning our first rehearsal. The restaurant was overly ornate, with black lacquer tables. Terry's plan was to shoot the scene over and over again and do wipe dissolves in the editing room to show time passage. What he wanted more than anything was a pullback to end the scene, but we had no crane and no time to rig one for the wonderful scene we had planned during our technical scouts. When Terry found that he couldn't achieve the shot he had planned, he studied what could be done and altered it. He improvised his blocking to fit the new location, and the crew spontaneously invented the equipment that could pull it off — punters all.

The key grip and dolly grip especially came through. Grips are in charge of the crew that rigs the shots. They set the flags that diffuse the lighting, lay the track, and push the dolly cart on all moving dolly shots. They move everything but electricity. That's for the gaffers. The grips work for camera; the gaffers work on light. Rigging difficult shots requires enormous practical ingenuity as well as the experience to know what has worked in the past and the talent to make up something new. This key grip was a star punter. He jerry-rigged some bungee cord and a camera arm into a crane so that Terry could have that delicious long pullback that ended the scene, revealing the romantic foursome in isolation. It was the most poetic camera move in the movie. The spontaneity of the whole process infected the actors and freed them to play. Everyone worked at peak capacity. It came off better than we had ever dreamed because Terry never lost his vision. He knew how to punt. What began as a perilous moment became a genuinely thrilling moment, contagious for the entire cast and crew. It was the least-produced scene in the movie; the scene made itself and it was a triumph.

When you are constrained by reality and you have to be economical, often a better solution emerges than if you just threw money at your problem. This is why, paradoxically, it's not always preferable to have all the money in the world to make a picture. (Though you must never admit this to a suit.) Without necessity as a guiding principle, things often get bloated. When the filmmaker doesn't have to rethink a shot, he can lose a degree of critical edge. (Think *Waterworld*. Can you imagine the Morse code on this movie? BBBBBBBBBBBBBBBBBBBBBBBBBBBBBBBBBBBBBBBBBBBBB BBB.)

Some production problems are small problems disguised as big problems, and some big problems are disguised as small problems, such as late delivery of dailies — the rushes from the prior day's shooting. This problem arises when the film is being shipped around and misses a plane. It feels like a small problem, but when you start losing negatives — no one knows where they are, and the editors fall behind — it's really a Big problem.

A cover problem (having a set to shoot in bad weather) is a problem that can be very big or small, depending on the show. Having no portable telephone transmission on location, as was the case recently in Bracketville, Texas, when we shot *Bad Girls*, is a big problem disguised as a small problem. But after the hysteria subsides, no phone can have a lot to recommend it. ("You were trying to call me? To tell me to cut that scene? Damn! I missed the call and we already shot it!")

All bets are off in a hard show. *Bad Girls* was a continuous migraine. The Morse code was like a nuclear disaster, reminiscent of *Waterworld:* BBBBBBB!!!!! *Bad Girls* was born in disaster — the show had wrecked before I got there.

There I was one morning, innocently enjoying a private yoga class, my true luxury, when the phone rang. No one in my office ever calls me during yoga so I dismissed it. The phone kept ringing and ringing. Irritated beyond belief, I excused myself and answered the phone. It was Peter Chernin, chairman of Fox, with whom I had closed a production deal just that month.

"Lynda, I need your help. Jonathan Kaplan has been hired to be the new director of *Bad Girls* and he's balking. I need you to help me convince him to take over the show. They're in hiatus, and it's a mess up there. The actresses aren't speaking to one another and the dailies don't work. I need to get the show back up and running. Can you get on a plane tonight?"

From yoga to production in fifteen seconds. This was a radical revving up of my engine. Could I say no? Could I look a gift horse in the mouth? Could I avoid the temptation of location? No way. It sounded like too much fun, the crucible test of the right stuff for a producer — especially when the chairman calls.

Bad Girls had become such a hemorrhaging disaster I never had a chance to worry about where to spend per diem (nowhere, as it turned out). Or where to live (in the house the director had left). No one has ever been able to properly collate the relationship between painful trouble during production and eventual success. Some say the harder the show, the better the end product, but *Sleepless* and *Bad Girls* prove that theory to be a lie. (Perhaps if we'd had more than three weeks to make the script work, *Bad Girls* might have proved the maxim right. It could have been hard and good too.)

I moved the second half of the show from Sonoma, California, to Bracketville, Texas, so Jonathan could have a large Western set and huge vistas and skies to shoot. The set that they had planned to shoot was tiny and had no "wild" (movable) walls, which terribly compromised shooting. Jonathan felt there was no way he could be constrained on that set for the entire story. The prior team had tried to make the movie as cheaply as they could while loading the top full of movie stars (Drew Barrymore, Andie MacDowell, Madeleine Stowe, Mary Stuart Masterson) who *require* expensive production value and have expensive production needs. Each star had her own set of hair and makeup artists who were always quarreling, her own trailer, assistant, and driver. All had very high weekly living expenses due to them contractually and to stay in shape they required trainers and a decent diet. The absence of any of these perks could spell trouble. Healthy food didn't exist in Bracketville, Texas (a dusty town in the middle of nowhere where a vegetarian is someone who eats vegetables), so I hired a real vegetarian cook. Meanwhile, the deals made by the prior team had impoverished the crew. This ill-conceived tactic was aptly described by our cinematographer as the cheap leading the stupid.

I had to go in and assess wreckage. Instinctively I had to sense what would fall apart if touched or challenged and where lay the untapped talent. That's part of what a producer does. I'm a divining rod. By then I knew where to look for help. On the way to the set the teamsters told me that they had known by day three the show would wreck. It took the studio — far away in L.A. — two long, expensive weeks to discover what the teamsters had known from the start.

Since *Heartbreak* I am always pals with my crew (they're the coolest). When you are friends with the crew you find out everything. When the production designer says the sets will be ready in a week, and a carpenter tells you he hasn't even gotten the wood yet, you know someone is lying. I cultivate many sources on a show; it's the intelligence gathering of production. The more actively involved you are, the more people feel that they can come and tell you things and the more informed and accurate your decision making can be. Being a democrat is an asset as a producer. Being imperious is not.

Being a good leader is critical too. A movie crew is like a family. I always think of myself as the mother and the director as the father, and when I'm working with a female director it's the same dynamic, but I degenderize it. Your actors and crew want strong parental leadership — just like kids. If there is no central leadership, the center does not hold and anarchy prevails. When I arrived on set at *Bad Girls*, the production office looked like the night of the living dead. People were staring blankly into space, and no one knew where any of the actors were. It was postapocalyptic. In the absence of a strong central authority, everyone had turned on everyone else, and there were no clear winners.

The first thing I did was whip the production office into shape. No actor was allowed to travel without my authorization (first they had to be located so we could inform them), travel memos keeping production aware of the cast and crew's itineraries had to be widely distributed, and no one was to give permission for anything without first consulting me. There must be negative accountability; when a show is disciplined everyone works better.

But there must be positive reinforcement too, in the form of praise given for a job well done. Approval. Always attend to the wellness of the cast and crew. And no matter the catastrophe, psychic or otherwise, don't panic. Panic is hell. It makes everything go from bad to worse. Do not let anyone or anything panic you. Every problem can be broken down to handleable components. If the actors or crew see you panic, you're dead, finished. They'll really give you something to panic about. Like I said, it's just like kids. There are benevolent mommies and mean mommies, demanding, abusive, and withholding fathers and supportive, inspiring ones. Just like life. You must balance one role against another to provide security. This is the director-producer relationship. If someone can't go to one of you, he should be able to go to the other. Family.

Bad Girls finally got up and running in no small part because the director and I got along so well and were unified in our purpose. Jonathan Kaplan is a big bear of a man with inexhaustible ideas, a big temper, and an even bigger heart. He instinctively understood my strengths and used them to free up his time for storyboarding and scouting. I indulged my passion for wardrobe and production design by reconstructing and redesigning these departments. The movie was up and running in three weeks. It was like making four movies at once. I could make a movie hanging upside down while tomatoes were being thrown at me after that. There were births and deaths, tornadoes and fires, the coldest temperatures in history, the hottest temperatures in history, and snow for the first time in this century in that part of Texas. A variety of extraordinary things happened on this movie in the space of one week that never, ever had happened. Ever. In the end I loved it. The whole thing. I felt about it the way you might feel about a reckless teenage daughter who gives you so much trouble, who has wreaked such havoc in your life, but who is so talented and who all of a sudden grows up and turns into this terrific person. (Okay, a person.) You're amazed and proud that this errant, reckless teenager is you, and is standing and looking beautiful. (Or at least standing at all.)

THE PRODUCER-DIRECTOR DIALECTIC

A producer must marry her director, no matter the gender. In fact I've often thought that if I could be as good to my man as I am to my directors, my social life would be a radically different story. Your job in relation to your director is akin to waitress-customer, brother-sister, employee-employer, or employer-employee. But you must be bound. You are the responsible and protective daddy to the powers that be, while you must also protect the star of the family: the director. Your job is to make his day work so he can make his day (get all the scheduled shooting done). His favorite food must be provided, his nap at lunch; the time he likes dailies is the time you show them. Because no matter how hard your struggles are, his torment is greater. This makes it okay. On set is the only place I am willing to play long-suffering wife and like it. I am cheerleader, coach, therapist, ally, killer. If the director thinks someone has got to go, it's my job to cut the cord and make it painless for him. I keep the studio dragons at bay, hating them vociferously on his behalf. I am a tireless promoter and provider.

Listen carefully: *If you don't support your director, you're out of the loop. If you're out of the loop, you're out of the show.* (The only exception here is if *you* are the loop and your director is out of it. This means he's a hack, and you are in trouble. This is a very bad sign.)

What not to say to a director: Anything negative.

What to say to a director: Any compliment.

And if you feel compelled to suggest something to a director, think three times. Be sure you're right and then say it to someone else.

The relationship between director and producer is so intimate that many top directors come already assembled with their own producers so they don't have to suffer the indignity of a forced marriage. Many of these producers are the early line producers who've earned their stripes and permanent credits with loyal past service. These alliances work for the director as they have no internal contradictions: The producer is beholden to no one — and owes his job to no one — but the director.

In more typical arrangements (like mine) wherein the producer hires a director onto material she has developed, the resulting alliance is like an arranged marriage: all of the responsibility but none of the romantic history. Sometimes these alliances work okay; sometimes they don't. It's a kind of roulette, or like pot luck.

In arranged producer-director alliances, the people didn't really choose each other — the material did. And the producer's experience on the movie is identical to her relationship with the director — this unpredictable chemistry is everything. If there's no chemistry, the producer suffers. Sometimes even the director suffers. But every so often, just as with arranged marriages, something clicks. In these cases, with equal parts luck, similar taste, and mutual self-interest, creative teams are born. Like Nora and me. And with Michael Hoffman *(Soapdish, Restoration)*, the director of *One Fine Day*.

After reading Ellen Simon's hilarious first draft, Michael reached me on vacation in Texas. I remember driving around aimlessly in my pickup, trying to get reception on the cellular phone so I could hear what he had to say. "It's George Cukor . . . the battle of the sexes of the nineties," I heard through bursts of static. "He is me, fighting the fight for all baffled, contemporary men, and she is my wife, battling back. I live this script." It was the quickest Michael had ever committed to a piece of material, and he was notoriously picky. Not wanting to give him time to rethink, Kate Guinzburg (Michelle Pfeiffer's partner) and I put him on a plane to meet Michelle. He had already become our captain, and we wanted our star to embrace him too.

But I had no way of knowing then how much fun Michael would be. What delightful company in the trenches! Our vision of the movie was exactly in sync — the first premise of any decent collaboration. Our minds are highly compatible. We learned to trust each other's instincts implicitly. And I loved his extracurricular reading material: prostitution and midwives in the Middle Ages; books on architecture, art, history. His trailer in the mornings was like "Sunrise Semester." Talking with him — on scouts, at restaurants, at the monitor on set — was its own reward. And his design of the movie — beautiful, moving master shots and brilliant blocking — as he conducted two hilarious performances was masterful to watch. After my two years of director hell, Michael restored my faith in producer as waitress — he was a true pleasure to serve and he wanted me to put down my tray and enjoy the meal.

I always knew Nora would be a natural director. Her voice is original and sophisticated. She is enormously smart and instinctive, confident in her own point of view. This is why she is such a great collaborator. She is never threatened or undermined by another person's good idea. She is delighted. That's what a director is, the captain of the show's point of view. In working with Nora, the meal's the thing. As long as the catering is top notch, the show will run. In Toronto, on her directing debut, we held extensive catering try-outs. Everyone lost. We ended up hiring six different caterers for two weeks each. The other fun thing in producing Nora is that scouting equals shopping. After eating and shopping we work and conspire — the girlfriend quotient in our producer-director dialectic.

MOVIE STARS: CAN'T LIVE WITH 'EM; CAN'T LIVE WITHOUT 'EM

You may have heard that many movie stars are difficult. They can be, and let's admit it, it's their faces on the screen, and if the movie is a bomb their fortunes are vulnerable. (This is true for all movie stars except Harrison Ford, who can do anything.) It should also be said that some stars are absolutely heavenly and make production worthwhile. The lead actress in my first movie, *Adventures in Babysitting*, Elisabeth Shue (now of *Leaving Las Vegas* fame), became a great friend. Driving the roads of West Texas with Drew Barrymore under a starry sky listening to her sixties tapes was among the most exhilarating moments I ever spent on location. Meg Ryan and Tom Hanks are impeccable: real people in committed marriages (not with each other!) and with great values. And Robin Williams is genuinely an angel.

Before I tell you how much of an angel he really is, a little perspective is in order. No matter how much a producer likes or admires the star, no matter how much of a fan he is, his relationship with his movie star is work and his job is essentially ombudsman, travel agent, gofer, nurse, cheerleader, and manager in residence. He lives in the region between the star's needs and wants and his schedule and budget. I have never worked with an actor who refused to leave his trailer to come to set, but it happens, and it's big-time producers jail when it does. This is always the producer's fault (whether or not it really is): Shooting has stopped because the star is unhappy. The producer's job is to make the star happy. Some stars, just like some people we know, are never happy. Then the producer has a really hard job.

Some stars just take. They're used to it. Other stars *help* production. They work with the crew, understand schedule pressures, and they give. Then there's Robin. The night we were shooting the waltz in Grand Central Station, we were in production hell. It was a night shoot with a thousand extras, and we had to be fully wrapped and out of Grand Central at five-thirty A.M. for commuter traffic, no ifs, ands, or buts. The logistics on the floor with a thousand extras who had never waltzed before (we couldn't afford that many dancers) were close to catastrophic. At three A.M. the assistant director, whose job it was to direct and place the extras, threw down his walkie-talkie and quit (Big problem). By the time we got him back on the floor we had an hour to shoot the rest of the scene.

The extras had been waltzing continuously for eight hours. They were exhausted and thirsty. If we broke to distribute water to a thousand extras, we wouldn't make the scene. Production assistants were scattered all over the floor trying to dispense as much water as possible without forcing us to take a break. Robin took it all in. Without a word, he began to waltz through the crowd, asking every extra his or her name, taking a twirl with each, making each the most important person in the world. "Hello, you gorgeous nun. Come meet this randy sailor named Joe." The extras were electrified. They didn't need any more water to finish the scene. They danced ecstatically. When it was over, they all drank themselves silly. (Water, of course.)

There is no amount of time a producer spends listening to the problems of the star that is wasted. A star's belief in the integrity of the production is critical. The producer *is* the production. If the star thinks the producer is a piece of shit, then the show is a piece of shit and he has no reason to help, and you need his help constantly. The producer must get the star to ride his horse in the show's direction, because when they're riding in different directions, the show wrecks. Goodwill is good business.

HANDY TIPS FOR KEEPING STARS HAPPY

1. Give great commencement presents. Buy your movie stars something extravagant and thematic. If you are making a space movie, buy a telescope (if you can afford it). Maybe on my virus movie I'll send a microscope. On *Sleepless* Nora bought beautiful replicas of the Empire State Building encased in glass snowballs.
2. Care a great deal about the star's accommodations on location. (This includes housing, auto, cooks, trainers, all the accoutrements of a healthy movie-star lifestyle.)
3. When the star needs to leave location, do everything you can with your schedule to help. Then he'll come back. The more you go out of your way, the more the star will go out of his way. If you force him to stay against his will, it will be a rough day for everyone.
4. Give the movie star space. Don't be in her face or his trailer. Don't hustle. Be available.
5. Love the last movie the star made unless the star hated it. Then you must hate that movie and love the movie that the star loves. He loves; she loves — that's the mantra.

THE STUDIO GAME

During the entire production of *Bad Girls* the studio and I fought about schedule and money. (This is the "can I survive the stress of the next hour?" part.) I needed more time to fix the script we were rewriting before shooting, and they wanted me to start within two weeks because the overages were so huge. I wanted a longer shooting schedule; they wanted me to cut the script to shorten the schedule. The movie had cost them millions of dollars before we began, so every day was understandably a nightmare for them.

The Morse code was BBBBB. The budget and schedule hadn't been approved before we started shooting. This is a uniquely panicky situation for the studio, full of great leverage for the production, which is shooting out of town and holding the equipment. It was these fights that almost wore me down. Over and over I had to remember that it was a game. Not to take the fighting personally. And it was all the more problematic because the director had brought me in, but the studio was Fox, my home base.

I have a love-hate relationship with studios. I am a studio producer, and they know it and I know it. But regardless of the fact that they are the source of my paycheck, I am not merely their tool. This makes them both happy and unhappy. On *Sleepless* I was brought in by the director. When you're brought in by the director, your job is to protect the director and to negotiate between the needs of the director and the needs of the studio. The former take precedence over the latter. That's how you protect your movie. No one ever said after seeing a movie, "How great! And they brought it in under budget!" The studio forgives the budget overages of hits. If they're big hits. If the movie is a flop, no one remembers you were under budget. So you win by aiming for the bull's-eye, not by pleasing or placating the bank.

I have a philosophy during production that always works when I get into a pitched battle. When I am fighting with the studio over days or money during production, no matter how mean they get, I keep remembering, "I'm playing the role assigned to me by God, and they're playing the role assigned to them by God." They have to say the things they are saying, and I have to say the things I am saying.

It's a Mexican standoff. Interestingly, I lose if I capitulate, because then I'm not playing the role assigned to me by God. As much as they're acting as if they want me to capitulate, they really don't (even if they don't realize it). This is a game. A test of wills. You're not supposed to lose. As mean as they get, what are they going to do? Come down to the set and pull the plugs out of the wall? At the end of the day, they have to say what they have to say, and I have to say the things I have to say, and I don't personalize it anymore because I know there's an algorithm to the whole endeavor. I know it, and they know I know it, and they know I know they know it, and it makes them feel better to know that I'm not going to collapse. They will never admit it, though.

I have heard that Mark Johnson, a well-respected producer (*Rain Man, Bugsy, A Little Princess*), has an expression he always uses when he is potentially going over budget. "I share your concern," he says gravely. He looks stoic, concerned, attentive. And likely does what he was planning to do.

When "they" (the other side; it gets like this at times) instinctively understand that I will maintain my position no matter what they say, in a funny way they know the picture is going to be okay — that I'm strong enough to do my job. If I act weak and scared with them, they fear I'll be weak and scared with the director and crew. They want me to win even though they are fighting me. Even though they are trying to get me to do what I don't want to. Note: This does not hold true if the show is out of control and you don't otherwise know what you are doing.

I can maintain my position in a budget dispute if I maintain my credibility. Being a week behind schedule *is* my problem. Appearing to care — even actually caring — by addressing things that can and should be cut is reasonable and responsible. It's not right to be a pig about it. Just a mother lion.

This is how I survive the most brutal budget wars and the ugliest moments of conflict in production. I don't take any of it personally, so I can maintain what's left of my sanity in the place where I live: between a rock and a hard place.

Here is a sample conversation with the production exec, the keeper of the producer's tight leash, who is assigned to the producer to say no.

Exec: I've been trying to get you all day!

Producer: Really? I've been on set.[1]

Exec: Great dailies.[2] Look, we're very concerned about the schedule. You guys haven't been making your days. You've got to cut something.

Producer: Any suggestions?[3]

Exec: Yeah. How about the scene in the mall?

Producer: Shot it already. Good idea, though. We were thinking of dropping the montage sequence.[4]

Exec: But that was my idea! My favorite scene.[5]

---

1. She's ignored three calls.
2. Dailies are always great.
3. Half serious — part jerk-off, part fishing expedition.
4. Wherein the exec sees that the producer is really trying to play ball.
5. That's why we suggested it. An excellent tactic.

Producer: Damn.[6] Then we can't cut that.

Exec: What about the train wreck?

Producer: Impossible. Critical for back story. Anyway, we already paid for the train.

Exec: Well, you have to cut something. We're a hundred thousand over budget, and everyone is freaking out.

Producer: We'll cut it in post.[6] Don't worry. Today we're making our day, and you'll love the dailies. You get what you pay for.[7]

FINAL WORDS ON LOCATION AND TEMPTATION

The thing that's addictive about production is that it's so concrete. You made your day — got all your scheduled filming done — or you didn't. If you didn't, you either cut the work you couldn't get to, cut something else it can replace, or you fight to extend your schedule to accommodate the scene you didn't complete. You had a bad day or a good day. You got the shot at the golden hour or you missed it. No room for interpretation. In production even time is measured in absolutes: day forty-three, sixteen to go. Then you wrap and head home to Hollywood, where you find that the very ground beneath you isn't stable and remember that you are living and working in a world in which increasingly, it seems, nothing makes sense anymore. Sound familiar?

---

6. Producers always say this. They've caught on.
7. How's this for disingenuous?

Chapter 10

HOLLYWOOD'S CERTAIN UNCERTAINTY PRINCIPLE

"Expect the worst. It's a Sicilian thing."

— *Martin Scorsese, 60 Minutes*

"Here I go up in my swing
Ever so high.
I am the King of the fields and the King
Of the town,
I am the King of the earth, and the King
Of the sky.
Here I go up in my swing . . .
Now I go down."

— *A. A. Milne,*
"Swing Song,"
Now We Are Six

I T WAS THE BEST OF TIMES, it was the worst of times." You're up, you're down. You're the queen of the ball, you're a shred of dirty shoelace on the ground. Sometimes you need to take a step back and try to remember what the point of the whole enterprise is. Why do I do what I do? Why do I put myself through this? Do I really need this aggravation? It's what

I wonder at the end of almost every day, except the good ones, when for some reason the question doesn't come up. But there are never enough of those.

Lately it seems as if work is the best and worst of times within the same day, the same hour, the same moment, and then within the same instantaneous frame. The velocity of change is so staggering it creates a kind of turbo-Darwinism, a revved-up struggle for survival in which one must constantly mutate to survive. I think this is why the movie business is equally popular as a spectator and participant sport; it is a mirror that only slightly exaggerates our visceral experience of life in the nineties, when nothing is certain but uncertainty.

In the old days you had time (or you remember it that way) to absorb the different blows, time to steep in each aspect of your multiple lives. But now the dissonant collisions give you no time to respond. It's hard on the system. So it's time to eat, and you're not hungry. You laugh at sadness and cry at commercials. You feel fragmented, inappropriate in your reactions, suspicious of anything claiming to be for your own good. Our heroes have feet of clay or, worse, of mud. Our protective warning system tells us that anyone willing to run for office is by definition unworthy of the office, so we have abandoned the hope that someone will save us. We are the stunned victims of a public serial melodrama, acting out our collective neurosis: A devoted mother drowns her sons and blames a black man, then it is revealed that her Christian Coalition–leader stepfather, paying for her defense, had had a sexual relationship with her while locally promoting family values. We reel from the riveting psychodrama of a black football idol arrested at his Bel Air home for murdering his blonde wife, à la *Columbo,* and we form a rapt national audience for his replaying of *The Fugitive,* complete with sidekick, passport, fake beard, and cash. And then he pleads not guilty. *The Defenders* episode follows. He wins. Is it real? Is it Memorex? Nothing is what it appears to be, yet there's no time to look deeper with everything changing so quickly.

So you analyze from the surface: the car, the clothes, the title, the credits, the family, the watch, the face, the body. Thoughtlessly we come to glib and dangerous conclusions. Little girls starve themselves to be beautiful, and middle-class boys emulate gangsters. Good news is always accompanied by strange news: Michael Jackson cavorts in his locked bedroom with children. . . . Michael Jackson marries Lisa Marie Presley. . . . Lisa Marie divorces Michael. News? Or PR? You know the cynical context and you play the game along with them anyway, relishing the unspoken subtext, each startling item earning the same offhand shrug. You live with a backbeat of danger, police helicopters patrolling celebrity weddings, people dying over stolen hubcaps or pulled out of their cars for their Rolexes. Life feels absurd, hilarious, tragic. So you find yourself consulting the psychic hot line, scanning horoscopes as if they were the trades. You have conversations in which no one is surprised to discover that Orange County went bankrupt because its controller was being advised by bad astrologers on the investments of the county's pension plan. You are only surprised that better astrologers weren't selected to recover the lost loot.

You try to narrate the chaos, to make sense of it. Some rely on formulas for success: Jim Carrey + comedy = hit, except *The Cable Guy*; Arnold + ammo = hit, except *Last Action Hero*; Sharon Stone + nudity = hit, except *Sliver*; you get the idea. Formulas lie. The stunned, long faces of execs every Christmas attest to the failure of surefire formulas even though such formulas give you momentary assurance that you're basing your whims on something concrete. Deep down you sense that life will stubbornly refuse to conform to your needs and you suspect that like a big cosmic joke, chaos, not order, rules.

But oddly, movies have rarely reflected the fragmentation of culture and daily life we are all experiencing. Movies are the last bastion of the old-fashioned world, reassuring us that everything will be fine and make sense in the end. Making movies is delving into the wishful mythmaking process that repeats its reassuring message like a perpetual motion machine: b follows a; effort is rewarded; the underdog wins; justice prevails. Together we indulge and invest ourselves in the enormous artifice of storytelling convention, the formula we learned from movies: After the darkest hour of our brush with death or terror comes the light, the healing time. We keep waiting for the music-up climb from the depths that tells us the credits are about to roll.

When we see a movie that reflects what we experience — the

nutty roller coaster of contemporary life — we can't stay away, and the movie hits the bull's-eye. This accounts for the remarkable success of *Pulp Fiction*. I watched fifteen-year-olds sneak into the movie behind the backs of their parents standing in line, all of them like lemmings following an almost pop-porn compulsion. The movie's nonlinear narrative confidently snubs the need for cause and effect. Its dissonant mix of terror, philosophy, comedy, gloom, and pieces of brain is a joyride of blind turns where the end precedes the middle, a metaphor for what it feels like to be alive right now. Like the characters in the movie, we are spiritual gangsters, terrified, looking for divine intervention. We couldn't look away.

We feel the strangeness on every level. The movie business itself is undergoing such enormous change it seems to have gone haywire, a function of an insane simultaneous acceleration of almost every possible factor. The most obvious source of chaos is the agent wars, launched by Mike Ovitz's departure from CAA. In the wild goose chase for everyone else's clients in this climate of instability, star salaries have gone, as we say, ballistic.

In 1995 Sony paid Jim Carrey $20 million dollars for the movie *The Cable Guy;* so what do we pay Tom Hanks, Tom Cruise, Harrison Ford? Sandra Bullock's fee careened from $4 to $11 million in a matter of months in the same year, and as her agents' fortunes rise as well as those of her business managers, cash trickles down through her entourage like a Republican fantasy, out the window of our budgets. All of this is fraught with radical consequences that will affect the quantity and quality of the movies we make. It's gotten to the absurd point that a studio head–friend confided to me that he lies awake at night wondering how it is possible for the studio to make money in the contemporary marketplace. Even the landlord has the blues.

A wild free-for-all has gripped the business like a gang war. The agents who try to impress and sign the stars that open the movies, the studios that need them to open their movies, and we producers, who need them to make the movies, are all climbing over one another for a start date. In this struggle's most vulgar application, the stars are evaluated (worse, self-evaluated too) by their fees: Whoever has the biggest one is the best. Their "slots" — their seasons of availability — are competed for in a frantic frenzy of bidding worse than the hottest auction because a bloated and expensive movie is thought to be better than no movie at all. So we fight over them, and they win (and lose) because whoever pays the most money wins. Period. Until the movie is a disaster and someone loses big — and brings down the studio. Remember *Heaven's Gate* and United Artists? Now think of it industry wide. You need hits to stay big, ergo, take no chances. The cycle is swelling to a crescendo no one fully understands. We simply know that the race is on, that we're panting for a pause that will never come, and that the competition has never been so fierce and so bone crushing, so constantly enervating for those of us on the racetrack together.

All of this makes managing the process nearly impossible. No one, no matter his leverage, is immune to the chaos that roils beneath everything we do. It creates a hundred little disasters for everyone every day. Thus natural selection, the survival of the fittest in its most glamorous incarnation.

THE THIRD-ACT CRISIS

"Love is a song that can never go wrong, and I am Marie of Romania."

— *Dorothy Parker, "Comment"*

When we make movies, when we engage in any high-stakes work, we willingly place ourselves on a roller coaster upon which our identity is tied to the dramatic highs and lows of every hour. This ranging sense of self is both exhilarating and terrifying. One day I am given inappropriate attention in restaurants, the recipient of almost unctuous fealty in the most unexpected places. Everything seems possible. The next day all my plans have been dashed and nothing seems possible. No sooner do we construct order out of chaos, victory out of loss, than triumph changes frames and turns out to be hollow or, worse, comical. Working in the movies is a condensed version of contemporary life. And conversely, the movies have insinuated themselves into everyone's thinking.

As a form of unconscious stress relief, we set a place in our lives for the third act, with its answers and resolution. But like Elijah, it never comes. And so we wish and hope — and then we discover that third acts are merely temporary illusions. If we're lucky there's a fourth and a fifth and a sixth act.

Because I am the kind of person who relentlessly tries to figure things out and see the prettiest picture of the present, I find that I unconsciously constructed a three-act story for my work life. I had it all figured out: *Contact*, like Prince Charming on horseback, would gallop in and save me (the damsel in distress) from the tragedy of *Hot Zone* (the dastardly betrayal). The making of *Contact* was to heal my wounds, justify my hard work. We would all be standing at the Academy podium next March: George Miller, Carl Sagan, Annie Druyan, and me.

George Miller returned from Australia to prep *Contact* and told the studio he couldn't cut the budget unless they let him rewrite the script — after it had taken us two years of constant work to secure Jodie Foster's commitment. The studio declined, and he was no longer part of the project. Although change is the nature of the process, I was still unprepared for the erasure of the two years of grueling, high-pressure work; of the captain I had selected for my ship; of the camaraderie I had established with George; of our start date, which I needed financially as well as emotionally; of the fantasy third-act ending that would have, at least financially, if not emotionally, salvaged the loss of *Hot Zone*. In actuality, the salvaging fourth act began when Robert Zemeckis came on board as the new captain.

Movies make us anticipate the happy endings that elude us in real life. We have happy-ending *moments*, but then the wrecking ball inexorably swings our way, and we have to do our best to duck.

SURVIVING THE WRECKING BALL

"Wear something pretty to the Wrecking Ball."

— *Emmylou Harris*

No sooner do you build a house (or a movie, or anything) than the wrecking ball tears it down, revealing a pile of cardboard note cards scribbled with our intentions. A Potemkin village is what we make, a set, a faux reality, and we cling to its illusion of permanence. Even the stars in our Hollywood firmament are not fixed. We watch with morbid fascination as the mighty ones tumble while new stars rise, and the skies themselves transform. If these stars can ascend to the great heights, so can we. If they can fall, ditto. The speed of fate makes us giddy.

When *Contact* stumbled off its white horse that fateful weekend when George left, something crystallized for me. It was different than when *Hot Zone* collapsed. I knew I wouldn't fall. The bogeyman is a shape-shifter, but even though he looks different each time, he gets less and less scary. No matter how important *Contact* seemed to me, I knew that it was a temporary framing of my life, not a tent pole of my identity. My anchor would have to be something inside of me that no movie could undo. The good stuff. Life. Real life.

Right after my work world threatened to crater again, a few really interesting things occurred to me. First, I was suddenly free to work on my son's college applications with him (time flies when you're having fun, they say). A precious period before he left home for college, this turned out to be the most wonderful transitional phase of his life — and I thankfully didn't miss it. He moved from constantly booming music I loathed from his room to jazz and reggae, and we listened together. He gave me the greatest work pep talks. He started writing stories and reading them to me.

I also found more time to spend in Texas, surrounded by wonderful friends, none of whom cared whether or not any of my movies was shooting. Ever since *Heartbreak Hotel* I had dreamed of moving to Austin, to the point that Nora used to tease me, à la Chekhov, "Austin, Austin, some day ve vill be in Austin." Finally, because of the cash deferment I received when *Sleepless* became a hit (thanks to Nora), I was able to buy my dream house, a cozy country home of limestone, mortar, and log in the hills outside Austin. It has become my respite, my place to write, entertain my family and friends, and just relax.

Now that I was in Texas, I could rest (a little, I still had *One Fine Day* shooting in the spring) and finally figure out what had actually happened during the past season of ordeals. First, I noticed that I was still standing. I was so relieved that my second round with the wrecking ball — *Contact* — hadn't knocked me down that I found my optimism again.

Each time the wrecking ball finds you it's easier to get up. It's not just the lesson of "Next" but the lesson of "So, this again: I survived it before; I'll survive it this time." As surely as the wrecking ball will come, so too will it swing away. The trajectory of the pendulum eventually pulls you back toward something fine.

So the trick is hanging in there. Endurance beats the wrecking ball because the hits get easier and easier to take. It is the secret of every pro, at work or in sport. A career is like a very long game, one in which, it often seems, the goal is just to get to continue playing. (Think Bill Clinton.) All weekend after George left, I worked out incessantly. During my workouts I realized that what I needed as a gymnast was exactly what I needed at work. (The very same thing I needed as a person.)

FEAR OF FLYING

"Once I might have thought, 'Uh, oh, what if I don't
make this shot and the whole team hates me?' Now I think
of the times I've been in this situation and hit this
shot before. I think, 'I've done this a million
times. Just do what you know how to do.' And — boom —
the ball goes through."

— *basketball star Jennifer Azzi*

In order to pull off my back handspring I need to relax and focus. I can't think about work or anything else, for that matter. (My consciousness needs to be hijacked to take a break.) Just to do it, to risk breaking my neck or dislocating my elbow or tearing a tendon, takes all the strength and courage I have. No competing thought or instinct can rush in, no mind infiltration about what problems tomorrow might bring, or I would get hurt. I have to galvanize my strength and approach the move with confidence, without tensing up from wanting it so much.

That's the hard part. As a grown-up rationally concerned for the survival of my neck, I pull back. My fear of making a mistake leads me to choke and not use all of my strength. My various gymnastics accidents (I was on crutches from a torn ligament during the entire scout of *Fisher King*) have all been precipitated by sudden bursts of fear that threw me off balance and made me think instead of act, undermining my approach. I realized that *not* using all of my power was more likely to get me hurt than working full throttle. Full throttle is the only way to build up sufficient momentum. Even when all the kinetic physics are working for you and making the process effortless, full throttle can't be accessed when fear is present. Full throttle needs a wide berth, forged by relaxation.

As I find the ability to relax and play, I throw a great back handspring. I fly. My confidence floods back. I smile, less scared. It's obvious: *The only way I can access all my strength is to relax.* I once read an article in which a skating coach described this phenomenon, observing that "if you get results obsessed, you get so gnarled up that you can't play. You have to enjoy the battle as much as winning."

The paradox is that you must learn to be relaxed while using all your power. Pure athleticism equals total relaxation: This is the secret that all great athletes know, as well as the secret to surfing through Hollywood's uncertain waters.

This is the principle (even better, the practice) that would fuel all of my projects on the front and back burners. Relaxed, I wouldn't crumble with that rock that I had named *Contact*. If I could relax and focus, a new, great director would come aboard our foundering *Contact,* as the studio assured me.

That's what seems to have happened, so far, with *Contact.* I fear to jinx it because everything I ever thought out loud about *Contact* suffered a form of unplanned obsolescence — like if I say it, it will die. But the return swing of the pendulum has brought a spectacular shot at the brass ring. So it seems that the highs are as great as the lows. Robert Zemeckis, one of the best directors in the world, is its director now, the knight to ride *Contact* to its hoped-for glory.

The skill to managing a crisis is viewing it as a simple mess — a working debacle — that can be recycled and tilled into fertile new ground for more work. And so it goes.

KILLING DREAD

"Whoever can see through fear will always be safe."

— *Tao Te Ching*

What turns a work crisis into a life crisis is the infusion of dread. Dread is generalized, nonspecific fear, when it feels like someone is stalking you with a knife but there is no specific someone and no specific knife. I've been thinking a lot about dread, and I can identify three different kinds that get to me. First, there is the primal level of jungle-survival dread, the flight-and-fight adrenalized reactions that are genetically encoded for response in times of danger. The fact that business culture acts and feels like the primeval jungle keeps us stuck in our reptilian brains, slaves to our fear instincts.

Then there is what I call midnight pogrom–like dread, the "jig is up" dread, which I don't think is particular to Jewish people, though we certainly specialize in it. All my life I have been seized at unexpected moments by the irrational terror and apparent foreknowledge that someone dear to me is in mortal danger. (Usually it's my son, and now that he's a teenager, it is almost rational.) Hollywood exacerbates pogrom dread with its frequent middle-of-the-night emergencies — waking up to fires when you have to grab your belongings and run. Like the time in New York when, on a fun trip on my studio president's largesse, I woke up to discover that he had been replaced the day before in L.A.

Underlying all of these kinds of dread is familial psychological dread. This dread is a factor of how safe you felt as an infant inside the family structure. This is the one you take with you. Because we assign parental roles to our bosses, our partners, and our collaborators, we are constantly projecting our familial dread onto our workplace.

If we can't do anything to control the unpredictable hairpin turns of our careers and we have to live with the anxiety of radical, constant change and disappointment, at least we can try to subtract from work the dread we bring with us, the stuff that has nothing to do with work, with our battles, issues, or efforts. Unresolved and unaddressed, these ancient issues of dread magnify our realistic fears, making them loom far too large.

As my mother used to say, quoting Matthew, "Sufficient unto the day is the evil thereof." When it happens, then you can worry about it. There's already enough to worry about for today. Emergencies will come, they will go, and we don't have to make everyone else's dramas our own. Inevitably someone will get fired, someone we like less will replace him, and green lights will collapse. The wrecking ball loses force as it swings. And sometimes it misses you entirely for a while.

AMY AND LYNDA'S SURVIVAL MANUAL

"The way to solve the problem you see in life is
to live in a way that makes the problem disappear."

— *Ludwig Wittgenstein*

So how do we make a life among the half-built houses in which we live? How do we construct a nonillusory sense of stability, sacrosanct from the ups and downs of our destinies, independent of our logos? As Wittgenstein says, we have to live in such a way as to make the problem disappear. We have to reframe.

I was discussing how to live a quasi-normal life while pursuing big game in Hollywood with my pal Amy Pascal. She sat down in her elegant office at Turner Pictures, asked her secretary to hold her calls, and poured some tea. Our monthly tradition. We love to discuss the sociology of the business, and on this day we both found ourselves in the common contemporary state of exhaustion. She was trying to organize getting married the same year she was given the job she always wanted. Discovering the wisdom of the old adage "Be careful what you want, for you may get it," she was being pulled in all directions, afraid of being partly there for each aspect of her life, as I was. So we shared our version of recipes and we created a checklist for the future. For *a* future. Here it is:

1. Develop your life apart from work: a husband/wife, girl/boyfriend, child, home out of town, cause, hobby; anything that provides unconditional support and is not an extension of business. (Aspen doesn't count.)

2. Eliminate financial dread. If you're not independently wealthy (who is?), try not to care too much about money; spend little, need less; or if you're in an earning cycle, put enough money aside for when you aren't. Don't inflate your overhead. (This is my business manager speaking through me.) Play the game like an aristocrat by being able to walk away, push a start date, or play hardball with impunity, by not living for the fee. Survival takes the fun out of the game, and the whole goal is to keep playing. You can't play in the jungle if you can only stalk or be stalked or be a victim of the food chain. You can't find the game or free yourself up to play it when the stakes are so high.

3. Create an escape route that allows you to be dependent upon no one else's whims within five years. This looks different for everyone, but it is the same: freedom.

WHERE MEANING CAN BE IMPOSED

"What can be done?"

— *Lenin*

When *Contact* imploded I was close to a midlife version of a collegiate existential crisis, convinced that I'd knocked myself out for nothing. Then my friend Ingrid Sischy (author and editor of *Interview* magazine) helped me reframe. She showed me some photographs by Dorothea Lange. Slightly crippled from polio, Lange traveled the West and recorded the grim realities of the Depression, arousing crucial public sympathy for the social programs of the New Deal in the America that also inspired the genius of Steinbeck and Dos Passos: the dispossessed, the hungry, the marginal, those that the Dust Bowl and the Depression had left behind.

In her most famous photograph, *Migrant Mother,* Lange transforms a hungry farmworker holding a child into a Depression pietà in a pea pickers' camp. In others: A working man's calloused and eloquent hands make a statement of his determination though his head is half sliced from the frame; a simple ramshackle frame house lined with an interior door, the floor draped by a sleeping homeless man, a picture inside a picture, a frame inside a frame, in a profound blending of form and content.

I was transfixed by the integrity of her vision. Only one photographer could have taken these enormously diverse pictures. What gave them all such pathos — house, face, hands, gas-station sign — was the way she saw things and what she chose to see. Then I turned the page.

A Hallmark-type, well-fed Kansas hausfrau was brightly greeting me, hand outstretched. Saying nothing. Maybe hello. The next, last pages had none of the power of the photos before. I looked at the dates on the next group of pictures: 1956. There were some touching shots of dirty Irish children, a world-tour-like effort to recapture a beat. It was as if two completely different photographers' work had been compiled: one group infused with purpose and conviction, and one, whose author had seemed to have lost her sense of purpose sans the Depression, working its way toward the clichés of UNICEF shots.

You could see that when Lange could affect the world with her work, the material was elevated into art, though she didn't call it that. To her, photography was about connecting to the pulse of the people. In this way she is like us. When we do work that is connected to our original reasons for wanting to hook into the guts of the culture, our work has meaning.

Look at Steven Spielberg. After decades of reigning as the king of mainstream directors, serving as an inspiration to thousands of young filmmakers, he used all his leverage to delve into something considered untouchable for popular entertainment: the Holocaust. But one only had to look at the tearstained faces of his family in the audience at the Academy Awards, the faces of the Holocaust researchers who helped him make the film, and the eyes of the director himself to feel that the Academy had withheld its most prestigious award for the filmmaker as if it collectively knew that a more important moment would come: *Schindler's List,* the story of an ordinary man becoming a hero in extraordinary circumstances. The movie was a product of the connection of the man to his roots, a creation sourced from issues that profoundly motivated and moved him, and these forces forged his best, most accomplished work. It was his gift to us from his soul.

Like Spielberg's, our work is meaningful when we make movies about the things that move us, provoke us, inspire us, that *engage* and compel us. These personal issues are the source of our deepest and purest intentions. They are the mine from which we can excavate meaning and then, rightly, bring it to our work, whoever we are, no matter the work. We replace fairy-tale endings with purpose.

If the products of our efforts reach the screen, the bookstore, the public in any way — regardless of whether they are hits or flops — and they have some kernel of fineness, some ineffable, original first-rateness that only *we* could have provided, it all will have been for something worthwhile. Like that of the mythical Sisyphus, perhaps the first true producer, our work has meaning when we're pushing our boulder uphill. We're lucky to have a shot at the top of the mountain.

When I first wondered whether the last Monday had finally come on *Hot Zone,* I understood the notion of "final" only in the most limited framework. I had already learned, à la Yogi Berra, that "it isn't over till it's over" and I was an old pro with the movie business version, "It happens when it happens." But I still saw making the movie only in one time framework, the creatively compromised context of the race with *Outbreak.* When the competing project started shooting and my cast moved on, that ended *that* set of Mondays only. But that moment turned out to be only the temporary end of making *Hot Zone.* Round 47. The material still lives. The success of the book was the salvaging momentum for the movie. There goes that pendulum again. And *Hot Zone*'s eventual gift to me will have nothing to do with its outcome. *Hot Zone*'s legacy will have been the understanding of the illusion of finality. The myth of the final Monday.

There truly is no last moment, save the Big One that stops us. We can be derailed, subverted, slowed down, and discouraged. But we cannot be stopped if we have passion, a reason, like Dorothea Lange had, to go on.

Writing this, I am struck by something Abe Rosenthal said on the fateful day I told him I'd be leaving the *Times* for Hollywood. He looked dismayed but resigned. "You know what I always think of when I think of Hollywood?" he asked me. "Gertrude Stein's line 'There's no *there* there.'" At the time I was certain he was right. (About almost everything.) But certainty being what it is these days, I have come to see that Abe was probably wrong that time. There is very much a *there* here. *There* is a kaleidoscopic tragicomedy of contemporary manners performed by a cast of characters clamoring to create and achieve, to find meaning, hope, and acknowledgment against odds skewed by competition, chaos, and chance. Just trying to keep their boulders from barreling down the hill on top of them.

They are us. There is here.

FRIENDS FOR LIFE

One day recently, Nora Ephron called. She was about to shoot *Michael*, a delicious romantic comedy she and her sister Delia rewrote, in Austin, Texas. I was thrilled to hear that she would be spending time in Texas; it was working on *Sleepless* that had enabled me to buy my beloved house near Austin, which I'd been telling her about endlessly. She could never understand why I hadn't moved back to New York (easy answer: no escape from the dominance hierarchy, and $$$), and the charms of Texas had thus far escaped her. I was doing my chamber of commerce thing, giving her a list of my favorite haunts, stores, restaurants, BBQs, when she politely interrupted.

"Rosie O'Donnell isn't available to direct *Friends for Life*," she said. She was referring to a movie about girlfriends we had been developing together as producers. "What about you to direct?" she asked.

I was so moved I almost wept, but I didn't. She would have really hated that. Instead I told her how flattered I was, regardless of whether or not this turns out to be the right project for me to direct. She had been my mentor, then I had been honored to be hers when I produced her directing debut. Now she was offering me the opportunity to be produced, taken care of, by my closest mentor. The karmic kickback was actually kicking in.

There *are* friends. Just not as many as you had hoped when you began. And there *is* joy, just not unmitigated joy. There are instincts free of strategy and rewards apart from power. We can grow here — from girls and boys to pros, from pros to human beings capable of creating enduring relationships that make it all worthwhile, even fun. We stabilize ourselves with the help of these relationships, with equanimity in the face of the turmoil of our work, because we know now that everything is not suddenly going to get better or start making sense by itself.

The Buddhists say that facing the fear of death and the suffering of life is the beginning of enlightenment. That is, if we face it, embrace it, we can make peace with reality. That's what's there. No more, no less. The fracturing of illusions may be painful, but they're growing pains. It's a lie that people are whole; we have many selves and identities. When we embrace the complexity and accept the fragmentation, it is a tremendous relief. Breakthroughs, in art, in culture, in personality, come when tackling the unexpected.

Change is good, or at least constant and unpredictable. Railing against it, summoning nostalgia, clinging to an illusion of permanence, may feel safe but can never be satisfactory, because it is false. Why cling to an illusion that isn't there and never was? Strength lives in facing what is. If it feels meaningless, bring your own meaning. At least we can get another shot at another boulderless mountain. Our lives are gyroscopic. We can't control the drunken careening of fortune, but we can find an internal center of gravity that holds. This is where real meaning — not externally determined, status-driven meaning — is generated.

People once might have thought that life prepares you to work in the movies. In fact, it's the reverse. Making movies prepares you for life. It's a guerrilla version of postmodern existence, an exercise in surviving the mood swings of life in the nineties. To misquote Frank Sinatra, if you can take it here, you can take it anywhere.

AFTER OVITZ

When I began writing this book, Mike Ovitz was the undisputed King of Movie Moguls, despite his number two ranking on the perennially irritating Premiere Power list. As head and founder of the preeminent Creative Artists Agency, he changed the nature of agenting, packaging, and deal making in Hollywood over the course of the '80s and '90s. When I completed the book in 1996, he had fallen to number seven as president of Disney and supposed heir apparent to Michael Eisner, chairman of Disney, the largest media conglomerate in the world. This decision quickly led to personal anguish for Ovitz: After a year of denying rumors of a rift, both the long-term friendship between the two men and their efforts at forging an alliance at the helm of Disney were abandoned. The best-laid plans of mice and men (as it were) had come to nothing more than "a mutual decision."

At the time Ovitz left for Disney, I was optimistic about Mike's prospects, naively so as I have come to see. I had understood his decision in terms of the expansion of his work palette — an ambition to challenge himself by extending his deal-making skills into corporate culture, a sign of the growing power of the studios over the agencies, the encroaching influence of the media conglomerate in an entrepreneurial industry.

But I underestimated the zeal of the industry reaction. From the moment he left the top perch at CAA for a number two spot, the town loudly and unanimously disapproved. In the move, he had been subsumed, ipso facto, by Michael Eisner. "Mike Ovitz isn't Mike Ovitz anymore," David Geffen was quoted as saying soon after. "He is a guy who works for Michael Eisner." This summed up the local realpolitik.

A conscious decision to be number two after being number one in a power-as-a-spectator-sport town like Hollywood appears irrational: It disturbs the ethos of the dominance hierarchy. Those striving for oneness — not cosmic oneness but solitary number oneness — saw the aperture and wanted to fill it. We heard it wasn't working at Disney almost immediately. Within a year, the constant leaks of Ovitz's demise became fact — and perhaps inevitably self-fulfilling prophesies.

To be sure, there were legitimately angry people left in Ovitz's wake, most notably his former partners and employees at CAA whose own careers were upset by the indecisive process of his departure and his earlier muddled negotiations with MCA. And there were plenty of ignored, stepped-over, formerly marginal players who saw an opening for their own advancement with his bottleneck on power broken. Then there were his former co-combatants — studio heads and executives, competing agents, belittled producers, talent who claimed to have felt the heat of his so-called foot-soldiers keeping them in line — those who had been at the receiving end of his leverage. Out from under his power, they smelled his weakness and went for the jugular.

The frenzy is called "Who is going to be number one, now that the title holder of the past decade and a half has been unceremoniously decapitated by his long-time enemies and former friends?" (When friends become enemies, the worst kind of enemies are made: personal ones.)

The high-pitched squeal of the media frenzy bleated from the pages of customarily saner magazines and newspapers: *Vanity Fair, Los Angeles, The New Yorker,* the *Wall Street Journal.* No compunctions inhibited the largely unattributed slugfest. The background tune of the attempted annihilation was "Let's get back at Ovitz for having wielded so much power, so aggressively, for so long." Ovitz had been circumspect to the point of paranoia with the press in his heyday, inventing the modern agent's mantra "Never get your name in the newspaper. The client is the star." He had used this excuse to avoid on-the-record conversations for years, and the formerly shut-out press pack was literally aching to get at him: A field day had been declared on the notoriously untouchable target. Sources were coming out of the woodwork. The normally low-key but pervasive local attitude of wishing others to fail went haywire.

There is a kind of enthrallment with the newly permissible "get the guest" atmosphere. Pot shots at the previously reigning deity became a kind of cocktail sport. Heads of rival agencies couldn't have invented a scenario that would have given them more glee. Every man who had battled Mike and lost — friend and foe — was delighted to see him fall, and then wanted to push him into the ground, alive.

The tenor of the character attack was sealed early with gleeful pronouncements of his demise. "The Antichrist," former NBC hon-cho Don Ohlmeyer called him in the *New York Times*. Those at his feet for years, almost literally sucking up, begging for a phone call, an acknowledgment at a restaurant, they are all finished with him now. They have determined that he has no future, they begrudge him his powerful past.

Many say that the number and force of the hits are not business as usual but are instead a consequence of the *way* Ovitz wielded power at CAA — using maximum leverage, unilaterally. Ovitz described this strategy very succinctly. You were either inside the building or outside the building, he said. Inside, you would get the maximum protection, power, and influence of the agency exercised on your behalf. Outside the building, you got nothing. He said this last phrase matter-of-factly, but in a way that made it very clear it was cold outside that building. Though often tempted, I had never been a client. But as he spoke I felt myself running for the confines of the Oz-like IM lobby. You'd have to be a fool not to want the warmth of that lobby and all it represented.

The perception of this myth was very strong for a very long time. The unique power that Ovitz and his agency manifested was in large part the perpetuation of that mystique. Otherwise, according to Ovitz, the agency business was merely a service business, and there was no way to differentiate one agency from another. Without the myth of the agency itself, there would be an avaricious free-for-all, with each man, agent, and client alike only out for himself. Thus the building of the myth was a considerable part of this phenomenal success of CAA and the building came to symbolize this. Those outside the house did not like this world view. They lived to burn down the house he built.

Agents are now clearly more free to move their clients around, now that Ovitz has shown the way toward self-interest *uberalles*. So we have seen a year in which powerful individual agents act as feudal lords moving from one agency to another with important clients in tow. This has created a climate of disloyalty and instability, and a perception that the playing field has been leveled. But after the shooting has died down, CAA has lost no more than 5% of its former client list and signed as many as were lost, the rate of attrition in a "normal" year. In the absence of myth, the low-key, team-oriented process that Ovitz innovated, before the emergence of the foot-soldier myth, prevails. Perhaps it, with all of its Beta overtones—the client really *is* the star these days—was the real secret of CAA's success. The king is gone, the castle stands.

Like some Aztec ritual, Hollywood is tearing the heart out of its former king. Regicide. It is the animalistic destruction by the pack of the weakened leader, its former Alpha male. The scent of vulnerability has been given off, its source, its bleeding heart, must be eviscerated.

The laws of the jungle say kill or be killed, and when the lion has gone down, all the weaker species come out to feast on his body. Hollywood is a community fed by the desire to dethrone, defrock, denude its victim of any remaining power or life. This, along with the public's repulsion at the scale of the salaries paid for work undone, is the source of the outcry upon learning of Ovitz's enormous golden parachute — the millions he took for himself to survive. Survive? Who said he could survive the loss of power? And with millions?

For Ovitz to have gone from Hollywood's most powerful icon to its most despised in the space of a year is truly astonishing. The plummet is yet another instance of the near-psychotic pace of change in contemporary Hollywood. The sound barrier was broken by the implosion of his own well-cultivated mystique, and the force of the shock waves are a consequence of how deeply his mythology defined an era. He was not just an agent, he was *the* agent, the Godfather. Defrocked, he was the guy behind the curtain, suddenly illuminated in his mortal manipulations. No more wizard, Oz wanted him out. And where the stakes are the highest and the most envy and resent- ment have been bred, the fall is the most precipitous. To experience within one lifetime the utter obeisance and contempt that Ovitz has ranged through this year is almost incomprehensible.

I guess what I don't understand boils down to this. I'm pretty competitive and everything, and no one has ever mistaken me for a shrinking violet, but what's this thing about men and their constant need to stratify into Alphas and Betas — the leader of the pack and his followers? This need to stratify appears to be genetically hard-wired and generates driven, compulsive behavior. I might be proven wrong by later anthropological studies, but my anecdotal experi- ence of women in power is very different. Though highly competi- tive on their climb into positions of prominence and conflicted about what is being given up along the way, once they succeed they have no need to destroy or subsume their competition. Once differentiated, they are a band of nurturers who love to bond with other Alpha females. Like female chimpanzees, they spend hours grooming one another emotionally by minutely comparing all points of convergence. When one fails, or is fired, or is sick, they all show up, ready to help. I know there are exceptions, women who feast on the carcasses of other women, just as there exist contented Beta males, but the generality proves the rule.

One of the neurotic applications of Alpha-male behavior is often seen in the inability for an Alpha to pick an heir, a successor. The prospect of choosing a successor is traumatic for successful entrepre- neurs. I've seen three inelegantly handled ones, all by wildly successful and original men. Abe Rosenthal at the *New York Times* had such a difficult time choosing and breeding his successor that many assumed it was management who ultimately chose Max Frankel for him. Com- mon wisdom has it that Roone Arledge destablized ABC in his reluc- tance to find an heir apparent, and he finally chose his boss, David Westin, who was willing to keep him in a power-sharing partnership. And what we witnessed at Disney was certainly in part at least a failed attempt by Michael Eisner to pick a powerful successor.

You've got to give Eisner credit for choosing such a formidable candidate. He had been accused of losing Jeffrey Katzenberg over his refusal to give him the president's position, and such a bold choice as Ovitz — the other most powerful man in town — was a brave and daring one. Was it a need to subsume his only potential competitor? Was it an unconscious effort to eliminate anyone who might exceed him? Or was it a straightforward recognition of his own failing health (he had recently endured triple-bypass surgery) and Ovitz's obvious stature and abilities? Whatever the intention, he chose a successor with such a high profile that not only was the entire Disney power structure fundamentally disturbed by Ovitz's sudden arrival but it created a dark shadow of mortality for Eisner, who stepped up his work activities in the wake of bringing in Ovitz.

What is this about? Death. Fear of same. Picking an heir means your time will soon be up, or at least it acknowledges that your time is finite. With this much money and power, how can a mogul admit his mortality? His struggle for dominance is a disguised struggle for survival. For those personalities who require power over others, survival is a precarious thing. It requires the articulation and identification of number oneness to breathe. To even live. Let alone to prosper.

What a pleasure it is not to have to be number one. There was a time in my life when I was confused about power, about how much I wanted and could have, and about what it felt like to have so many people have power over me. But when I detoured to find the power in the work (as opposed to in the marketplace), I unwittingly saved myself from this Alpha struggle, one I surely would have been too weak to have won. It is a relief to be content with the amount of power my work has accrued, just enough to do the work I want to do. (Most of the time, anyway.)

I watched 76-year-old Sol Zaentz pick up an Irving Thalberg Lifetime Achievement Award at the 1996 Academy Awards as well as the Best Picture Oscar for *The English Patient*. To get the movie made, he battled two studios for an iffy cast. (One studio, which will remain nameless, wasn't too sure about Kristen Scott Thomas). Fifty years of picture making, and he could stand roundly at the podium in triumph and say, "my cup runneth over." I wondered as

I watched him from my location home in Austin (happily skipping all the festivities): Who is happier? Michael Eisner or Sol Zaentz? Who sleeps better? Are all the Alphas vying for Mike's old spot as happy and contented as Beta Zaentz? His struggles are on behalf of a movie. His efforts have a material object, an end, a purpose beyond the bending of others to his will (that too, but at least for a purpose.) To prosper, for Betas, is not to dominate, win, or triumph over adversaries. It is to achieve an achievable objective, making something fine finer. It is the protection of the small kernel of art inside our business — the "movie" in "movie business" — from the pernicious compromises of business itself.

Do I count out Ovitz? No way. I count out no one, particularly those with iron constitutions and a lot of powerful friends on Wall Street. The only thing that kills players is the loss of will, and I'm sure he's too angry to lose any of that. But I wish him sanity, the ability to enjoy the process above the rewards. Work does not have to be a jungle. Maybe it can be a kinder, gentler jungle populated by enlightened-type chimps, playing and fighting and fornicating and grooming. It helps when we start rewarding the Betas as much as the Alphas. Remember: 1996 was a bad year for Alphas. Or maybe Hollywood can be sort of, almost, a community of humans. It just takes a little empathy, a little civility, and the grace to wish others well.

—L. O.
June 1997
Austin, TX

INDEX